Remotely Global

Remotely Global

Village Modernity
in West Africa

—◁○▷—

Charles Piot

The University of Chicago Press · Chicago & London

The University of Chicago Press, Chicago 60637
The University of Chicago Press, Ltd., London
© 1999 by The University of Chicago
All rights reserved. Published 1999
Printed in the United States of America
11 10 09 08 07 06 05 04 03 02   3 4 5 6 7

ISBN: 0-226-66968-8 (cloth)
ISBN: 0-226-66969-6 (paper)

Library of Congress Cataloging-in-Publication Data

Piot, Charles.
  Remotely global : village modernity in West Africa / Charles Piot.
      p.   cm.
  Includes bibliographical references and index.
  ISBN 0-226-66968-8 (cloth : alk. paper).—ISBN 0-226-66969-6
(paper : alk. paper)
    1. Kabre (African people)—Social life and customs.   2. Kabre
(African people)—Government relations.   3. Kabre (African people)—
Politics and government.   4. Villages—Togo—Kuwdé.   5. Kuwdé
(Togo)—Social life and customs.   6. Kuwdé (Togo)—Politics and
government.   I. Title.
DT584.45.K33P56   1999
966.81—dc21   99-11071
                                                                    CIP

For Kalina

Contents

Acknowledgments

This project belongs to many others, as much as to myself. Literally every page contains the traces of encounters, both small and large—a conversation with a friend late at night, a remark by a teacher years ago, a reader's suggestion, someone else's inspired writing on a particular problem, and, needless to say, a multitude of conversations and experiences with Kabre interlocutors. Words are unable to express my profound gratitude to all those who have changed me and enriched the text.

My fieldwork in northern Togo was generously supported by the Social Science Research Council, the National Science Foundation, and the Wenner-Gren Foundation for Anthropological Research. To each I am most thankful. I also gratefully acknowledge the Togolese Ministère de l'Education Nationale et de la Recherche, and the Direction de la Recherche Scientifique, for research authorization and support throughout my several stays in Togo. At the University of Chicago Press, David Brent was a terrific editor, shepherding the manuscript through the review and editing process both expertly and expeditiously. The press's two reviewers, Alma Gottlieb and Paul Stoller, made many perceptive and important suggestions that have made this a much better book than it was. Copy editor Evan Young and production editor Leslie Keros skillfully helped me put the finishing touches on the manuscript.

In Paris and Lomé, many people contributed in myriad ways to making my research both possible and pleasurable. In particular, I wish to thank Jean-Claude Barbier, Kodjo Batema, Sid Bliss, Jacques Delord, Marty Havlovic, Kokou Kansoukou, Bakolea Karma, Anne-Marie Pillet-Schwartz, Alfred Schwartz, M. K. Simtekpeati, and Raymond Verdier. Bassari Ebia was an indispensable help with the orthography of Kabre words, and has been a constant friend and source of insight into the culture and politics of present-day Togo.

In the north of Togo, my debts run deeper and extend to more individuals than I could begin to enumerate. The people of the village of Kuwdé were extraordinary hosts throughout my various visits. Without the support and sage advice of Chief Halatakpendi Tedihou and Chief Palabéi

Kansoukou, my research would never have been possible. The two families with whom I have lived, those of Halitoké Korakoma and Tamouka Anamissi, and their wives, Kpèm Basséliki and Mama Kpénkpé, were inordinately generous and gracious in accepting me into their lives. Most importantly, without the friendship and research assistance of Nnamnawé Atakpai, Kouwènam Basséliki, and Tikénawé Gnossi, my research would have been unthinkable. To these three I owe much more than I am able to return.

Many teachers, students, friends, and colleagues in the United States have nourished me intellectually over the years, and especially throughout the long gestation of this project. The members of my dissertation committee at the University of Virginia—David Sapir (the chair), Chris Crocker, Fred Damon, Joe Miller, and Roy Wagner—were inspiring teachers and scholars, and forever challenged me to exceed my own expectations. Fred Damon, in particular, deserves special mention. He schooled me in the enchanted world of gifts and commodities and contributed to my growth as a scholar in ways that are too many and varied to enumerate. Marilyn Strathern's provocative work, especially *The Gender of the Gift,* has played a vital role in my own thinking about problems anthropological and her influence runs throughout the pages that follow. Dennis McGilvray and Paul Shankman were special friends and fabulous colleagues during my years teaching at the University of Colorado. Orin Starn read every chapter of the manuscript and, in his own inimitable way of combining compliment with critique, offered incredibly smart commentary that has enhanced the text immensely. For many years, this project was Nancy Ehrenreich's as much as my own. Without her keen interest and support, her embrace of Kabre culture, her fine ear for the language, and her tireless editing of earlier versions, this would have been a very different—and a much diminished—book. Its authorship is in many ways hers as much mine. There are many other friends and colleagues whose influence is in the text, either directly or indirectly: Lee Baker, Barbara Bianco, John Chernoff, Don Donham, Carrie Douglas, Susan Erikson, Kathy Ewing, Eric Gable, Jane Guyer, Jennifer Hasty, Danny Hoffman, Karla Holloway, Ralph Litzinger, Don Moore, Mack O'Barr, Susan McKinnon, Marc Schloss, Barbara Voorhies, and Teresa Wilkins.

Finally, I wish to acknowledge the support of my families. Early on, in myriad often-unsuspecting ways, my parents, Pat and André Piot, schooled me in the challenges and pleasures of trafficking across various cultural divides. Their unfailing support of my unorthodoxies has always been an inspiration. Anne Allison has not only been an astute reader and critic but also an incomparably supportive partner. She made the struggle to complete the manuscript not only possible but also pleasurable. My debts to her, both intellectual and personal, have no end. *Remotely Global* is dedicated to my daughter Kalina—Kuwdé pelo ("Kuwdé girl"), as many in Kuwdé like to call her—whose calm presence, sweet smile, and boundless energy forever fill my imaginings when we are apart.

Note on Kabre Orthography

In the text that follows, I have retained the French spelling that is used in Togo today for the proper names of people and places. All other Kabre words are rendered in the dialect of the northern massif (Lamatessi), where Kuwdé—the community in which I lived and conducted research—is located, and are phoneticized according to International Phonetic Alphabet conventions. Thus, consonants correspond to their standard English pronunciations, except for 'c' which is pronounced like the 'ch' in "charming," 'ḍ' which is pronounced like the 'dg' in "edge," 'ŋ' which is pronounced like the 'ng' in "sing," and 'ɣ' which is a throaty "r" like that in the French "très." Vowels are pronounced as follows: 'a' like the 'a' in "far," 'e' like the 'a' in "skate," 'ɛ' like the 'e' in "hen," 'i' like the 'e' in "be," 'ɩ' like the 'i' in "it," 'o' like the 'o' in "hotel," 'ʊ' like the 'o' in "come," 'ɔ' like the 'ou' in "ought," and 'u' like the 'u' in "flute." Bassari Ebia, a Kabre linguist at the Institut National de la Recherche Scientifique in Lomé, and a native of Faren in the northern massif, very generously helped me with the phoneticization of Kabre words.

One

....

INTRODUCTION

Images and Power

This study is an attempt to retheorize a classic out-of-the-way place
(Tsing 1993)—a society in the savanna region of West Africa where
Meyer Fortes, Jack Goody, and Marcel Griaule conducted their ethnographic research. These scholars analyzed Tallensi, LoDagaa, and Dogon societies as if they were timeless and bounded, located beyond the
space-time of the colonial and the modern. By contrast, my own analysis
of a society in this savanna region—the Kabre of northern Togo—will
argue that this place has long been globalized and is better conceptualized as existing within modernity.[1] To claim as much is to argue against
appearances, however, for this is a place that has all the earmarks of a
still pristine African culture: subsistence farming, gift exchange, straw-
roofed houses, rituals to the spirits and ancestors. Moreover, many of
these elements of "tradition"—the ritual system, the domain of gift exchange—have flourished and intensified over the last thirty years. And
this during a time when the president of the country, who hails from this
remote ethnic group, has vigorously pursued a modernizing mission.

I want to suggest that these apparently traditional features of Kabre
society are in fact "modernities" (Dirks 1990, 1992; Comaroff and Comaroff 1993)—that they were forged during the long encounter with Europe over the last three hundred years and thus owe their meaning and
shape to that encounter as much as to anything "indigenous." Moreover,
it is in terms of these features that Kabre comfortably, if not always
seamlessly, inhabit today's world. I thus join other scholars of Africa
(S. Moore 1986, 1994; Mudimbe 1988; Ferguson 1990; Comaroff and
Comaroff 1991, 1993, 1997; Appiah 1992; Apter 1992; Cohen and Odhi-

1

ambo 1992; Gable 1995; Hutchinson 1996; Weiss 1996; Barber 1997; Shaw 1997) whose work seeks to unsettle the orientalizing binarism—and conceit—that associates Europe with "modernity" and Africa with "tradition" and has long informed scholarship about Africa and other places non-Western.

There is more than mere scholarly debate here, however. Demonizing images of Africa circulate in the press these days with startling frequency. In a rash of recent articles in leading U.S. newspapers and journals, under headlines that invite the sort of prurient voyeurism that has long accompanied Western interest in places Other—"The Coming Anarchy," "Our Africa Problem," "Tribal Ritual on Trial," "Persecution by Circumcision"[2]—Africa, and especially West Africa, is portrayed as a place where democracy and development have failed, where drought and disease run rampant, where nepotistic ethnic politics is the norm with genocide right around the corner, and where "traditional" cultural practices such as polygyny, spirit worship ("animism," as the popular press refers to it), and clitoridectomy (often referred to as "female genital mutilation") still hold sway. In short, it is represented as a place where modernity's signature institutions and beliefs—democracy and development, monogamous marriage, individualism and secularism—have failed to take root. Moreover, in many of these articles the blame for this failure is placed on the tenacity of "traditional culture." Such an explanation—striking for its inattention to history—resembles the refrain I repeatedly heard from people working in development in Togo during the 1980s when yet another project of theirs had failed—namely, that it was the local "culture" that had prevented the group in question from changing its ways. Here, of course, the contrast is particularly sharply drawn: "traditional" (anti- or non-modern) culture retards the embrace of modernity.

◄O►

I sat eating lunch with a high official from the American Embassy on the patio at Marox, a German-owned restaurant that was a popular hangout among expatriates in Lomé. Beyond the railing of the patio, the pock-marked street was flush with pedestrians and taxis dodging huge puddles left by a drenching dawn rain—smartly dressed women heading to the Grand Marché; food vendors with piles of fish, fruit, and vegetables on platters on their heads; peddlers selling watches, sandals, and cigarettes.

A large man with a wad of money in his hand and deep scars on his cheeks—a Yoruba from Nigeria—stopped at the railing and asked if we wanted to change money. "Marks? Dollars? I can give you a better price than the banks."

I had just returned to Togo in the summer of 1996 for a short trip to the north and had met the official in a hallway at the embassy while I was "registering" before heading upcountry.[3] When he found out I was an anthropologist who worked among Kabre (Kabiyé),[4] the minority group from the north that has held power since 1967, he proposed lunch—to talk, he said, about Togolese "cultural politics" (a phrase oddly reminiscent of leftist academics describing the struggles of subaltern groups against dominant cultural and political-economic orders; yet here—employed by an embassy official surveilling a troubled postcolonial context—it seemed to have a disturbingly different sense). "I've read some of your work," he said. "Got it off the Internet. But it doesn't address the current conflict between Kabre and Ewe and I'd like to hear your take on it."

He was a slight man who seemed cut from the same cloth as many of my (white, middle-class) students at Duke—clean-cut, smart, easy to talk to, conservative. His job at the embassy was to advise the ambassador and the State Department on local politics. It was he who monitored Togolese elections and who kept tabs on the simmering conflict between Kabre and Ewe, the country's two most powerful ethnic groups—a situation he kept describing, mantra-like, as "another potential Rwanda." He was also in charge of gathering information about the case of a Togolese woman seeking asylum in the States. The case had flashed across the pages of U.S. newspapers during the spring and fall of 1996, and had become a cause célèbre in American feminist circles.[5] The woman, Fausiya Kasinga, originally from a small village in the north, had fled Togo—first to Germany, then to the United States—because she was in danger of being forced by her family to undergo clitoridectomy at the time of her marriage to a businessman in the south.

I myself had become keenly interested in the case when it was first reported in the press that spring, and had used a *New York Times* article on it in a class I was teaching to point out once again how orientalizing the press was whenever it wrote about Africa. The background images that framed the *Times* piece—images of Togo as poor, patriarchal, oppressive, illiterate—dominated and overwhelmed the story of Kasinga herself. It seemed more an article about Africa's Otherness than about either the plight of a woman caught in a nasty local dispute or a difficult and complex issue that defies easy resolution. Demonization all over again.

"Why," I asked, "was the embassy involved in Kasinga's case?"

"Because it's a high publicity case that could affect U.S. policy not only in Togo but also throughout Africa. There are proposals in Congress to tie development money to the eradication of FGM [female genital mutilation]. There's a big debate going on in the State Department right now over precisely this issue. And, it's not all one-sided: there are strong advocates of noninterference in 'cultural' matters, people who are arguing that it's wrong—a type of imperialism—to impose our values on others. The U.S. courts also worry that if they grant asylum in a case like this, the floodgates will open and anyone claiming cultural persecution of any kind will be granted asylum. This is a very sensitive case. We need to make sure we've got our ducks in a row."

Our discussion of the Kasinga case ended (the official wanted to move on to other issues) with his relating a strange twist that had emerged from his undercover work: one of his local sources—a woman in the Togolese government—had told him that Kasinga's claim was almost certainly a cover for the fact that she was a member of an international prostitution ring that worked the Togo-Germany-United States triangle. "Whenever these women get caught," he had been told by this woman, "they use this as their alibi."

Sipping a strong German ale, my companion switched the subject, probing to find out more about my work. He wanted to know how much time I'd spent in the north, where I lived, whether I spoke the language. But he was especially interested in those aspects of northern culture that bore on the current political situation. He wanted to know how much support Eyadéma, Togo's Mobutuesque president, had in his home region and seemed surprised when I said that it was decidedly mixed. He also wanted to know more about the young men from the north whom Eyadéma recruited into the military and police force. As the most visible arm of the state—clad in olive-green uniforms, brandishing AK-47s, they work the many checkpoints throughout Lomé and along the national highway that stretches to the northern border, often harassing drivers who seem suspicious or whose papers aren't "in order"—they had been the target of intense criticism in the Togolese press during the early 1990s. They were also widely assumed to have "disappeared" members of Eyadéma's political opposition. The press portrayed them as thugs who knew nothing but blind loyalty to the president and the power of the gun—and who were the product, it was suggested, of a "culture of violence" that festered in the rude backward regions of the north.

I calmly but persistently tried to disrupt the stereotype, pointing out how those youths I knew in the north are not the thugs portrayed in the southern media, that Kabre are markedly nonviolent (and indeed always struck me as more so than any people I'd ever known), that Kabre and Ewe, the two groups at odds during the 1990s, have lived side by side in southern Togo since the early colonial period and there get along extremely well. I also suggested that the current conflict between the two groups was explained less by primordialist assumptions about ethnic groups—what the press was fond of calling "tribalism"—than by understanding the volatile mix of processes of underdevelopment with postcolonial power configurations, and that the international community was as responsible for this mix as anyone else.

It was the totalizing, essentializing cultural categories—the "Kabre" and their "culture of violence"—within which this official operated that I found particularly troubling. While he seemed well-meaning, he was the victim of a State Department policy of extraordinary hubris that rotates officers from one country to the next every two years. He thus had had little time to learn much about Togolese and their history, and by default fell back on ethnic stereotype. Most sobering of all was the fact that he wielded enormous power: at his suggestion—by the circulation of a single memo suggesting that Togolese were unwilling to engage in the electoral process or to eradicate clitoridectomy—millions of dollars in aid money, money a country like Togo relies on just to stay afloat, could be cut off overnight.

This encounter underscores the insidious and volatile way in which image and power feed off one another in this postcolonial context, and the enormous stakes involved. It also calls attention to the types of global processes and interconnections that seem ever more commonplace as the century draws to a close—processes that draw into the same tight circle a hill people living in a remote corner of French West Africa, a civil servant from the world's most powerful country, and a Western anthropologist whose work can be downloaded off the Internet at the click of a mouse (and put to use in ways that are beyond his/her control). Clearly, the need is as pressing now as ever to write against power and against the images it deploys in legitimating imperialist agendas.

A Critique

> The fact of the matter is that, until now, Western interpreters as well as
> African analysts have been using categories and conceptual systems which
> depend on a Western epistemological order. (Mudimbe 1988: x)

If one of the aims of my account is to criticize orientalizing images by
showing the way in which an apparently traditional African society is
within, and has been shaped by, modernity, another is to remain mindful
of the point made by postcolonial scholars (Nandy 1983; Mudimbe 1988;
Prakash 1990, 1994; Young 1990; Chakrabarty 1992, 1994, 1997; Chatterjee 1993; Bhabha 1994): that we problematize Eurocentric epistemologies when theorizing such places. Thus, these scholars are committed
to writing histories that disrupt the conventional grand narratives of
Western scholars—those universal Histories, whether from a modernizing or a Marxist perspective, that center the West and deny agency to
subaltern groups—the so-called "peoples without history." In so doing,
postcolonial scholars aim not only to give voice and agency to the subaltern but also to refigure the way in which subaltern subjectivity has been
constructed by Western scholarly discourses in colonial and postcolonial
contexts—and thus to rethink the humanist subject and the type of history that is written with that subject in mind.

It is this latter point that keys my own study—but in a very specific
way, and more from within anthropology than postcolonial studies.[6] I
take my cue from some of the work of Marilyn Strathern who, working
in Melanesia (a place where many a Western theory has foundered), has
recently engaged in a radical epistemological critique of anthropological
theorizing there. In *The Gender of the Gift,* for instance,[7] Strathern criticized the way anthropologists had used conventionalized categories like
"society," "agency," "gender inequality," and so on in describing Melanesian social processes. These analytical categories, she suggested, are
deeply informed by Euroamerican commodity metaphors, property assumptions, subject-object relations, and individualistic views of the person, and thus operate at some distance from local conceptions of the
nature of persons and social life.

Melanesians, Strathern argued, develop their forms of identity and
symbolization through the "gift" rather than the commodity form. Thus,
the types of person/thing separations capitalist societies enact (as represented, for example, by commodity fetishism) contrast with the manner
in which persons and things are intertwined in Melanesia. To wit, the
identities of Melanesian persons are constituted through, and forever

entangled with, the transactions of gift-objects (and the relationships such transactions signify); conversely, objects themselves only have meaning in relation to persons and relationships. For example, the exchange-value of things/gifts is not so much (as with commodity transactions) the measure of the things exchanged—a ratio of congealed labor, a determination of relative utility—as it is an index of a specific relationship between persons (Foster 1995: 10). Thus constituted through exchange, persons in such societies are better thought of as "relations" than as discrete essences, as "composite"—the site of a plurality of relationships—rather than autonomous and individual. So, too, unbounded persons are not "objects" manipulable by other persons ("subjects"). Attending to the dynamics entailed by such an understanding of persons/things, Strathern suggests, is where an analysis of Melanesian social life ought to begin. And, I might add, where an analysis of Melanesian engagements with colonialism, modernity, and the global should commence as well.

But to do so means having to abandon analytic frameworks derived from much classic (Eurocentric) social theory. If there are no "individuals," then thinking in terms of the fundamental problematic of much Durkheimian social theory—how to tie the "individual" to "society"—misses the mark. And if persons (and groups) are not divided by social interest—and thus cannot be theorized through a subject-object view of social relations—then interest-based theoretical accounts of social inequality, such as those proffered by Marxists and feminists, are also inapplicable. These various models—which are simple transformations of one another (Strathern 1988)—subscribe to a deep-seated individualism rooted in the social and political experience of Western societies.[8]

A Place

The present work carries such arguments to the African context. Like Strathern, I am concerned to show that analyses informed by classic Euroamerican social theory (in both Durkheimian and Marxian versions) do not adequately capture the meaning or nature of social life in other places. In particular, I aim to show that such analytic frameworks fail to get at local understandings of social relations—and of gender, power, agency, history, and modernity—in societies of the Volta basin area of West Africa.

This region would appear to be a privileged one in which to examine such issues, for it has been home to some of the classic analyses in the history of the discipline. Foremost among these, of course, were those by adherents of the British school—Meyer Fortes, Jack Goody, David Tait, and others. These anthropologists offered dense, and in their own way brilliant, sociological analyses of Voltaic kinship systems and attempted to build a generalizable theory—"descent" or "lineage" theory—that would account for not only the specific shape of local kinship practices but also the variation in such practices from one society to the next. Their analyses were seminal in generating the questions that would inform a generation of anthropological research into systems of kinship and descent across the continent.

A French anthropological tradition has also flourished in this savanna area, focused less on kinship and more on systems of meaning. The most celebrated work in this tradition is that of Marcel Griaule and Germaine Dieterlen, whose writings on Dogon myth and ritual described symbolic systems of stunning complexity. But this area of West Africa has produced many other prominent French anthropologists as well. Scholars such as Michel Cartry, Françoise Héritier, and Michel Izard—all more influenced by Lévi-Strauss than by Griaule—produced elegant, if detached, analyses of systems of initiation and sacrifice, conceptions of personhood, and, in Héritier's (1981) case, "semi-complex" systems of marriage alliance (a work that led to her succeeding Lévi-Strauss at the Collège de France).

In the 1970s and 1980s, other anthropologists working in this area produced important work inspired by the Marxist critiques then current within anthropology. Olivier de Sardin, Pierre-Phillipe Rey, and others (Seddon 1978) took earlier anthropologists to task for their inattention to issues of power and inequality (between juniors and elders, between women and men, and between the societies being studied and the larger colonial system) and offered analyses that placed such concerns center stage.

My own initial research among the Kabre was influenced by these Marxist critiques and entailed an attempt to rethink some of the work of British descent theorists such as Fortes and Goody, as well as that of French scholars focusing on ritual and meaning, from a Marxist perspective. Drawing on the work of French anthropologists Claude Meillassoux and Emmanuel Terray (both of whom worked in West Africa, just outside the area of the Volta basin proper), I sought to analyze the sources of social inequality in Kabre society. It appeared from the literature on Kabre, for instance, that male elders came to sit atop various hierarchies by controlling the labor of others—of women and children through the practice of polygynous marriage (which added laborers to the home-stead's workforce, and thus might benefit those males who were in charge), and of younger men through a system of work groups (which was run by male elders and, it appeared, might be exploited to their advantage).

What I found, however, was quite different. Men who married polygynously had to work harder, not less, since Kabre women do not farm. Thus, a man with two wives (and the additional children adding a second wife brings) had to work twice as hard, since he was the sole provider of cultivated food for the family. As for the work groups, I found that they were in fact set up to *prevent* individuals, or groups of individuals, from benefiting from the labor of others. If, for instance, someone tried to "call" the work group to achieve any end other than the feeding of his family (e.g., enhancing his personal wealth), the work group would simply refuse to work his fields.[9]

I later came to realize that my perspective was flawed not only empirically but also theoretically. I was applying a type of Eurocentric logic to social and productive relations, and indeed to the whole question of inequality. I was assuming that the structure of Kabre society could be analyzed as if it entailed a type of contest among individuals for scarce resources (labor) in which certain of those individuals (male elders) had triumphed, using others (women and children) as pawns in their grab for power.

But for Kabre, as I aim to show, things are other, and more complicated, than this. Persons are not the autonomous, contesting "individuals" that such theories might have us believe. An instrumentalist, subject-object view of persons—in which active, authoring "subjects" are seen as treating others as passive, acted upon "objects"—does not capture Kabre constructions of the nature of the person or serve to explain the structure of society.

Africanist Discourses

Evolutionism, functionalism, diffusionism—whatever the method, all repress otherness in the name of sameness, reduce the different to the already known, and thus fundamentally escape the task of making sense of other worlds. (Mudimbe 1988: 72–73)

In order to frame more adequately the analysis that follows, I turn briefly to an examination and critique of certain theories of society that have emerged within Africanist anthropology. My discussion of these theories focuses especially on the way individualist assumptions, subject-object relations, and Euroamerican property metaphors lie embedded within and inform their explanatory models.

Structural-Functionalism

Structural-functionalists, whose theory dominated African studies from the 1940s to the 1960s, viewed African societies as composed of segmentary lineages or descent groups. These lineages were "corporate" in nature and therefore had, to quote Fortes (1953: 25), a "single legal personality." Each could be regarded as a "single person." Lineages were also property-owning units, possessing land, cattle, or various immaterial forms of "property" like ritual knowledge. The message these theorists convey, then, is that African groups are like Western individuals—each with separate identity and interests, each owning his separate property (and I use "his" advisedly, for a lineage's property was said to include its outmarried women).

A central "problem" in structural-functional theory, given its view that society was composed of bounded, property-owning units in competition with one another, was to determine how the units were kept together. This question seemed particularly important and intriguing in the African context, since many African societies were acephalous: they lacked a coercive state apparatus. The solution to the problem of cohesion varied from author to author, and from place to place. For Evans-Pritchard (1940) it was the feud; for Fortes (1936, 1945, 1949), ritual and complementary filiation; for Middleton (1960, 1963), the cult of the dead and witchcraft beliefs; and so on.[10]

There are many problems with the theory. As critics have long pointed out, the cohesion argument is circular: since the analyst sought out mechanisms of solidarity, and since it was assumed that the society being observed was solidary, whatever the people did was said to have produced such solidarity. The argument is also indeterminate: it does not explain why one form of cohesion is found in one place and a very different one obtains elsewhere; nor does it account for the internal logic and complexity of the social practices described in any particular case. For example, the rituals Fortes (1936) described as promoting cohesion among the Tallensi were always more detailed and complex than would be necessary to fulfill the function he attributed to them. Similarly, the witchcraft beliefs described by Middleton (1963) as controlling the behavior of Lugbara elders are more elaborate and nuanced than his theory can account for.

Other critics (Kuper 1982, 1988: 190–209; Jackson 1989: 10–11; Gottlieb 1992: 46–71) have pointed out the gap between descent theory constructs and local categories. Thus, for example, there is no Nuer word for "clan" (Evans-Pritchard 1940: 195), no Tallensi word for "lineage" or for the segments of the maximal lineage (Fortes 1949: 9–10), no Lugbara term for "lineage," "segment," or "section" (Middleton 1965: 36), and so on. And yet, these descent theorists argued that it was the groups defined by these categories that constituted the basic building blocks of the social structures they analyzed.

Finally, from the perspective being suggested here, the model has deep roots in a Euroamerican view of society: the structural-functional notion that individuated, property-owning lineages become part of the larger whole due to the existence of coercive mechanisms bears transparent resemblance to the Enlightenment idea that autonomous, self-interested (property-owning) individuals must be coerced—or convinced, depending on your perspective—into giving up some of their self-interest to join society. I am suggesting not only that structural-functionalism conceived of African groups as Western "individuals," but also that their central problematic—how to tie the individuals together—is one produced by an individualistic society.

There is a certain irony in the idea that descent theory was influenced by individualistic notions, since structural-functionalists saw themselves as very much opposed to such a perspective—opposed, for instance, to Malinowski's utilitarianism (Fortes 1957) and to the idea that there was anything like the Western individual in Africa. Africans had identity, Fortes claimed, only insofar as they were members of groups (1953: 26, 1973: 315). But what structural-functionalists attempted to transcend at one level, I am suggesting, reemerged at another.

Marxism

Marxists, beginning in the 1960s, proffered a different view of African sociality. Meillassoux initially suggested that power relations, rather than concerns with social solidarity, were at the heart of African social practices. Further, he argued that those in power—male elders—acquired and maintained their status by controlling the means of reproduction—subsistence goods and the circulation of women in marriage (Meillassoux 1981: 49; see also Terray 1972; Coquery-Vodrovitch 1972; Dupre and Rey 1973; Rey 1975, 1979). For instance, among the Gouro, the Côte d'Ivoire people studied by Meillassoux, it was the elders who at the end of each agricultural cycle retained the surplus seeds needed for the next round of agricultural production. Thus, to obtain a livelihood, juniors were of necessity bound to the elders (their fathers) and forced to work for them. Junior males also depended upon their fathers in order to marry, for the latter controlled the bridewealth goods (iron bars) needed to obtain a wife. In this analysis, women were little more than pawns of men. The major lines of authority and power in the Gouro system, then, consisted of those between elders and juniors, and between men and women, and these were manifested and reinforced through the control of property (Meillassoux 1964, 1972, 1973, 1981).

Meillassoux's formulation has been criticized and reworked many times (see Terray 1972; Coquery-Vidrovitch 1972; O'Laughlin 1977; Harris and Young 1981; Donham 1985), though its influence has remained unusually strong in the works not just of Africanist anthropologists but also of historians. I focus here on one recent use of Meillassoux's model, Donald Donham's (1990) analysis of the Maale of Ethiopia, since it is, I feel, the most sophisticated attempt to apply and expand upon that model.

Donham suggests that while there are problems with Meillassoux's original formulation—for example, that households, at least in the Maale case, are part of more inclusive structures not analyzed by Meillassoux, and that it is the domain of production rather than that of reproduction that dominates (1990: 83, 94, 102–3)—a revised version of the model is nevertheless useful in analyzing Maale society.

The major lines of authority in Maale are those between king (and chiefs) and commoners, between lineage heads and their dependents, and between male household heads and their wives and children. These hierarchies are defined and articulated by the movement of labor and products up the hierarchy, and the beneficent effects of ritual down the hierarchy. The king, for instance, performs rain rituals for the kingdom as a whole, thus fertilizing the land, and receives sacrificial animals and labor tribute from commoners in return. Lineage heads perform first-fruits ceremonies to the ancestors and have formal ownership of all the property of the lineage (land and cattle) and ultimate say over its disposal. Finally, household heads, through their ritual powers, ensure the fertility of the household and its in-married women and receive sole benefit from any surpluses produced. At the level of the lineage and the household, surpluses are often converted into animals and land, which the heads of these units then use to attract more followers (Donham 1990: 89–123).

For Donham, the central question posed by this system is how such hierarchies are reproduced. How does such a configuration of unequal access to power and property persist? Why do dependents acquiesce in their exclusion from power? Donham provides two answers. First, in a move reminiscent of structural-functionalists like Middleton (1960), he suggests that the compliance of dependents is produced by Maale beliefs about misfortune—since certain types of sickness are said to be caused by mystical retribution for resisting the authority of seniors (for example, by refusing to work the fields of the king, or by failing to provide sacrificial animals to a lineage head), people generally comply with hierarchical norms. Donham's view, then, is that the belief system operates as a social control mechanism that, in the absence of coercive state power as it is known in the West, serves to reinforce the social and political hierarchy (1990: 98–99).[11] *fear, Chomsky's manufacturing consent*

Donham's second, and (for me) more interesting, answer to the question of how Maale power inequalities are perpetuated draws on Marx's analysis of commodity fetishism in capitalist society, though Donham suggests that in Maale it is not the power of things that is fetishized so much as the power of persons. He claims, for instance, that in believing fertility to be produced by ritual, Maale misperceive its true source (their own labors and sexuality), and so give up power and control to those in charge of the rituals. Thus, through a type of false consciousness or mystification, Donham suggests, Maale power inequalities are created and reproduced.

While provocative, such an account of sociality and ritual is nevertheless problematic. The view that one can account for social practices (in this case, fertility rituals) in terms of their role in reproducing power inequalities is similar to structural-functional explanations, with power substituting for cohesion as the explanatory, and functional, ground of social practice and belief. As such, it is plagued with many of the same conceptual problems of that earlier theory: with tautology (the circularity that attends attributing a function to a particular social practice) and indeterminacy (the inability to account for the complexity of meanings surrounding the practice in question). In other words, since correlation does not establish causation, how would one ever know whether fertility rituals served the needs of power any more than of cohesion, and how would one account for the fact that the rituals are so elaborate?

There is also a chicken-and-egg problem with the "rituals produce power" argument: Donham assumes that hierarchy and power in this system result from elders' control of ritual and property rather than the other way around—that is, that their control of these domains and resources emanates from their authority. But why is the latter not the more plausible position? If, as among other African peoples, hierarchy is considered an irreducible first principle of social life, then it need not be seen as built up from, or caused by, the fact that elders control more property. This latter might instead be viewed as a manifestation of their power. Presumably, even without property and ritual, elders would still have power.

An additional problem with functionalist explanations of rituals such as this is that they necessarily displace local understandings: Maale conceptions about the source of fertility (ancestors/spirits) are assumed not to be real (for the Marxist, they represent a form of false consciousness) and are instead said to serve some other interest (in this case, the mystification and reproduction of hierarchy) of which the local people are apparently unaware. Thus, the analyst here claims access to a "real" beyond Maale words that only he is able to grasp.[12]

A more general problem with this type of interpretation is contained within its initial premise: namely, the assumption that the general structure of (Maale) society may be accounted for in terms of property relations—who owns what and who is excluded from that ownership. A different version of the same approach is found in the works of those Africanists (Bloch 1982; Murphy 1980, 1991) who treat ritual and/or knowledge (e.g., secrets) as "property" and suggest that it is the control of these nonmaterial resources that produces hierarchy in the societies they study. In this view, then, individuals are seen to control others as they control resources—both material and nonmaterial. But such a propertied view of persons and society—closely associated with the rise of industrial capitalism in Europe—assumes the existence of autonomous persons (and the particular types of agency such persons are believed to possess) as well as a split in the person/thing relationship (and, thus, the fetishized attitude toward property such a split entails). In short, it assumes an entire Enlightenment-capitalist cosmology.

Again, there is an irony in the fact that Donham's analysis adheres to Western individualistic and property assumptions, for he explicitly recognizes that the conception of the person is different in Maale than in the West:

> No Maale man . . . conceived of himself or was conceived by others as an isolated "individual" set against other individuals. Rather, each man was a constituent member of a lineage descended from an original founder, set within a particular chiefdom, set within the kingdom. And depending on his place within this array, each man exercised only relative control over his "own" property. To those to whom he was indebted for his very physi-

cal existence, to those who begat him—the ancestors along with living members of his lineage closer to the line of eldest sons of eldest sons, and the chiefs and king—a person was bound to defer various kinds of control over property that otherwise he referred to as his own. For it was the fertility and generative power of these others that was responsible, *it seemed,* for the property in the first place. (Donham 1990: 105, emphasis added)

Donham seems here to recognize a less individualistic theory of fertility, power, and property. However, instead of following out the implications of this understanding, he resorts to an analysis in which the power of certain individuals over others is seen as based on their exclusive control of property (and on the fetishistic understanding such a configuration apparently necessitates).[13]

Practice Theory

A more recent version of what I see as a similar set of assumptions is found in the works of practice theorists. Indebted to the writings of Pierre Bourdieu (1977, [1980] 1990; Bourdieu and Wacquant 1992),[14] practice theory has been increasingly influential in the works of Africanists since the late 1980s. While I find this theoretical move generally salutary—especially as it aims to move beyond a static structuralism toward a more historically informed, processualist anthropology that focuses on the pragmatics of everyday practice—it nevertheless relies at its core on a conception of persons and the social that is deeply Eurocentric.

One of the main thrusts of Bourdieu's analysis in *Outline* (1977) is showing how Kabyle individuals strategically manipulate social rules and norms. Others working in the same tradition have attempted to map cultural categories onto individual and group interest: whose interest, such analysts ask—elders', juniors', men's, women's—is being served in any instance of wealth formation, of the operation of taboo, of knowledge that is secret? Moreover, in such cases, "interest" is said to account for the meaning of the categories themselves.

In the view of these theorists, social life is seen as a field of open and indeterminate contests for power, and social practice as the site of interested individual strategies and manipulations. Culture (kinship, ritual, secrecy, etc.) thus becomes a terrain controlled by different individuals and interest groups: some possess more, others less; some are centered and dominant, others are marginalized.[15]

But such a view remains firmly embedded within the Durkheimian duality of "individual" and "society"—here "agent" and "structure." And within this duality we remain wedded, on the one hand, to a reified, nondiscursive, ahistorical view of the subject (as everywhere-and-in-every-society voluntaristic, strategic, and manipulative), and, on the other, to a view of culture-as-commodity (as manipulable, ownable, and owned by individuals).

Further, practice theory's stable of conceptual terms—"strategy," "interest," the "accumulation" of "symbolic capital," and so on—not only is hard to pin down analytically (how, for instance, to decide when and for whom "interest" is operating and when it isn't; how to define it in other societies/places[16]) but also betrays a self-evident economism. As Raymond Williams (1976: 143–44) has suggested, we ought to be suspicious of using a term like "interest" for "attraction" or "involvement" which "has developed from a formal objective term in property and finance . . . and . . . is saturated with the experience of a society based on money relationships." The economism of practice theory's view—as well as its battlefield imagery—certainly captures a sense of a late twentieth-century, late capitalist, cultural terrain, and of a certain cultural politics within that terrain; but does it adequately describe sociality elsewhere/everywhere?

—◀○▶—

To summarize, I am suggesting that a series of Euroamerican conceptions of self and society lie at the heart of these various theories. The person/individual (or the group as individual-writ-large) is variously conceived as autonomous, propertied, self-interested, accumulative, and having independent agency—measured in terms of its power or control over others. This individual's interest is seen as opposed to both the interest of other individuals and that of the larger social whole. With such a conception of the individual in mind, it is little wonder that Euroamerican social theory has been centrally preoccupied with determining how different societies attend to the opposition between such "individuals" and "society." And if different theoretical schools have focused on somewhat different questions—how the solidarity of "individuals" is brought about to produce "society" (structural-functionalism), how "individuals" manipulate "culture"/"society" to achieve their own ends (practice theory, Marxism)—they are nevertheless all variations on a common (functionalist and individualist) theme.[17]

An additional problem with each theory is that it assumes a bounded society—and thus presumes that it can account for social practice by reference to dynamics that are strictly internal to the society at hand. Its theorists assume, for instance, that the nature of kinship, gender relations, ritual, or the domestic economy among the "Tallensi," the "Lugbara," and the "Gouro" are the product of forces that are local—village- and place-bound—rather than of forces that stretch beyond the local to the larger region and the global, to the national and the (post)colonial. Wittingly or not, such theorists have committed themselves to a type of orientalism—to the positing of an "outside" or a beyond, a pristine space unaffected by history and the colonial/postcolonial order of things.

Reinscribing Persons

At the risk of totalizing, I want to review some of the literature on personhood in various African societies, for this literature presents a very different set of understandings from those contained in these Africanist theories. I should emphasize here that I fully believe that both "Africa" and the "West" are not single, that they are as internally diverse as any other place, and that the categories themselves, and the way in which they naturalize an association between term and place, are unstable and shifting. I thus employ these terms provisionally and strategically. These are my "fictions" (Strathern 1988), invoked to critique a certain type of anthropological theorizing about African societies, and to enable a reconceptualization of "society" in terms other than those of relationships among "individuals" and between "individuals" and "groups."

Persons, we are told over and over again,[18] can never be considered apart from their ontologically prior social context—from the community of relationships into which they are born and within which they live (Jackson 1982, 1990: 63; Riesman [1974] 1977, 1986). To abstract out the individual—and his or her "interests" and property—would seem, then, to be an inappropriate starting (or ending) point for theoretical analysis. Further, the divide between individual and society presumed by these theories is not part of the construction of sociality in many African societies. Indeed, Riesman suggests that, for the Jelgobe Fulani of Burkina Faso, the concept of society as an abstract entity—as something other than, and coercive of, the individual—does not exist: Jelgobe have no term for society; the closest, *gondal,* simply means "being together" ([1974] 1977: 162). "Being together" implies, among other things, a radical reliance on others, rather than self-reliance. One way Riesman explicates its meaning for Fulani is by telling how they found certain aspects of his own behavior puzzling. "When people talked about us, I heard, 'But they don't ask us for anything,' as if it were something astonishing" ([1974] 1977: 182). Riesman further elaborates the point by telling about the time he was making a Fulani cloak for himself and ran out of thread. His initial thought was that he would wait until the next market day to purchase more. When he told this to those who were helping him, they suggested instead that he ask one of the women in the community who had extra thread. After some initial hesitation—checked by his own sense of self-reliance—he did ask, and found not only that she gave it to him with pleasure but also that at this moment his relationship to those he lived with changed dramatically.

We are thus dealing here with persons constantly involved in, and defined through, relations. But if one's relations are always with others, or between oneself and others, then so too is one's "interest." It does not reside so neatly within the self as established theoretical models would have it. Further, as Riesman, and many others, have pointed out, it would be a mistake to see such relationality as ultimately motivated by self-interest—as, for instance, rational choice models presume. Not only is such a claim tautological (Cancian 1968), but it also demands seeing the human subject as an entity apart from the relationships of which it is constituted, as somehow having an agency that is outside those relationships. If, however, social relationship is presupposed, if the person is always an aspect of various relationships, we should see this person as composed of, or constituted by, relationships, rather than as situated in them. Persons here do not "have" relations; they "are" relations.[19]

The reality of such a relational self—of a self thoroughly penetrated by the external world—manifests itself in the ontologies, cosmologies, and psychologies of African peoples in myriad ways. For example, in many African societies, a person's bodily state—his or her physical well-being—is seen as influenced by, and therefore as a register of, that person's relationships with others. Sickness, in these societies, is often thought to be produced by a breakdown in social relations, and its cure is effected through a restoration of those relations (Evans-Pritchard 1937; Berglund [1976] 1989; Jackson 1982: 28–29; Riesman 1986: 77). Or, to take another example of this less individualistic conception of self-other boundaries, among the Beng of Côte d'Ivoire spirit retribution for a wrong may be inflicted not on the individual who was directly at fault but instead on another member of his or her matriclan (Gottlieb 1992:

57). And among the Dinka of Sudan, thoughts themselves are seen not as internal representations of external realities but as aspects of those things themselves (Lienhardt 1961: 150). Finally, among the Kuranko of Sierre Leone, what a Westerner would take as attributes of the individual are instead relationally conceived. Thus, a Kuranko individual's "personality" is thought of not as that unique aspect of the self that sets it apart from its social background but rather as the embodiment within an individual of the types of relations he/she has with others. Someone who is generous and mindful of others is a "true person" or has "personhood beyond the telling," while an unsociable person is said to be "not a person" (Jackson 1982:15–16). "Intelligence" for the Kuranko is defined not so much as some abstract quality possessed by individuals as knowledge one has about one's social world (Jackson 1982: 22–23). The list of such examples is potentially endless.

Not only is the self in these societies tied to other human beings; it is also diffusely spread into the nonhuman world of spirits and ancestors. The visible body is often connected to an invisible, and more mobile, "shadow" (Gottlieb 1992: 20) or "double" (Zahan [1970] 1979: 87) that roams away from the body. The self is also tied to ancestors, bush spirits, totemic animals, and the divine creator (Jackson 1982, 1990: 64). All of these other beings influence and have intentionality toward the individual, and vice versa. A person may also use these beings, or their powers and magical properties, to amplify his or her own powers and affect his or her relations with other humans (Jackson 1982: 22).

Jean Comaroff (1980: 644) captures many of these themes in discussing the South African Tshidi Tswana sense of self:

> No interior entity exists which sets apart the experiencing self and exterior impingements upon it. Memories, dreams, and much of thought are rendered as the products of external forces acting upon the person. Tshidi depict the self as enmeshed in a web of influences, a field of relations with other people, spirits, and natural phenomena, none of which are set apart from the self as static and objectified states of being and all of which are linked to the self in terms of continuous strands of influence.

In short, this diffuse, fluid self—a self that is multiple and permeable, and infused with the presence of others, both human and nonhuman—is not captured by much Euroamerican social theory. Only with difficulty, then, can "the individual" serve as the basis for anthropological theories of society—and of gender, power and history—in such places.

Orientalism?

By thus suggesting that Africans are different—are nonindividualistic—
I risk erecting a polarized divide (between the West and Africa), thus
producing once again an orientalist Othering of the term Africa and of
Africans. The standard critique here is that such binary representations
have served as a foundational premise of the West's domination of its
Others and that challenging the imperial order requires overturning such
polarities (Said 1978, 1993; Coronil 1996). Despite the instrumentalist-
functionalist claim inherent in such a view—the suggestion that a complex "culture" (the discipline of anthropology and its theoretical discourse) is little more than a reflex (i.e., serves the interests) of a "political
economy" (global capitalism)—I would not want to deny the importance of that critique. Othering has unquestionably been one of the major ideological bulwarks of Western imperialism, and certain anthropological depictions have just as undeniably fed the imperialist agenda.
And yet, how is one to avoid the—to my mind, even more colonizing—
characterization that everyone everywhere is just like a (European)
bourgeois individual: maximizing, self-interested, property-seeking, and
so on?

My own view is that individualistic theories not only misconstrue others but also misrepresent the West itself. Westerners appear to me far
less individualistic and self-authoring than our ideology and our theories
suggest. I would thus challenge orientalism's polarized and hierarchical
conceptions not by showing how individualistic Others are—one of the
strategies of orientalism's critics—but instead by pointing out how nonindividualistic (non-"Western") Westerners are.

Further, much recent feminist, diaspora, and critical race theory has
alerted us to the fact that while difference can be entrapping, it can also
be empowering (Lorde 1984; Gates 1988; Gilroy 1987, 1993a, 1993b;
hooks 1989; West 1990; Butler 1993; H. Moore 1994; Appiah and Gates
1995; Crenshaw et al. 1995). Thus, appropriating different conceptions
of identity, of social relations, of aesthetics, and so on is seen throughout
this literature as allowing individuals and groups to challenge the hegemonic discourse of bourgeois individualism and explore alternative, and
potentially transformative, visions of social life.[20]

Surely it is possible to proffer a more nuanced—post-orientalist—
view that would not regard all perceived differences as equally othering
and would not see similarities and differences as necessarily mutually

exclusive. Thus, a person's difference from another in one domain need not imply that they cannot be similar in others. There is no inherent reason, for instance, why someone who believes in spirits should not also be able to embrace the spirit of capitalist enterprise; or that diffuse, unbounded selfhood should be incompatible with entrepreneurial behavior (cf. Ewing 1990). Indeed, if current characterizations of post-Fordist capitalism (Harvey 1989; Jameson 1991; Dirlik 1997) are at all accurate, there is reason to believe that those who come from places where the self is less bounded may be better suited to life in a globalizing, postmodern world than those Westerners weighed down by modernist and unitary conceptions of selfhood. Witness, for instance, the apparent ease with which West Africans from remote villages adapt to life in metropolitan centers like New York and Washington (Coombe and Stoller 1994; Zukin 1995; Stoller 1996; Perry 1997).

But I am not arguing here for some autonomous space outside of global capitalism—a pristine society, an "original" culture, unaffected by European colonialism. Rather, I am arguing for an oppositional space—an alternative modernity (Gilroy 1993a, 1993b; Comaroff and Comaroff 1993; Escobar 1995; Appadurai 1997)—within capitalism. Indeed, it is easy to show that whatever Kabre are—including the very name "Kabre"—has been fashioned within, not outside, the encounter between Europe and Africa, as well as within the encounter between Kabre and various non-European others. Thus, as alluded to above, and as I detail below, everything one might consider most un-European and "traditionally African" about Kabre—their prestational economy, their ritual system, their kinship system—is arguably the product of interactions between Kabre and various others (particularly Europeans) over the last 300 years. Recognizing such entanglement should also force us to acknowledge the two-way nature of processes of transculturation (Comaroff and Comaroff 1991, 1997; Thomas 1991; Pratt 1992). Not only has Europe been part of Africa; Africa has been an integral part of Europe over this 400-year period. Not only did African peoples like Kabre supply the plantation labor that helped create Europe's wealth in the Americas; they also contributed cultural practices—music, cuisine, social sensibilities—that became central to the culture of modernity (Philips 1990). By this line of reasoning, modernity's roots lie in Africa as much as in Europe. Acknowledging such mutual influences, however, should not prevent us from appreciating the critical and transformative possibilities such spaces as that of Kabre hold out. To use an example closer to home, while under capitalism labor—the working class—is undeniably the product of capital, this does not mean that it cannot also be a site of opposition—and potential transformation.

Cosmopolitans in the African Savanna

There is one more image of an African society my study seeks to unsettle—that of the small, bounded, static society at some remove from the tumult of global history: a society defined by its very opposition to all we mean by the term "cosmopolitan." In spite of the now orthodox critiques by Wolf (1982), Fabian (1983), and others of earlier anthropologies that subscribed to the notion that non-Western societies were static ("cold" in Lévi-Strauss's ([1962] 1966) terms), this image keeps reappearing in many of the latest metropolitan theorizations both within anthropology and beyond.

Thus, theorists of the postmodern like Harvey (1989) and Baudrillard (1989) repeatedly draw contrasts between the object of their analyses—late capitalist, postmodern society—and other—modern and premodern—social formations. While the postmodern for these theorists is characterized by fluidity, instability, heterogeneity, contradiction, and so on (features they see as reflecting post-Fordist conditions of flexible production/accumulation under late capitalism), the modern/premodern is thought to be all the postmodern is not—more bounded, stable, and homogeneous. Within the latter category, it is often the classic anthropological community—the small village at some remove from the centers of global capitalism—that figures as exemplar.[21]

Perhaps even more surprisingly, the same image of a static, homogeneous Other reappears in the literature of one of the newest, and most exciting, areas to emerge recently within anthropology itself—that of transnationalism. Thus, Appadurai, in his widely cited and otherwise extremely stimulating 1991 essay, "Global Ethnoscapes: Notes and Queries for a Transnational Anthropology," contrasts the "ethnoscape" of today's transnational world—characterized by flux, improvisation, new forms of fantasy, the breaking down of old boundaries—with those ethnographic sites and societies traditionally studied by anthropologists. The latter he describes as "tightly territorialized, spatially bounded, historically unselfconscious, and culturally homogeneous" (Appadurai 1991: 191). There, "social life was largely inertial . . . traditions provided a relatively finite set of 'possible' lives, and fantasy and imagination were residual practices" (Appadurai 1991: 198).[22]

Both attempts to secure legitimation—of the category "postmodern" by theorists like Harvey and Baudrillard, and of the "transnational" by theorists such as Appadurai and Hannerz—rely on a neo-evolutionary master narrative in which the postmodern/transnational sets itself against and displaces that which it is not—the "traditional," the "pre-modern," the "local." Here Theory is reinscribing the oriental as its Other.

I aim here to challenge such characterizations from beginning to end. I know of no bounded, culturally homogeneous African culture. Nor do scholars of Africa suggest that one ever existed (Kopytoff 1987; Wilmsen 1989; Amselle 1990; Vansina 1990; Young 1994; Iliffe 1995). Kabre—a group of cereal farmers living in the heart of the West African savanna at some remove from today's centers of global commodity production, and thus a group bearing all the markings of the most traditional of anthropological communities—is nevertheless, I would argue, as cosmopolitan as the metropole itself, if by cosmopolitanism we mean that people partake in a social life characterized by flux, uncertainty, encounters with difference, and the experience of processes of transculturation (cf. Hannerz 1996: 102–11; Abu-Lughod 1997: 123–27). For one thing, living in a world in which half of life's co-inhabitants are invisible spirits and ancestors who communicate their desires to humans through non-verbal signs that require elaborate systems of interpretation/divination makes for a world of ongoing ambiguity and uncertainty. For another, living in extended, polygynous families in which members are constantly coming and going, in which conflict and divorce are high, and in which the fostering of children is routine means a life of constant human shuffling. Moreover, this is a world in which the very constitution of the self and of communities is based on a never-ending dialectical incorporation of that which is outside (of spirits, other humans, neighboring groups, colonials)—a set of processes that destabilize and decenter as much as they control and contain.

Nor do those Kabre I know see their culture as antithetical to modernity. Indeed, and in spite of appearances, they welcome and appropriate many things Western—tin roofs for their houses, Western clothes and medicine, radios and cars, a moneyed economy, certain forms of Christianity—and relish the spectacle of a (Kabre) president of the country who flies from community to community in his helicopter to attend the wrestling matches of male initiates. Cultural mixing here, as elsewhere in Africa (Amselle 1990; Comaroff and Comaroff 1993; Weiss 1996), is seen not so much as a loss of culture as an addition to it.

Politics and Anthropology

A final note on the politics of Africanist anthropology. As critics have long pointed out (Asad 1973; Hymes [1969] 1974), anthropology has always been, if not the handmaiden of colonialism, at least enabled by colonialism's institutional structures. The example of Germany—whose anthropology died when it lost its African colonies after World War I— illustrates this only too well. Nevertheless, the precise nature of the relationship between anthropology and colonialism has been highly variable, and I do not find plausible the instrumentalist charge that certain schools of anthropology (most notably British structural-functionalism) directly facilitated colonial rule by providing knowledge about African polities, and thus about the management of colonial subjects for colonial administrators (cf. S. Moore 1994). Indeed, Asad himself has recently rejected this view of the relationship between anthropology and colonialism:

> The role of anthropologists in maintaining structures of imperial domination has, despite slogans to the contrary, usually been trivial; the knowledge they produced was often too esoteric for government use, and even where it was usable it was marginal in comparison to the vast body of information routinely accumulated by merchants, missionaries, and administrators. Of course, there were professional anthropologists who were nominated (or who offered their services) as experts on the social life of subjugated peoples. But their expertise was never indispensable to the grand process of imperial power. As for the motives of most anthropologists, these, like the motives of individuals engaged in any collective, institutional enterprise, were too complex, variable, and indeterminate to be identified as simple political instrumentalities. (1991: 315)

Anthropology's complicity with imperial culture, I would argue, lay more in its ties to an epistemology of the Enlightenment, and thus in its colonizing theoretical gaze. As I have attempted to show, Euroamerican anthropological theory has often done little more than project itself onto Africans. Without suggesting that there could ever be an act of unmediated translation of another ethnographic/cultural world, I nevertheless suggest that by critically, self-reflexively tacking back and forth between Euroamerican and African knowledge practices—at once doing an ethnography of Kabre *and* of Europe—we might open a productive space that allows for the interrogation and unsettling of longstanding anthropological assumptions. Part of such a process, I would also suggest, involves writing texts that confront the difficulties of their own making (Clifford 1983, 1988; Clifford and Marcus 1986) and that acknowledge the fraught nature of conducting research in a colonial/postcolonial setting in which metropolitan scholars translate into text the lives of subaltern others.

A Position

I have a personal set of commitments I should make clear at the outset. The years I have spent living among Kabre have unquestionably been among the most challenging and compelling of my life—both intellectually and personally. Not only was I overwhelmed and awed by the complexity of Kabre culture—the endless proliferation of ritual, the intricacies of a gender system that seemed at once more rigid and more fluid (and both more and less hierarchical) than anything I was familiar with, the uneven weave of a society spread across and complexly sutured into a contested national culture, the paradoxical mix of modernity and tradition at the heart of almost everything, conceptions of value and history that confounded any standard anthropological understandings—but I also found the everyday humanity, dignity, eloquence, and humor of those Kabre I came to know—their ways of dealing with one another, and with strangers such as myself—deeply affecting. This is not to say that there were not certain aspects of Kabre culture, and certain individuals, that I found less appealing. Nor is it to suggest that my presence in the community where I lived was straightforward and uncomplicated. In fact, as I describe below, alongside the extraordinary politeness with which I was received, I was also greeted by some with a good deal of suspicion, and the nature of my presence in their midst was under constant negotiation. Nevertheless, while I recognize the danger of writing overly celebratory, romanticized images, and have tried hard to avoid them, my experience was overwhelmingly positive, and this has no doubt informed the view of Kabre culture I present in the pages that follow.

But there are other more pressing, more political concerns that motivate my account as well. At a time in Togolese history when images of the "savage" nature of the peoples from the north circulate promiscuously in the local press—and among diplomats in the embassies—and produce acts of brutality against northerners on the streets of Lomé, silence too easily slips into complicity. If I aim, then, to convince the reader that Kabre are interesting and complex people, cosmopolitans in their own way, "moderns" who have much to contribute to an ever-refracting modernity, I do so out of a sense of urgency born of the current political moment.

Two

HISTORY

From the Black Atlantic to the Banality of Power

Rainmaking

In the middle of July 1996, in the Kabre region of northern Togo where I work, and in the midst of a season otherwise notable for its heavy rainfall, the rain suddenly stopped, and a haze that resembled that of the harmattan season in December (when wind-blown dust from the Sahara fills the skies over West Africa) descended upon the farming communities of this mountainous area. After two rainless weeks, and amid mounting fears that the dry season had returned out of season, a diviner was consulted and revealed that a spirit, upset over the way a funeral had been performed the previous February, had stopped the rain. To calm the spirit and bring back the rain, the diviner instructed, the funeral would have to be repeated, this time as it should have been done previously. Members of the house responsible for the ceremony agreed to redo it, and on the day they finished a week later, the rains returned.

The funeral that raised the ire of the spirit involved a man from the house of rainmakers in Faren, the highest-ranking Kabre community where all rain ceremonies take place. This man had migrated south many years previously to work in the fertile agricultural belt of southern Togo where many Kabre currently live and farm coffee, cotton, and cocoa—cash-crops that do not produce well in the more arid north. When he died, the man's sons did as was expected and returned his body (actually his symbolic body[1]) to his natal homestead in the north, where they performed the funeral ceremonies. However, they refused to carry out the sacrifices on the ancestral stones that would have begun the process of turning their deceased father into an ancestor, claiming that since he had become a Christian, he would not have wanted to mix his new religion with ancestral worship. This refusal, the diviner claimed, aroused the spirit's ire and so caused the rains to cease.

These events speak not only to a society that takes seriously its spirits and its ceremonial procedure—thus raising a set of venerable anthropological questions about modes of rationality/sociality[2]—but also to a society spread across a vast national, and indeed international, landscape whose history is complexly engaged with various modernities and nationalisms. Thus, to understand a case like this requires exploring not only the lineaments of a local cosmology but also the more encompassing contexts of colonial and postcolonial history—the migrations, cash-cropping, commoditization, and Christianity that have been integral to Kabre culture since the early colonial period. Further, it would be a mistake to assume that this drama was merely the concern of a small number of more "traditional" northern Kabre. When, for instance, I was travelling south in a bush taxi shortly after the diviner had been consulted, Kabre soldiers who stopped us at checkpoints along the way asked what the problem was with the rain in the north. And wherever I went in Lomé, the coastal capital, Kabre of every stripe—market women, civil servants, researchers at the university—not only had heard that the rain had stopped but also wanted to know whether, since I had just come from the north, I knew what the diagnosis of the diviner had revealed. Here, then, is a clear example of the cultural mixing I referred to in the last chapter—the inextricable interweave of modernity and tradition in the life of Kabre—for not only do those "fetishists" from the north, as they sometimes defiantly refer to themselves, live in and embrace a world circumscribed by commodities and migrations; city-dwelling Kabre—many educated and Christian—possess a worldview that includes spirits and divination.

The "métisse" (Amselle 1990) nature of this culture cannot be overemphasized: living in their mountains, in a remote area, engaged in subsistence agriculture, still practicing elaborate rituals to the spirits and ancestors, Kabre have all the appearance of a culture untouched by history and the modern world. Indeed, when I first arrived in Togo, I was repeatedly told by others that of all the country's ethnic groups, Kabre seemed the purest and most resistant to change. "They still do all their ceremonies—to a degree I have seen nowhere else," I was told by a French anthropologist with years of experience in West Africa. Another, a missionary who spent fifteen years among Kabre, told me that they were "an ancient people, with very old customs," and speculated that they might be the lost Hamites. (His point was not how un-African they were—the Hamitic hypothesis—but rather how old.) Yet another, an Italian romantic searching for the primitive, a middle-aged man with glazed-over eyes, showed up in the community where I lived one day, led to my house by a child. He announced that a friend in the capital had told him that this was where he could find the "real Africa," and asked whether Kabre still practiced "voodoo." Needless to say, such images of Kabre as pristine primitives could not be farther from the truth. Not only have Kabre been deeply influenced by their engagement with Europe and things European during the colonial and postcolonial periods; the very origin of Kabre culture itself is rooted in the slave wars that ravaged this area during the time of the Atlantic slave trade and, thus, in what Paul Gilroy (1993a) has aptly characterized as one of modernity's defining moments.

This chapter sketches the history of Kabre, and of the larger area—the Volta basin—within which Kabre are located. Understanding this history will provide a context for coming to terms with events like those surrounding the rain's disappearance, and with the sprawling mongrel culture to which such events allude. The history I propose, however, is hardly a neatly linear one. It is composed of fragments—stitched together from myths and oral traditions, colonial documents that are sketchy at best, published accounts, and conversations I have had with Kabre both north and south. It is thus a history told from many angles and with many interests in mind; and, as with all histories, it is far from politically innocent—though whose politics its different tellings serve is not always readily apparent.

Origins

Kabre recite a myth about the time when they first settled in the mountains in northern Togo. According to a man named Sikpetro whom I interviewed about Kabre history in the mountain community of Faren in June 1989,[3] the myth goes as follows: the first Kabre human, Kumberito, descended from the sky to earth, landing in the plain between the two mountain ranges where Kabre currently live. His footprints, Sikpetro claimed, are preserved in a bed of rock at the spot where he landed.[4] (When I asked how long ago Kumberito fell to earth, Sikpetro said simply "in the time of the ancients"—the Kabre expression for the distant past.) After his descent, Kumberito lived in caves and wandered in the plain for several years until frightened by the hooting of an owl-like bird (*mututukuɣu*) at night. The bird's calls suggested that danger was imminent—that enemies were coming to kill him—and he sought refuge in the mountains. Feeling safe, he decided to settle down in the present-day community of Faren, where he gave birth to many children. ("Did he have a wife?" I asked. "Oh yes," Sikpetro improvised. "Who came down from the sky with him?" "Yes." However, she is nameless and is never mentioned as part of the narrative.) Some of Kumberito's children stayed in Faren while others set off to found other communities. Thus, one of his children, an older son, moved across the ridge to Boua, and another, a younger son, settled in Kuwdé just up the ridge from Boua. A subsequent generation of Kumberito's "children" founded Wazilao and Somdé, two communities in the center of the massif, and, in time, one of Wazilao's founder's sons settled in Asiri, a community on the massif's northern edge. Later, descendants of Kumberito moved across the plain to the southern massif, where they founded those communities—Kouméa, Tcharé, Piya (the president's natal community), and others—inhabited by present-day Kabiyé.[5]

◄o►

As first pointed out to me by Ebia Bassari, a Kabre linguist/anthropologist who has spent much of his life working at a research institute (INRS) in Lomé, the myth's evocation of a time of flight from enemies is almost certainly referring to the period during the seventeenth and eighteenth centuries when societies throughout this coastal hinterland were heavily raided for slaves sent into the Atlantic trade and many, like Kabre, sought refuge in mountain areas. This was a defining moment in the larger history of the Volta basin—a time when the political and cultural landscape of the area was dramatically transformed.

Located 400 km from the coast, the savanna region where Kabre live—a vast plain blanketed with tall grasses and cereals, and filled with sprawling farming settlements—was part of the hinterland for, and on the cusp between, two of the great slaving complexes in West Africa—Ashanti and Dahomey. By the mid-eighteenth century, those kingdoms looked to this hinterland zone for the majority of their slaves. Indeed, it was from this area that many—perhaps as many as one million—of the slaves came in the period from 1700 to 1850 when the Atlantic trade was at its height. While the coastal kingdoms were the main protagonists in the trade, and while most of the slaves taken in this area eventually made their way to these coastal entrepots, those kingdoms themselves did little raiding in the hinterland, leaving that to various societies of the inte-

The plain where Kumberito landed; in the distance, the southern massif, President Eyadéma's home; Kuwdé, July 1985

rior—Mamprusi, Dagbamba, Mossi, Bariba. These predatory savanna states—possessors of what Jack Goody (1971, 1978) has called the "means of destruction" (guns and horses)—raided not only one another but also, and especially, the area's less centralized polities—who, in turn, often sought refuge in mountainous (or riverine) areas.

Kabre, one of these less centralized groups, still today have vivid memories of this time of raiding. Elders can recall stories told by their parents and grandparents of raids by a group of fierce, mystically powerful warriors from northern Benin called Samasi (Bariba). Armed with guns (obtained from Europeans at the coast for slaves) and on horseback, they rode into the mountains, sacking homesteads and snatching people. However, while initially successful, Samasi were eventually turned back by Kabre—not only because the mountains were difficult of access but also because Kabre possessed greater mystical power (*hama*). (Other acephalous societies from this region widely known to anthropologists—Tallensi, Dogon, LoDagaa, Konkomba—were also targets of raiding by the more centralized polities and similarly fled to more easily defensible locales like the massifs and outcroppings where Dogon and Tallensi live today, or along the banks of rivers where the Konkomba and LoDagaa are located [Goody 1978].)

While predatory raiding was the dominant form of slave acquisition,

Kabre within the larger region

it was by no means the only one. Some societies instead paid slave tribute—anywhere from dozens to hundreds of persons a year—to the centralized polities. Agreeing to tributary relations of this sort may have had
the advantage not only of allowing those societies to avoid the killing
that attended raiding, but also of giving them greater control over who
was enslaved. Slaves were also sold on the open market by various
peoples—by noncentralized groups like the Kabre, as well as by kingdoms seeking to dispose of their captives. People today still recall the
large marketplaces in the savanna where slaves were purchased by private merchants, who conveyed them to the coastal kingdoms of Dahomey and Ashanti. Such sale, like slave tribute, may have been a strategy
to keep raiders at bay and to ensure greater local control (see Piot 1996).

Needless to say, these slaving practices produced massive dislocations
and movements of people into and out of various polities in the area and
beyond—the flight of many into refuge areas; the incorporation of others into expanding states; and, of course, the dispatching of hundreds of
thousands south into the Atlantic system. As a result of these movements, by the end of the slave era (c. 1850), the Voltaic area was characterized by a distinctive political geography—it possessed two discrete

types of polities inhabiting markedly different locales. On the one hand, centralized polities (those who had profited from raiding) were found in low-lying plains areas; on the other, noncentralized polities (those who had fled from raiding) were located in mountainous (and riverine) areas (Goody 1978). Despite having been subjected to repeated raids, the latter were inordinately densely populated (and indeed, more so than anywhere else in West Africa with the exception of some of the Nigerian city-states). This bipolar contrast was strikingly apparent to the first Europeans into the area at the end of the nineteenth century. They remarked again and again that they there found two types of peoples—those with "organized government," who were easier for them to deal with; and "barbarous tribes," who resisted their incursions and threatened them with attack (Ferguson 1895, cited in Goody 1978: 538–39).

This, then, was the cultural landscape studied and written about by British anthropologists of the colonial era—Rattray, Fortes, Tait, Goody. The famous distinction between acephalous and centralized societies that became the cornerstone of Africanist anthropology at mid-century (Fortes and Evans-Pritchard 1940)—an anthropology that assumed that social forms could be analyzed as if they were pure Durkheimian types, untouched by history—was, in this area at least, the product of a quite distinctive history. If anything, these two types of polities suggest a morphological contrast between societies on two sides of the slave divide—those who were raided and those who did the raiding.

◄○►

Little is known about Kabre before this time period, the time of the mythical Kumberito. Were Kabre truly autochthonous, as the origin myth claims? Or, if not truly autochthonous, had they already inhabited the massifs they live in today for many centuries, even millenia? Or conversely, were they recent migrants into the area? There is some evidence that the latter was the case—that is, that it was during the period of slaving itself that Kabre first came to their mountains. A Kabre researcher told me recently that in 1975 he went to the town of Kete Krachi in Ghana to investigate a seemingly far-fetched suggestion in the writings of the renowned turn-of-the-century German explorer/ethnographer Leo Frobenius, that the language spoken there was related to Kabre. This researcher was astonished to find not only that the language was indeed lexically and morphologically cognate to Kabre but also that it was largely intelligible to him when spoken. Further, he was told by an old man that oral traditions there suggested that Kabre had left Kete Krachi for northern Togo during the Ashanti slaving wars (of the seventeenth and eighteenth centuries). However—in an episode that gives a glimpse into the nature of ethnic politics and of the politics of representation in a postcolony like Togo—on returning to Lomé, and as he was preparing to publish his findings, this researcher was discouraged from doing so by a more senior Kabre scholar. The president, he was told, would not look favorably on such a finding, for it was not in his interest to promote the idea that Kabre might not be indigenous to Togo.[6] If he persisted, this senior scholar told him, he would likely lose his state-funded research position. Needless to say, he chose not to publish.

As he was telling me this, I recalled a time in the mid-1980s when I went with an American archeologist who had worked in northern Togo to visit a Kabre scholar at the Université du Benin who also happened to be the head of the president's cabinet. As serendipity would have it, this archeologist had been a Peace Corps volunteer in Togo many years earlier and had taught this now prominent Togolese scholar/cabinet head when he was in high school. We were intending to apply for research support, we told him, for a project that would combine archeological and oral historical research about an area of northern Togo that included Kabre, and we wanted to know whether the Togolese government would support such a project—not only granting research permission but also perhaps providing us with a vehicle. This cabinet head told us that he was certain the government would look quite favorably on such a project, since both he and the president were convinced that Kabre were the oldest inhabitants of Togo—and that our study would prove as much!

As I walked away from this meeting I was—to say the least—unsettled by the clear coerciveness of the situation; even today I find myself unable to fully sort out my feelings about the government's interest in our project. I certainly had no intention of allowing my research to be affected by the state's political interests—of becoming a type of government anthropologist. But, then again, who was I—an outsider with little at stake in the very real political futures being contested in Togo—to decide what research I would conduct and what history I would tell? Indeed, if there is no neutral history—if histories are always contingent and multiple, and if their telling is always tied up with a politics of the present—why should I be so put off by the government's interest here? It was not as if mine could be the only "real" history. Moreover, it has been precisely over questions of origins that intense struggles by indigenous peoples with real political stakes have taken place, struggles that have sometimes—one thinks of many recent Native American cases—brought them into conflict with anthropologists. But this particular Togolese example complicates the usual dichotomy between dominant (powerful, majority, colonizing) and marginalized (powerless, minority, colonized) groups that often operates in such cases (as, for example, when Native Americans have contested those histories written about them by scholars). Here Kabre are the group in power, and the history the president hoped we would write would have supported that power. It is also clear from my researcher friend's experience that there is no single Kabre viewpoint—that different Kabre may be at cross purposes. Indeed, his willingness to tell, and have me write, his story now and not earlier reflects recent shifts in Togolese politics—a Kabre president who is still in power but who has lost many followers because he hasn't delivered on his promises, a 1990s political culture that is more open and "democratized," and so on. So, in the face of these contradictory pressures, what does one do? I have no easy answers. And in this case, conveniently perhaps, my archeologist friend and I lost touch with one another when he took a teaching job in Gabon, and the project never materialized.

Renaissance

For the societies of the Volta basin, the period between 1850 and 1900—that is, between the effective end of the slave trade and the onset of colonialism—was almost certainly one of cultural efflorescence. Able to channel their energies in more peaceful directions, Voltaic societies evolved highly complex productive and social systems. This was especially true for the acephalous groups living in mountainous areas such as Tallensi and Kabre. There, the constraints of locale—people piled on top of one another amidst challenging terrain—produced pressures that led to novel adaptations. Thus, many of these societies developed "intensive" agricultural systems (Netting 1968, 1974)—permanent cropping regimes on terraced, manured, continually weeded fields—on a scale that was virtually unprecedented for sub-Saharan Africa. When, for instance, Frobenius passed through Kabre in 1909 on one of his many transcontinental treks, he marveled at "the most remarkable type of agricultural system known in Africa" ([1913] 1961: 101). "No other people in Africa," he continued, "work their fields as intensively as Kabre"; here was a "black people of Africa ... who have attained the heights of science" ([1913] 1961: 139, 140).[7] Indeed, such praise of Kabre agriculture, and of their "work ethic," would become a constant refrain in subsequent writings on Kabre by colonial administrators and researchers—and, in a cruel irony, would later lead to their being nominated to become the colony's main labor force.

The Kabre system of intensive cultivation Frobenius and subsequent writers (Sauvaget 1981) have described is still the agricultural mainstay in the village of Kuwdé where I lived.[8] Though it was never central to my own research, I too have been continually fascinated by this system, and spent many hours interviewing Kabre about their cultivation techniques and the complex labor arrangements that accompany them. Whenever I return to Kuwdé, I enjoy spending an entire morning touring the fields of a friend and assistant of mine, Atakpai Nnamnawé. Beginning in his velvety sorghum fields high on the mountain, we descend through well-groomed plots of millet and corn intercropped with the small ("female") variety of yam, before ending up in the lush soggy "bas-fond" at the base of the escarpment where the large ("male") yams grow in rows of cone-shaped buttes, mixed with cassava, rice, and okra. To repeat: what irony that a regime and achievement such as this was produced by the ravages and pressures of slaving—and that it led to Kabre being further "enslaved" as workers during the colonial era.

Fed by the productive vigor of the post-slave era, the Volta basin's markets expanded as well. Thus, the periodic markets for which this area of West Africa is well known (Bohannan and Dalton 1962) multiplied and became interconnected in new ways—producing ties that not only cross-cut the societies of the area but also fed into the trans-Saharan trade. This expanded marketing system owed no small debt to the commercial networks established by the earlier traffic in slaves and to the existence of a currency—cowrie shells—that flooded the area during the slave trade era (Hogendorn and Johnson 1986: 104–9; Manning 1990: 99–102). (Cowries were used as ballast for slave ships sailing to West Africa, before being exchanged at the coast for slaves. They then made their way into the interior, again in exchange for slaves. It is reported by Frobenius ([1913] 1961: 154), for instance, that Kabre received 150,000 to 200,000 cowries per slave.)

If the cramped conditions imposed upon Voltaic peoples during the era of slaving produced agricultural and commercial innovation, the same conditions produced enormous creativity in the social arena as well—generating, for instance, the extraordinarily complex kinship and cosmological systems famously described in the works of Fortes, Goody, and Griaule. The incessant elaboration of ties of descent and affinity for which Voltaic societies became known to anthropologists was no doubt in part a consequence of having to come to terms with the dense flows of people into and out of these polities and the complex accommodations to land and resources such flows necessitated (Hart 1978: 187–88).

Another Origin Story

For Kabre of the northern massif, the colonial era opened (c. 1898) with an event that has left a lasting impression. One day a German horseback battalion appeared in the plain. Its mission was apparently simple reconnaissance—making contact with Kabre for the first time, and informing them that they were now under German rule.[9] The German battalion rode up into the mountains and camped in Kuwdé. There, one of the officers went looking for food for his horse and helped himself to some sorghum in a field. Or, as others tell it, he entered and stole grain from a granary. Upon hearing this, the field's/granary's owner, a man named Mahate, took an arrow and his bow, sought out the German soldier, and shot him through the heart.[10]

The Germans immediately fled and the people of Kuwdé dealt with the body as they had always dealt with outsiders they killed—they buried it in a sacred forest. Shortly thereafter, however, the Germans returned with reinforcements—according to the French historian Cornevin (1961: 96), there were three separate German battalions crisscrossing Kabre territory at this time—and, in apparent retaliation for the killing, began torching homesteads and shooting people with their guns. Overcome with fear, the people of Kuwdé fled to the other side of the mountains. After several weeks, however, recognizing that they could not match the power of the gun, they decided to return to Kuwdé and submit to German rule, willing to cede their autonomy in return for being allowed to regain their homes and fields. (This moment is referred to in the colonial documents as "pacification"—needless to say, an obscene choice of term in this context.)

Interestingly, when I was discussing this history with people from Kuwdé, it often blended into that of Samasi (the slave-raiders from northern Benin). Indeed, certain people I spoke with said it was a Samara, not a German, who was buried in the sacred forest. Initially puzzled by the inconsistencies in the accounts I was getting, I came to realize that such elisions/conflations in the historical memory of Kabre made perfect sense. Not only are there striking factual similarities between the two cases—both witnessed the arrival of powerful outsiders who possessed guns and horses; both invaders were light-skinned (Samasi, I was told, have "red" skin almost as light as mine)—but also it is not difficult to imagine why Kabre might conceptually equate the predations of the slave trade with colonization, and thus one predator with another. One might also add here that both moments were watershed periods in Kabre history, associated not only with extreme violence but also with a dramatic reworking, even revitalization, of Kabre culture.

A humorous sequel to this story reveals the types of contestations that fill Kabre quotidian life as well as the way in which the global seeps into the local. Sometime in the 1970s, several Kuwdé "lycée" students, doubting the veracity of the elders' burial account, stole off to the sacred forest in the middle of the night and began digging—to see if they could find the bones of the mythical invader killed by Mahate. In the very location where the elders said the body had been buried, they were astonished to find a set of teeth and some pulverized bones. After some debate, they decided that they were indeed the teeth of a human, though they could not tell whether they belonged to a European or not. When word got out about what they had done, the elders became upset for fear that digging in the sacred forest would anger the spirit who resides there, and they convoked the transgressors to the chief's. There the youths were chastised, fined, and made to rebury the bones (which they did—apparently without ill effect). Upon discussing this droll set of events in 1996 with some of the youths involved, I jokingly suggested that were I to take the teeth home with me, I could have them analyzed by a colleague, a physical anthropologist, to determine whether they were the teeth of a European or a Samara. Taking my suggestion more seriously than I had intended, however, and no doubt imagining a new riposte, they asked the elders whether I might be allowed to do so. Not surprisingly, the elders refused. And, in a fitting denouement, when on my return to the States I asked my colleague whether he would have been able to settle the issue, he said that dentition is an area where differences between Europeans and Africans do not show up—thus, science could not in this case help decide the veracity of the elders' story. Nor—my point throughout—can it save us from the contingencies of history.

◄O►

In February 1909, Frobenius passed through northern Togoland and spent two weeks among Kabre. He recorded his impressions in a fascinating document (published in 1913 in his *Und Afrika Sprach*), which is interesting not only for its remarkably detailed, and in many cases accurate, descriptions of Kabre but also for what it reveals about the way Europeans of the colonial era viewed African cultures.

Frobenius's account is framed by what now read as a series of quaint typifications of customs and rituals. Much of the text involves a meticulous documentation of ceremonies—age-grade, marriage, funeral—and religious beliefs. There is little trace here of the tumultuous history Kabre had undergone, of their dynamism since 1850, of their brutal pacification at the hands of the Germans, of the way in which by 1909 they were already enmeshed in the colonial order. As such, Frobenius's "ethnography" removes Kabre to a timeless past, configuring their culture as a textual museum in which customs are neatly boxed, catalogued, and displayed.

In addition to expressing the othering gaze of the orientalist (*we* have history, *they* have quaint customs), Frobenius's document clearly served more immediate colonial interests as well. As the first post-pacification document to offer a detailed description of this people of northern Togo, it provided a type of up-close witnessing—indeed, of surveillance—for colonial administrators anxious about the management of their subjects. Those at the coast who ran the colony possessed virtually no knowledge about those in the interior—those northern peoples whom they had defeated through a series of armed interventions between 1898 and 1902. Were such people orderly or anarchic? Who were their leaders? Were they armed? Rebellious? Would they be hostile to the Germans? And so on. In thus naming, describing, cataloguing, and inventorying all that it could, Frobenius's text rendered Kabre knowable and nonmysterious. Its minute descriptions of Kabre material culture—of the crops Kabre grew, as well as those sold in the markets (and the price, in cowries, they would fetch), of the many different pots used by women in cooking and the various hoes used by men in cultivating, of the numerous implements (necklaces, bracelets, anklets, rattles, gongs, flutes, and so on) used by initiates during their ceremonies—all help to create a normalizing/familiarizing effect.[11] So, too—and reassuringly so—does its detailed inventory of Kabre weaponry. Here, in one of his few references to history, Frobenius tells the reader, deploying a striking colonialist euphemism, that many of the iron weapons Kabre possessed were lost during the "fight for independence" and then, after their defeat by the Germans, "remade into hoes," a swords-into-ploughshares motif, and "are no longer made today."

Finally, as mentioned above, there was another instrumentality at work in this text. Through its praise of the Kabre work ethic—of Kabre farmers as industrious, enterprising, and hard-working, but also, crucially, as a people living in an area that was overpopulated—the text generated images of Kabre that directly led to their subjugation as laborers in the colonial workforce. It was Kabre who built most of Togo's roads and railroads—and it is their industriousness and high population density that are repeatedly cited in colonial-era documents as justification for coercing them into this calling. Frobenius was quite direct in expressing his thoughts on this subject in the preface to *Und Afrika Sprach:* "The working capacity of the socalled "negro" population of tropical Africa represents the highest asset possessed by these lands . . . [and] cannot be emphasized too strongly" (Frobenius 1913: vi).

If this was ethnography, it was clearly ethnography in the service of empire.

The Making of a Diaspora

The colonial era for Kabre, as for many West African peoples, was one of continual movement and circulation beyond their borders. Early on (c. 1910), when the Germans discovered that cash crops would not produce well in the arid north, they sought to turn the northern territories into a labor reserve. They began recruiting groups like Kabre as workers—both to build the colony's roads and railroads in the south and to work in mines and plantations. (Taxation, as throughout much of colonial Africa, was the method used to coerce people to seek work beyond their borders—for taxes had to be paid in colonial currency, which could only be secured at these sites of colonial production.)

In the 1910s, Kabre men began migrating on foot to southern Ghana (500 km away) to work in the mines and cocoa plantations. (Vestiges of this experience remain embedded in the Kabre language—in loan words that derive from English rather than German or French, and thus inscribe the traces of migratory movements that made problematic the imposition of colonial boundaries and frustrated colonial-era attempts to fix groups in manageable, bordered spaces.[12]) During the same time period, Kabre were transported to southern Togo—ten to twenty men from each village for two-week stretches of time—to build the Lomé-Blitta railroad and to begin work on the colony's road system (Verdier 1982: 145).

As Meillassoux (1981) has pointed out for other areas of West Africa, it was also colonial policy in Togo to leave the home communities of migrating workers largely intact, so that those communities, and not the colonial government, would bear the costs of social reproduction. The Germans (and later the French) evolved a system that required Kabre to leave their communities for short periods of time only (a few months at most, more typically several weeks) before returning home—to produce food, bear children, care for the elderly, and bury their dead. In this policy of noninterference, then—a policy whose sole aim was the cheap reproduction of labor—lay the roots of the Kabre's moniker as the most "traditional" of peoples. This "tradition" has long served the interests of a southern colonial-capitalist sector, and indeed owes its existence in large part to its intimate and ongoing connection to that sector.

As elsewhere in colonial Africa, the work-and-tax scheme of the early colonial period worked through indirect rule. The first Kabre chiefs were appointed by the Germans in the 1910s to recruit labor and collect taxes, and were in turn rewarded with tremendous wealth and power. They were also in many cases inordinately cruel, and, I was told, when colonialism ended, the homesteads of many of these colonial-era chiefs were destroyed by their people. "Our own chiefs were far worse than the Germans and French," I heard people say again and again.

By the 1920s, and as reprisal for losing World War I, Germany had been forced to cede "Togoland" to France and Britain, who divided it in half. The British half was incorporated into the Gold Coast, while the French half became independent (and was renamed "Togo"). Under the French, Kabre (who are conveniently described in documents of the time period as "over-populated"—Verdier 1982: 146,156) were once again recruited to the colonial project of road and railroad building. And, in a move that would dramatically affect their culture for the long term, some Kabre were forcibly relocated to a large uninhabited area of southern Togo—uninhabited because it had been a buffer zone during the slave wars between the coastal kingdoms and the peoples of the savanna. Once resident in this virgin territory, however, Kabre rapidly discovered that the soils there were more fertile and easier to work than were the rocky soils of the mountains in the north. They also found that they were able to produce cash crops (coffee, cotton, and cocoa) at considerable profit to themselves (Lucien-Brun 1974; Pillet-Schwartz 1984).[13] By the mid-1930s Kabre began migrating into this zone on their own, opening up scores of new communities—seventy by the mid-1950s (Verdier 1982: 146)—along a 200-km stretch of the national highway between Sokodé and Atakpamé. This migration continues to the present day, with more than 200,000 Kabre currently living and farming in this region, as compared to 120,000 in the north (Pillet-Schwartz 1984; Marguerat 1994: 65–88).

In spite of this northern exodus, and the long-term residence of many Kabre in the south, however, southern Kabre remain intimately tied to the homeland in the north. They return frequently—a steady stream of people filling the trucks and taxis that ply the national highway between north and south—not only to visit family and friends but also to initiate their children, to sacrifice to spirits and ancestors, and to attend funerals. When I returned to Kuwdé in 1996, I was struck once again by the steady flow of southerners into this northern community—even during the wet season when north-south traffic is at its lightest. Thus, the day after I arrived in early July, a group of southerners arrived for a funeral ceremony for a house member (and—a seemingly ubiquitous feature of these reunions—promptly got into a row for not inviting the right people to drink the beer they had purchased). The following day, a second party arrived from the south for another funeral. Others—seeking cures for various ailments—came to consult with diviners. And so on. Further, it is obligatory that all Kabre—even second- and third-generation southerners—return to the north at death, to be buried there and join the ranks of the ancestors. Members of Kuwdé, of course, frequently travel south as well—typically for short periods during the dry season months of December through March to visit family and make money, although a mass exodus occurs every July as well when school children, out for the summer holidays, head south to work for family members and make money to buy books and clothes for school.

Kabre culture is thus constituted as much as anything else by the constant shuffle of people and commodities between its two zones. These zones define complementary and interdependent spaces—the one a homeland associated with ritual, the other a frontier associated with money-making—and create a set of dynamics and sensibilities—comings and goings, pushes and pulls, longings, imaginings, ambivalences, and contestations—that today lie at the heart of whatever it means to be Kabre. This is a "traveling culture" in Clifford's (1997) sense of that term, in which identities are enacted at the interstices, and amidst the jostle, of these contradictory forces.

This imbrication of the colonial into the Kabre—of the colonial policy of resettlement into a defining feature of Kabre culture—illustrates the limitations of a colonial-era anthropology that ignored the effect of the colonial on Voltaic cultures (and indeed of the way in which the "traditional" cultures analyzed by anthropologists were themselves in part fabricated by the colonial system). Thus, Fortes's (1945, 1949) classic and otherwise masterful analysis of the Tallensi lineage and kinship system (c. 1930) presumed a bounded community where none existed—Tallensi were called to work in the south every bit as much as Kabre—and never took full account of the colonial presence. Fortes was, after all, interested strictly in the analysis of primordial social forms, uncontaminated by outside influence. But Europe had long been present in this area and had affected Tallensi as deeply as it had Kabre.

—◄o►—

There is a deep ambivalence in Kabre talk about the colonial era. On the one hand, they speak with intense anger of brutal beatings at the hands of the Germans and French, and of their lost autonomy. On the other, they see colonialism as having brought beneficial things that they would otherwise not have today. They value the roads, hospitals, and schools built during the colonial era, as well as the opportunity to migrate to the fertile lands of the south. Predisposed by my own leftist leanings to see colonialism as everywhere and always evil, but also informed by the knowledge that those Kabre I know are fiercely proud and independent (not only clinging tenaciously to certain traditions but also scorning state intervention into their lives), I have been puzzled by this attitude toward colonialism. Indeed, I have repeatedly tried pushing people in Kuwdé on this point when discussing the colonial era with them. "Okay, perhaps the fact that colonialism brought you roads is good because now you can travel to the south to make money," I concede, "but what about the fact that it was through uncompensated labor that you built those roads?" "It is true we were not paid to build them," would invariably come the reply, "but that is not so different from the arrangement we have with today's chiefs. You work for them in their fields from time to time because they spend their time judging disputes and dealing with the government. We built roads for the Germans and French and then were able to use those roads to migrate south and make money. But building the roads was even better than working for a chief because now the French are gone but the roads are still here!"

I remain unsettled by such responses, however, and have had to content myself with the knowledge that colonialism in northern Togo was apparently more benign than elsewhere. It was a remote area—two days on horseback from the nearest government outpost—with few resources to offer the colonial government. Thus, other than to recruit labor and collect taxes (both of which were in the hands of local chiefs anyway), the colonials were content to allow people to get on by themselves. When I shared my unease with Bassari, he repeated what others had told me and gave a pragmatic spin to their attitude: "We have things now that we didn't have before—roads, fertile lands in the south, hospitals," he said, "and we see this period in our history mainly in terms of its usefulness to us today." But, he added, that is only part of the story—his father and grandfather spoke with intense anger about the brutality of road-building during the early colonial period, and people today have simply forgotten.

The Banality of Power

> It is not surprising to learn that almost every foreign observer confesses to finding Togolese politics to be—if I may borrow a useful image—a wilderness of mirrors. Nothing is sure; nothing can be known precisely. Manipulation and deception are constantly suspected, and the role of what in the West might be called the supernatural is taken to be of prime importance. A powerful person is one who gives the impression of being in control of this complex array of forces visible and invisible. (Ellis 1993: 471)

In the 1960s, an unexpected event changed the history of Kabre—and of Togo—forever. A young Kabre soldier named Gnassingbé Eyadéma, who had fought for the French in Indochina and Algeria, returned to Togo at independence (in 1960) and sought entry into the newly formed national army. His request was denied, however—the government was run by southerners who, like their colonial predecessors, saw those from the north as inferior ("savage"—Yagla 1978: 107–12), and therefore denied them access to the government and military. Three years later, Eyadéma led a coup by a group of similarly disgruntled northerners.[14] These northerners replaced Olympio[15] (the first president) with Nicolas Grunitzky, who hailed from Togo's central region and whom they expected to be more sympathetic to their concerns—and, indeed, he turned the army over to them. However, four years later, still not satisfied, they led a second coup and placed Eyadéma in power, where he remains to the present day.

Eyadéma quickly concentrated power in the hands of a small circle of (largely) northern compatriots, and ensured that it would remain that way by stocking the army with northerners (Yagla 1978; Toulabour 1986). (Today 80 percent of the army is from the north, the majority Kabre.) Military control and dictatorial authority—a style of government that was largely, of course, an imitation of the brutal absolutist rule of the colonial era—was accompanied here as elsewhere, as Mbembe (1992) has so brilliantly described, by spectacle. Outrageously expensive government buildings and hotels were constructed less for their utility (the towering five-star Hotel 2 Février was almost always empty) than simply for ostentatious display. State rituals abounded. One of the more bizarre, called "animation," was enacted any time a high-ranking official or visiting dignitary appeared in public: the official/dignitary would be greeted by people, often school children, who lined the streets in bright matching outfits, dancing and singing the praises of Eyadéma and the government. And Eyadéma himself, as if pushing the logic of the spectacle a step farther, became a spectral fetishized presence, seeming at once to be both everywhere and nowhere. Images of him abounded—a smiling portrait in suit and tie on the wall of every public office and store, a daily picture on the front page of the government newspaper—and yet he was inaccessible to all except his closest advisors, and was rarely seen in public. I recall walking on a dusty Lomé street one noon in the mid-1980s when pedestrians were suddenly whisked to the side of the road by a policeman. Within seconds, a motorcycle with a screeching siren came roaring past at high speed, followed by the president's Mercedes. He was there and gone before anyone knew what had happened—leaving behind only a blurred trace: the scream of the motorcycle, the sleek quiet of the Mercedes, the cloud of dust that filled the air for a few moments before it, too, dissipated and disappeared. This spectral ritual is repeated every day at noon, always on a different street—as Eyadéma goes from the presidential palace to the military camp for lunch.

If manipulating images was a crucial element of Eyadéma's power, another—this one emanating as much from his subjects as from himself—entailed the creation of a spectacular presidential biography (cf. Toulabour 1986). Thus, after Eyadéma walked away from a plane crash in the north in the mid-1970s, stories of his invincibility and magical powers abounded, and the event was immortalized and inscribed into the Togolese cultural landscape: Sarakawa, the site where the plane went down, became both a national shrine/pilgrimage site and the name of a day of the week (in the north). When, a few years later, an assassin entered the presidential palace and shot at Eyadéma from close range, again miraculously, he walked away unscathed when the bullet lodged in a small notebook in his chest pocket. Then, in a classic power-enhancing move, one elaborated upon every time I have heard the story repeated, Eyadéma let the assassin out of prison on the first anniversary of the assassination attempt and invited him to dinner at the presidential palace.[16]

The spectacularization of power, however, could not mask the reality of a badly failing economy, and by the late 1980s, as the price of phosphates (Togo's main income-generating commodity) continued to fall on the world market, and unemployment steadily increased, there were serious signs of discontent. It was only a matter of time before ethnic politics reemerged. The major ethnic divide in Togo has always been that bequeathed to Togolese by the Germans and French—between the groups in the north and those in the south (Yagla 1978: 107–12; Toulabour 1986: 33–34). Eyadéma exacerbated the divide not only by appointing northerners to many key positions in the government but also by pouring as many of the country's meager resources as he could into the north (a move seen by northerners, however, as an attempt to right the wrongs of the colonial period during which the south, and the Ewe in particular, had benefited disproportionately from French rule). Government funds, for instance, built an international airport in Niamtougou, provided purified water and electricity to towns throughout the north, paved the national highway to the northern border with Burkina Faso, invested heavily in and built up the town of Lama-Kara in the president's home region, and, needless to say, financed private perks such as the mansion Eyadéma built for himself in his home village—a palatial residence that towers incongruously over the mud huts that surround it. All the while, the south went largely neglected, its rutted roads and run-down buildings symbolizing its plight.

When the wave of democratization swept the African continent in the early 1990s, southerners seized the moment. In fall 1990, Ewe students at the Université du Benin held a series of demonstrations against the government, demanding elections. The government refused and there followed several violent confrontations with the police. Key leaders of the student group disappeared, and when twenty-eight bodies were found in the lagoon in April 1991, Lomé erupted in violence. Vigilante groups took to the streets, vandalizing shops, decapitating government statues, and attacking northerners. (I heard horror stories about this time period from Kabre friends living in Lomé—of public humiliation, of homes sacked, of cars burned.) As many as half a million inhabitants of Lomé fled into neighboring Ghana and Benin. Amidst the bedlam, there were calls for a national conference to discuss the question of elections, and, reluctantly, Eyadéma agreed. After a tense, acrimonious round of meetings with the by-now large opposition (the students had been joined by prominent Ewe lawyers and doctors, and by returned dissidents—including Olympio's son, Gilchrist, who had been in exile in Ghana), Eyadéma agreed to hold elections in summer 1993. (It is interesting to note, in light of the Kabre origin myth mentioned above, that during this time period exiled dissidents were said—no doubt by Kabre—to have crossed the border into Togo as owls!—Ellis 1993: 470.)

It was widely assumed that Eyadéma's reign had finally come to an end, but, again miraculously, he rose from the dead. After a series of delays, the withdrawal of the main opposition candidate (who later became Eyadéma's prime minister), a boycott by the major opposition parties (who claimed that the election was fixed), the protest and early departure of an international team headed by Jimmy Carter that had been sent to monitor the election—after all this, the election was held and Eyadéma took 96 percent of the vote. In a provocative article, Stephen Ellis (1993), a political scientist who was in Togo at the time of the national conference, suggests that while intimidation and brutality have been important dimensions of Eyadéma's power throughout his presidency, he was nevertheless able to regain a surprisingly large following between the time of the conference and the election through more conventional political means. He did so by cleverly exploiting splits in various Ewe constituencies and, through a procedural argument, calling into question the legitimacy of the national conference: it had, he claimed (and many agreed), overstepped its constitutional powers. Eyadéma also managed to capture the "airwaves" of the all-important "radio trottoir" (literally, "sidewalk radio"—the streetside rumor mills). Rumors circulated as to his special powers—he was sighted in two places at once, he was seen consulting with diviners and was reported to have engaged in human sacrifice—that called up the stories of his past and lent him an air of invincibility.[17] Through these moves and maneuvers, Ellis argues, as much as through threats and intimidation, Eyadéma regained support and—in August 1993—took the vote.

Today, Lomé remains in a kind of limbo. In many quarters a deep antipolitics cynicism has set in—"after all the energy expended in the early 90s," I heard repeatedly, "nothing's changed—Eyadéma's still in charge, backed by his army—so what's the use." Furthermore, the economy suffered deeply during the political turmoil of 1991–94—development money fled, expatriates returned to Europe, shops were closed for months—and many are loath to risk returning to the privation of that time—"for what?" Thus, when Eyadéma claimed victory following a disputed election in June 1998, the widespread violence many had predicted failed to materialize. And when the opposition called for a series of strikes—"ville morte" (dead city)—during the weeks following the election, their exhortations met with mixed results. Some of this was due to intimidation and to the increasing, high-visibility presence of the Togolese police and military at checkpoints throughout Lomé following an August coup attempt—an attempt the opposition claimed was staged by the government. But it was also due to a deepening sense of hopelessness.

At the same time, however, ethnic tensions remain high and a palpable nervousness hangs in the Lomé air. Some Ewe I talked to imagine another Rwanda or Liberia if Eyadéma remains in power—and some Kabre fear the same if he does not. Many Lomé residents have reestablished ties with friends or family across the border in Ghana and Benin so that they can flee there if things get hot again. (The U.S. embassy official mentioned in chapter 1 seemed comforted by the fact that in Togo, unlike in Rwanda with its commingled Hutu and Tutsi, Kabre and Ewe come from different parts of the country. Thus, he said, if violence breaks out, there may be a few "difficult" days for those Kabre living in the south, but after they flee to the north, Ewe will not pursue them there.)

These events in the south have deeply affected life in the northern communities as well. Not only have many southern Kabre returned to the north—the Kabre town of Kara, the regional capital, has doubled in size since 1994—thus straining already limited resources, but the terrifying experiences of the early 1990s and uncertainty about the future have transformed the zeitgeist in the communities where I work. While in the mid-1980s the talk at work-group beer-drinking sessions typically centered on cultivation or local politics, it is today often dominated by national politics and the events of the early 1990s. And where returned southerners used to regale their northern family members with (often exaggerated and enmity-arousing) stories about the riches they were able to win in the south, they now speak of atrocities they witnessed during the time of the national convention. There is also deep northern resentment of those Western countries (such as the United States) who pressured the government into holding "multi-party elections" by threatening to withdraw foreign aid. Indeed, for many I spoke to, the term "democracy" has become synonymous with the violence that gripped their lives in the early 1990s.

◀o▶

Returning to the rainmaking episode with which I opened this chapter, we can perhaps now better understand the larger contexts and interpretive issues involved. Cast in terms of local cosmology—as indeed it is— the episode is also clearly about regional and national politics, and it cannot be fully understood outside of these contexts. Most obviously, it involves relations between northern and southern Kabre within the Kabre regional nexus. Thus, a central aspect of the case involved the negotiation of a set of constantly contested authority relations between northern and southern Kabre—of northerners trying to assert and maintain their (ritual) authority over their (wealthier) "children" who have gone south. Indeed, it was not so much the Christianity of the deceased that incurred the wrath of the spirit (many Kabre are unproblematically Christian) as the sons' refusal to place their father next to his ancestors in the north. "Everything is fine between us," a northerner told me in discussing those who have left the north, "so long as they do not forget us, so long as they continue to 'respect' us. It is at the time of the big ceremonies (initiation, funeral) that we see whether they continue to 'respect' [*nyamtʋ*] us or not." Here, then, we are in the realm not only of local cosmology but also of regional politics and, of course, of colonial history—for it was during the colonial period that Kabre migration to the south began and that 'respect' between northern and southern Kabre first became an important (and indeed a defining) issue within the Kabre diaspora.

Further, it is not just intra-Kabre relations that are being negotiated here, but also a certain Kabre nationalism. I was struck by the almost universal interest Kabre throughout Togo expressed in the case. (As mentioned above, when I traveled south shortly after the diviner had been consulted, soldiers along the way asked about the case, as did Kabre in Lomé.) I was further struck in discussions with these Kabre by the widespread consensus that the sons had erred in not properly returning their father's soul to the north. But why, in the face of a Kabre history of dispersal and cultural *metissage,* would there be such consensus about preserving this tradition among such far-flung and quite differently situated Kabre? Clearly an important part of the explanation lies within

Bassari: linguist, anthropologist, cultural critic; Lomé, August 1998

recent Togolese politics. Since the political unrest of the early 1990s, and the hardening of ethnic lines that has resulted, Kabre have a very clear sense that their survival depends on consolidating their identity. Indeed, in contrasting themselves with Ewe, many Kabre told me that it was their ethnic unity, and its lack among Ewe, that accounted for the fact that Kabre have remained in power to this day. Kabre know, too, that in some near future, the "return" of southern Kabre to the northern homeland may be more real than figurative.

◄o►

On the day I left Lomé in August 1996, I paid a visit to Ebia Bassari. I found him sitting beneath a shade tree in the dirt courtyard of his modest compound near the Ghanaian border. (Now in his seventies, he is recently retired from the INRS, and spends much of his time at home—still working on a grammar of Kabre.) Receiving me with the graciousness one becomes accustomed to among Kabre, he sent a child to buy beer for us at a nearby bar and we fell into conversation about mutual friends in the north, about recent Togolese politics, and about some of the historical material I had collected. A lifetime of culture-straddling has made Bassari an incredibly keen and articulate observer and critic.

Born into a high-ranking house in the community of Faren (the mountain community where Kumberito, the first Kabre, settled), he attended the first mission school in the north, served as interpreter for a well-known French anthropologist working on Kabre, spent a summer in Mississippi training Peace Corps volunteers bound for Togo, and then settled into a career as a researcher at the INRS in Lomé. Although a Christian who has spent much of his life away from the north, he, too, maintains ties to the homeland and seems perfectly at ease in either setting. He has returned to the north to initiate all of his children (at the same time that he has schooled them and sent one to study in France) and unhesitatingly states that he will be buried in his natal village in the north when he dies. As story bled into story—his views on the Kabre origin myth, his commentary on Kabre encounters with Samasi and the first Germans, his chilling account of life as a northerner in Lomé in the early 1990s and of his refusal to flee with his family to the north because he wanted to protect them from the humiliation Ewe soldiers were meting out to northerners at checkpoints along the way—I was reminded how a history that for me remains all too academic is for him not only palpably present but also a matter of life and death. At the end of our afternoon together, as he stuffed me into a crowded taxi at the border that would return me to the center of town, Bassari leaned over and, with a quizzical and slightly foreboding look, said, "You've lived in Kuwdé and know that all of life there is politics. The same is true of our country as a whole. It is simply a large village. But, as you know, in the village you never know what will happen next."

Three

....

EXCHANGE

Hierarchies of Value in an Economy of Desire

In this chapter I describe, and attempt to rethink, what anthropologists would call the "gift economy" (Mauss [1925] 1967; Gregory 1982; Strathern 1988) of Kabre. While my primary aim is to explore certain understandings about persons, hierarchy, and agency that operate in the exchange context, and thus to initiate a discussion that will carry into subsequent chapters, I also attempt to outline the history of this economy and of its distinctive modes of exchange. While the historical record makes it difficult to be certain exactly when such exchange modes came into being, there are grounds for suggesting that their origins—and certainly their present character—are quite recent. To suggest as much, however, is to go against the conventional view about prestational economies—namely, that their apparent alterity (as represented in the sharp distinction anthropologists have drawn between gift and commodity exchange) is a measure of their exteriority to capitalist modernity.[1]

Initiating Encounters

Beneath the surface of what at first sight appear to be static social forms and fixed rules of conduct, Kabre social life is a welter of movement, a world of persons and things in motion. Indeed the quantity and complexity of exchanges people are constantly involved in was for me as an ethnographer simply overwhelming. My own attention was initially drawn to this aspect of Kabre life through the relationships I myself entered into with Kabre—through the flood of gifts I received and, often clumsily and inappropriately, tried to reciprocate.

Immediately upon my arrival in the community of Kuwdé in November 1982 the gifts began. My wife and I were given chickens to welcome us. We were given meat and beer at the almost daily funeral ceremonies we attended throughout the months of December and January. (Most funeral ceremonies are held during these dry season months.) We were offered meat at ceremonies for the spirits in sacred forests. We were sent bowls of food almost nightly both by the family we lived with and by the family in the homestead next door, often, to our chagrin, after we had already finished our dinner. Children who killed birds and bats with their slingshots, and mice with rock traps, brought us morsels of their prey. And then there were the markets: in each of the two or three we attended every week, dozens of people from our community and others bought us calabashes of beer.

But what did these gifts mean? And how to respond to them? Were they just welcoming acts, and therefore not requiring a return? The chickens seemed to be, but what about the nightly food gifts? Surely *they* required a return. Still, should we reciprocate in kind, by sending back some of our own food as Kabre co-wives do to one another? That would not work in our case, we realized, when we saw the decidedly mixed reactions of homestead members to our sauces. Or were they expecting other gifts—money?—in return? Or could we—should we?—politely refuse the food? We decided upon this latter strategy at one point when we discovered that Kabre are constantly offering and refusing one another food gifts. For instance, a woman who is cooking will offer food to any outsider (non-family member) who enters her homestead at dinnertime. In such a case, the polite response is "I've already eaten, but tomorrow I'll come back and then we'll eat." We realized we had made a serious mistake when we tried this out one night on Kpèm, the cook in our homestead: our refusal of her food was met with her own refusal to speak to us for the rest of the night. *Within* the homestead you always accept the food gift, we were instructed. "You take it, taste it, and compliment the cook on the sauce." And then, we learned months later, if you are not hungry, you call in the children and give it to them to eat.

But while this solution eased our guilt over accepting, and sometimes wasting, unwanted food, we were still left with the problem that the gift remained unreciprocated. So we decided to give them other, mostly non-food gifts. Whenever we went to markets, we bought bread, tobacco, salt, and occasionally larger presents—cloth for the women, umbrellas for the men, sandals for the children. But there too we made mistakes. One day in one of the markets I bought what I thought would be a special gift for Halitoké, the head of our homestead—an uncooked piece of meat. When I gave it to him, however, he expressed surprise that I would give him such a gift. It turns out that such meat, as opposed to meat that has been sacrificed in the community, is not normally given as a gift.

Reciprocating beer gifts in the markets was easier to figure out—a gift of beer was met with a similar return. Once, however, after buying some beer for someone who had bought for me earlier in the day, I was lectured by Tamouka, the head of the homestead next to mine, on the inappropriateness of returning such a gift on the same day. You wait, he said, before making the return. But how long? A month? Two months? "There is no specific time. You wait for another market when you see the man who gave to you wandering around with no money in his pocket. *Then* you buy him back."

In this clumsy manner, then, we muddled along for months. My wife's and my conversation during that early period centered as much on the gift-giving we were involved in as on anything else. And while the meaning of much of what we were experiencing remained opaque to us, certain things about this flow of gifts nevertheless became quite clear. First, because we were unable at that point to communicate through spoken language—we were still struggling to learn the basics of Kabre and very few of Kuwdé's inhabitants spoke any French—gift-giving became for all of us a kind of surrogate language: the gifts were attempts to communicate, to bridge the gap between us, to express relationship. But they represented more than that as well. They were also probings of a sort—attempts to discover what we were like, how we responded to others, what knowledge we had of the proper forms of exchange. What kind of people are these, Kabre seemed to be asking, and how should we treat them? Such probing is not, of course, unlike what they do with one another when they exchange gifts: gift-giving is always a type of moral inquiry, an interrogation of the other.[2] And, finally, these gifts had, I now realize, one additional purpose. They were attempts to contain and control us. Gifts obligate and indebt, and in so doing they render the receiver subservient (Mauss [1925] 1967; Gregory 1982). What better way, then, to gain some mastery over an uncertain situation—over outsiders who often responded in surprising and unpredictable ways, who seemed to have a never-ending supply of money and material objects, and whose motives for living in this out-of-the-way place seemed enigmatic and suspicious—than through the gift?

Circulations

In order to give a fuller picture of the Kabre world of exchange and of some of its underlying principles, I begin with some examples of the types of exchanges of things-as-gifts (Gregory 1982) I witnessed in Kuwdé during the 1980s and 1990s.

In a year-long household budget survey I conducted in 1983, I found that 50 percent of all cash brought in by men from the sale of food surpluses in the markets was turned directly into gifts to other men, often beer gifts in the markets. Much of the rest of a man's cash income was ultimately given away as well, for he used it either to purchase sorghum to make beer so that he could thank the work group for working his fields, or to buy animals for sacrifice.

To give another example, a male household head gives away fully one third of what he harvests in his fields to women who help in transporting the harvested grain back to his homestead. For their aid, these women—up to a dozen affines and outmarried sisters of the man—each receive a basket of grain which they take home and put in their granaries to use later in the year to feed their families. What a household loses in this manner, however, its married women usually regain from the similar aid they give to their brothers and male affines. In the households I surveyed, these to-and-fro transfers of harvested grain roughly cancelled one another out. In addition, in June, during the period before the first harvest when food is short, the women who harvested from a man's field will often send him a small pot of beer in thanks. The recipient shares this beer with friends and other members of the household.

Things circulate around the community in other ways as well. All adults I knew repeatedly engaged in the bartering, or direct exchange, of products—seed yams for chickens, grain for animals, chicken baskets for hoe handles, and so on—with other members of the community. It was not uncommon to find that the seeds a man had planted in a particular field, the tools he used for cultivation, and even the field itself had been obtained through exchanges like this.

Another type of circulation, the borrowing of animals and land, is ubiquitous in Kuwdé. Every adult male and female I interviewed, for instance, was either borrowing an animal from, or lending one to, another person; in many cases, people were doing both at the same time. The same was true of fields. Thus, while all male household heads owned fields of their own, most also borrowed fields from *and* lent fields out to others at the same time. For instance, Nnamnawé, the one whose fields

I tour whenever I return to Kuwdé, was cultivating eight fields in 1996. Of these, he owned two and borrowed the remaining six. At the same time, however, he was lending two additional fields to others.[3]

All of these various forms of exchange—gift, barter, loan—are, Kabre say, motivated by the practical "need/desire" (sɔγɔlɪm)[4] of one of the parties. For instance, people borrowed fields because they didn't have enough of their own, or because they wanted fields closer to their houses, or fields with special soil types. Similarly, people exchanged subsistence products because they were in need of seed yams to plant, of a chicken to sacrifice, and so on. The same needs-based logic was equally true of beer gifts: people insisted that you only bought beer for someone when they were out of money themselves and, therefore, in "need."

But there were several interesting cases that led me to realize that there was more than just the exchange of utilities going on here. A particularly striking example involved a land-rich man in the community who owned twenty fields. Of these, he cultivated six for himself, loaned out four to friends, and left the other ten to lie fallow. However, he also cultivated two additional borrowed fields. When I discovered this, I assumed there must be a utilitarian explanation for these borrowings—that the land was more fertile than that in his fallow fields, or that it was closer to his house. However, neither of these was the case. In fact, some of his fallow land was better land closer to his house than the land he had borrowed. Rather, he borrowed, he claimed, because "it is not good to die without having eaten off someone else's plate." The metaphor here expressed a desire to establish social relations that lies behind much Kabre exchange (cf. Mauss [1925] 1967; Gregory 1982; Strathern 1988). Indeed, I would say that all of the exchanges described above, and others as well, have as much to do with relationships as with utilities.[5]

Persons and Things

The relational dimension of Kabre exchange is perhaps best illustrated through the following account given me in July 1985 by Karabu, a man in his late fifties with a body made hard and lean from years bending over the hoe. Karabu was describing ɪkpantʊrɛ, the friendship that can develop between two exchange partners over the course of many years through exchanges such as those described above. Every adult I knew in Kuwdé, both male and female, had anywhere from two to a dozen such relationships.

"With each ɪkpantʊ (friend) it is different," Karabu began, describing his own ɪkpantʊrɛ relationships. "With one, for instance, we started by buying each other beer in the markets. I bought him some beer one day and then, later, he bought me back. And so we went, back and forth. Then, one day he came to me when he needed something—a red chicken for a sacrifice—and asked if we might exchange chickens. I accepted, and he gave me his white one for my red one. Then, later on, I wanted to borrow a field and noticed that he had an extra field, so I asked if I could borrow it. Now we loan fields back and forth all the time."

"But there are many ways to begin ɪkpantʊrɛ," Karabu continued, drawing deeply on a pipe and releasing a pungent cloud of smoke into the air between us. "When I was young, I had an enemy from Tchi-Kawa [a community in the plain]. I was carrying on one day with a girl from his village. He took offense and insulted me. We almost came to blows. The insults continued for awhile, but then one day he bought me beer and we became ɪkpantʊna. Now, if either of us needs something, we may go to the other and ask him for it. For instance, I am borrowing a field of his down in the plain where I grow yams and he is borrowing one of my dogs. In another case, a woman I know became the ɪkpantʊ of another woman after she had squirted the other with breast milk in the market one day. It was an accident but, still, there is no bigger insult.[6] To cool the temper of the one offended, my friend bought her beer. They have been ɪkpantʊna ever since."[7]

"Two others—a man and a woman—may find ɪkpantʊrɛ over the selling of beer. He may go to her house often to drink her beer but may not always be able to pay. If she is nice, she will continue to serve him. For his part, whenever he sees her, he will remind her of his debt to her. Then, after the harvest, he will take her a basket of sorghum to pay off the debt. This will please her, and the next time she makes beer she may invite him to come drink. And, so, they become ɪkpantʊna."

"Many men here in Kuwdé found ɪkpantʊrɛ with men from other villages during the time of forced labor [1920–1955, when the French were conscripting Kabre to build roads for the colony]. The relationship often began with some small act—the help someone gave you lifting a rock from the road, their covering for you so you could slip into the bush while the "colon" was looking the other way—and grew from there. When we returned to the north, we continued the relationship." (In 1996, I asked another man with whom I was discussing exchange relationships whether the transborder relationships many Lomé residents developed during the political turmoil of the early 1990s were also a type of ɪkpan-

tʊrɛ, and he immediately agreed. "These are deep *ɪkpantʊrɛ* relationships that involve much gift-giving—and gifts that are bigger than those we give here in the north.")

"Each *ɪkpantʊrɛ* is different," Karabu continued. "Each follows its own path. Some of these friendships go nowhere, or they 'break' altogether. Perhaps your partner is so poor that he can never make return gifts, or perhaps you see something about him, something inside him, that you don't like and you stop sending him gifts. In any case, *ɪkpantʊrɛ* is costly and it is not possible to continue with everyone."

"With certain of your *ɪkpantʊna,* however, maybe two or three of them, you will build something bigger. One day, after many years of small exchanges, and much good feeling between you, an *ɪkpantʊ* may invite you and your family to his house on *sɪŋkarɪŋ* [the day of the harvest festival]. He asks you to sit and brings out food and beer. He has killed a chicken just for you and your family. Such an act makes a very strong impression. It is a sign of great friendship. The following year, it is your turn. You invite him to your house and serve him food and drink. If you can, you kill an animal that has more value [a guinea hen, a dog, a goat] than the one he killed for you, and you make a pot of beer that is bigger than the one he gave you. This shows that the relationship is growing. And so it goes, back and forth, each time a larger pot of beer and a more valuable animal. But it is the intention of the giver that is important, not the size of the gift. If my *ɪkpantʊ* cannot afford to increase the gift, he will come to me and tell me that he would like to kill a goat but can only afford a chicken. If he does this, I will accept and the relationship will continue."

The flexible nature of the exchanges Karabu was describing—and the premium placed on attitude and intention rather than object—is illustrated in an experience of my own, an experience that also reveals something of the complicated dynamics at work between myself and those with whom I lived and worked most closely. On a return trip to Kuwdé in 1989, I asked Tikénawé, a woman in her early twenties with an upbeat personality and a sugar smile, if I could pay her, as I had previously, to bring us water from the spring and do our laundry. She readily agreed to do the work but insisted that I not pay her this time. When I asked why, she said that the money I had sent as a gift the previous May had "saved" her at a time when she was low on food and out of money. She was returning my gift, she said, with one of her own—one that she hoped would meet *my* need. I remained intent on paying her, however, as I had the money to do so and knew that she did not have a lot. But she refused and said that if I insisted, I could find someone else to do the work. Needless to say, I relented but in the end I was able to get my way by converting the payment I wanted to make into the terms of *ıkpantʊre:* I made a separate "gift" to her at the end of the summer of the money I would have paid her along the way (though, of course, I never referred to it as anything other than a "gift"). This, it turned out, *was* acceptable to her.

Of course, I was delighted with all that Tikénawé's gesture implied—a paradigmatic display of gifting behavior, the apparent triumph of altruism over self-interest, a friendship that suggested a narrowing of the gap between myself (as outsider and anthropologist) and someone local, a refreshing refusal to commodify relationship—a refusal that was all the more striking given her meager resources. I also found refreshing the contrast between her attitude and that of Kouwènam, my main assistant. I had hired Kouwènam early on to help me learn the language, and then continued with him as interpreter when I began doing interviews. He was extremely bright and had extraordinary translation skills. He always seemed able, even in the midst of discussions about the most abstract and esoteric of topics, to quickly grasp what I was after and translate it into the local idiom, and vice versa. And yet it had always bothered me that he unfailingly wore his self-interest on his sleeve: I paid him well and almost daily gave him additional gifts of food and beer, but unlike virtually everyone else I knew in Kuwdé, he constantly pestered me for more. Needless to say, when I gave him money at the same time as Tikenawé, he did not make a gesture like hers.

I now realize, however, that Tikénawé's generosity was more complicated, and perhaps less altruistic, than it at first seemed. I have seen her befriend other Europeans and Americans over the years—a French nurse, a Peace Corps volunteer—and have been struck by her ability to easily win them over. In part it is her personality—self-effacing, coy, a quick wit and ready laugh; but it is also her demeanor—she seems to enjoy and appreciate friendship for its own sake, and will invariably decline a gift when it is first offered. Indeed, there seems nothing more touching for many European travelers to West Africa than to find friendship that seems "real"—and not always mediated by money and gifts. And yet these foreigners, like me, inevitably press things on her, and in the end she accepts. It is also clear that Tikénawé desires the material benefits that come to her as a result of such friendships, but that, unlike Kouwènam, she is simply good at concealing her desires.

What ironies, however: Kouwènam, the schooled cosmopolitan who

Tikénawé selling sorghum beer in the market; Kuwdé, March 1984

has always seemed ambivalent about his attachments to local culture and never misses an opportunity to befriend a European, is often less successful at making such relationships work than Tikénawé, the unschooled local who speaks much less polished French and has never wanted to leave her village. I find myself asking, however, whether my overwhelmingly positive feelings toward her—and, indeed my fascination with gift exchange more generally—are not the product of hers and others' inventions and manipulations, and/or of the mirror they hold up for me. Who's pulling the strings here?

I also find myself reconsidering my feelings toward Kouwènam—it is *my* cultural impulse to want him to be both translator/employee *and* friend, and to want him to at least occasionally conceal his self-interest. But he is all too aware of the gulf that exists between us. As much as I might want to deny it, I will never be a local in any typical sense of that term. Ours is forever an employer-employee relationship, fraught with the power differentials and tensions that inhabit today's postcolonial spaces. Kouwènam recognizes this and is perhaps simply trying to take advantage of the situation as best he can. Thus, if Tikénawé fulfills my fantasy of local affiliation, Kouwènam reminds me of certain undeniable political realities, and of the risks of self-deception.

But of course these thoughts came years after my conversation about *ɪkpantʋrɛ* with Karabu. "Sometimes, though not very often," he continued, "the relationship will grow even bigger. This happens if my *ɪkpantʋ* and I, after many years of exchanges like these, decide to arrange a marriage between our families. For instance, I might take the initiative and go to him one day and say that I would like my daughter to marry his son. If he accepts and the marriage takes place, the two houses now become tied together for many generations [through a series of obligatory affinal exchanges]. We say now that the relationship cannot be broken. But it is not good to let *ɪkpantʋrɛ* finish itself like this. It is better if there is another marriage between the houses, this time in the other direction. But not in the same generation—that would be returning the gift too quickly. The marriages of women who cross each other's paths in the same generation [sister exchange] do not last: if one woman leaves her husband, the other woman will side with her brother [the first woman's husband] and leave her husband as well. This way, you end two marriages at once. There is no 'respect' (*nyamtʋ*) in such marriages. It is best to wait until the next generation and try to get that woman's daughter to marry back, though if the daughter is unavailable any woman from the same house will do. This type of marriage [FZD] is called *ʋmɪla* ʋ-*kpeɖirɔɔ* ("she has returned to her [mother's] cooking stool"). When such a marriage occurs, we say that the two houses have become 'one' or the 'same.'"[8]

The Quality of a Gift and the Agency of Persons

As a type of total institution in the Maussian ([1925] 1967) sense, this system of exchange opens itself to the full range of human emotions and social dispositions. A set of practices at once material and meaningful, it collapses standard antinomies—structure and play, strategy and protocol, affection and enmity—and troubles analytic distinctions between the economic, the social, the political, the affective, and the aesthetic. At once utilitarian and mundane, it also embodies a certain longing for immortality: as Karabu put it, the aim of *ɩkpantʋrɛ* is to make something enduring, a relationship "that cannot be broken." It is also incredibly labile, operating in the villages and the cities, as well as in the borderlands between nations. What I wish to focus on here—since it bears on the themes developed in subsequent chapters—are questions of value and agency as they are made manifest in exchanges like these.

Karabu's narrative is more or less representative of the dozen such accounts I collected from different men and women in the community. In each case, the details would change—about how the person began *ɩkpantʋrɛ*, about the types of incremental steps made in the second sphere, and so on—but the general features remained the same. All, for instance, described a three-tiered system involving the exchange of food gifts (seed yams, beer, fields) in the bottom tier, wealth items (animals) in the middle, and women at the top.[9] All also described a set of alternating exchanges between two partners in which one person's "desire" was met by another, and so on, back and forth. This dyadic, alternating, hierarchical pattern is common to exchange wherever it is found in Kabre society.[10]

While this set of exchange practices facilitates individuals' access to things—in many cases utilities—it is clearly as much or more about relationships than about things. Indeed, it would be more accurate to say that persons use things to gain access to persons rather than that they use persons to gain access to things.

Moreover, consistent with the relational aspect of exchange is a focus on qualities rather than quantities. Thus, it is not so much the quantitative equivalency of objects exchanged that is paramount as whether or not an individual's desire was satisfied, and therefore whether a (qualitative) relationship between persons was created. For example, while there are standard numerical rates at which exchanges should be carried out— for example, one chicken is said to be worth fifty seed yams—very few actually are. Indeed, in the dozens of exchanges I witnessed and heard about, none was ever carried out at the standard rate! Sometimes thirty seed yams were exchanged against the chicken, at other times forty-five, and so on. And yet regardless of the actual rate of the transaction, all were deemed equivalent to the standard. In none of them, for instance, did one of the parties incur a debt of the sort familiar to a transactor of commodities—e.g., a twenty-yam debit that was carried over to a subsequent exchange.

The equivalence Kabre see in such numerically different exchanges is rooted in the fact that all that matters is whether someone's immediate need/desire was fulfilled. In some cases thirty seed yams met that need, in others fifty. In both, however, the subjective needs of the exchangers and the relational implications of the exchange—the fact that it creates a relationship between two individuals—remain unchanged. For those I spoke to in Kuwdé, these qualitative aspects of the exchange are all that matter. (In cases where the quantity was inadequate to the need of the initiator—where someone needed fifty seed yams instead of thirty—the needy party would simply seek out someone else.)

Comprehending this principle allowed me to understand a relationship whose meaning had puzzled me for many months. Tikénawé made "market beer" every Friday, and often sold to Palabéi, the chief of Kuwdé, on credit. Palabéi would, for example, usually only pay for half of the beer he drank. As a result, and because he loved beer, he accumulated a sizable debt with Tikénawé—1,100 francs CFA—over the course of a single year. (In the case of money transactions like this, debts *are* incurred if payment in full is not made.) At the time of the harvest, however, Palabéi gave Tikénawé three small baskets of sorghum which, she told me, had "finished" the debt between them. When I pointed out to her that, at the going market rate, the three baskets were worth only 750 CFA (thus giving Palabéi a windfall of 350 CFA), she responded that that didn't matter. "In such a case, you don't think about the market. He gave me what he could. All that matters is that he thought of me when he harvested his grain. We now have a relationship which goes beyond the market. If I need something some day, I can go seek him out."

Still not satisfied, however, I put the question differently. Was this not an example of a powerful senior man taking advantage of a younger

Chief Palabéi; Kuwdé, June 1985

woman? "Certainly not," she responded. "The opposite is true here: I had a chief who was in debt to me all year long. Because of this, he had to 'respect' me. Whenever he saw me, he reminded me of his debt to me. This is worth far more to me than a few calabashes of beer." Clearly, here, Tikénawé's focus was on the relationship engendered rather than on money credits and debits. One could hardly have a clearer example of what Gregory (1982: 42) claims is true of gift exchange generally, and of the way it contrasts with commodity exchange: "The distinction between gifts and commodities manifests itself as a difference between the exchange relation established: gift-exchange establishes a relation between the transactors, while commodity-exchange establishes a relation between the objects transacted."

The same principle—a focus on qualities rather than quantities—operates in many noneconomic domains as well. For instance, when sacrificing, Kabre may substitute quantitatively dissimilar objects for one another—not unlike the famous Nuer sacrificial substitution of a cucumber for an ox (Evans-Pritchard 1956). Thus, Kabre allow chickens to be substituted for goats, guinea hens for sheep, and, most astonishing to me, mice for cows. There is a tropic logic to such substitutions (chickens are figuratively similar to goats, guinea hens to sheep, mice to cows[11]) that renders the objects equivalent to, and thus substitutable for, one another.

However, when asked, what Kabre draw attention to even more is the intention of the giver. If a sacrifice has to be made and the "right" animal cannot be found, another appropriate animal will do, they say. In this way, the (qualitative) relationship with the spirits or ancestors to whom the sacrifice is being made is maintained. Quantities—the size or value of the type of animal used—make no difference (although they always prefer the bigger ones, if they are available, since there will be more meat to go around).

Understanding this principle obviates, in the Kabre case, a whole set of pseudoproblems that have dogged certain schools of anthropological theory. These anthropologists are fond of drawing attention to the gap between what informants state is the ideal pattern and what they "really" do. The ideal is then often ignored/discredited and/or explained as an attempt to mystify the real. But for Kabre the ideal is always the same as the real (or the ideal is the same as many reals): thirty yams is the same as fifty, 1,100 CFA is the same as 750, and so on. They are the same because in each case the type of relationship they create is the same. Focusing on quantities (what they "really" exchange) is misleading, and there is nothing to be gained by introducing here a theory of false consciousness.

If Kabre exchange centers on persons and qualities rather than things and quantities, it also aims to *create* difference rather than overcome it. For instance, it is always the case, those I spoke to claim, that two people who have engaged in an exchange are unequals—one is beholden to the other (cf. Mauss [1925] 1967; Gregory 1982) and therefore must show him or her "respect" (*nyamtʊ*). This is because the one was "saved" by the other (*oyapa ma-nyuɣu*, literally "he/she bought his/her head"), rescued by the other from his or her need. Thus, even when two people barter objects that have equal value—either identical products (a chicken for a chicken, a field for a field) or different products that have similar value (fifty seed yams for a chicken)—the exchange is still considered unequal. This is because one of the parties to the exchange had a serious need, causing him to ask his friend for help, while the other did not. The differing/unequal needs of the transactors create an unequal exchange of equal products.[12]

As mentioned earlier, the same theory of need/desire applies to outright gifts as well. Recall, for instance, Tamouka's admonition to me when I returned beer too quickly to someone who had earlier given to me. "You wait [to return the gift]," he said, "[until you see him in some future market] wandering around with no money in his pocket. *Then* you buy him back." The reasoning here is that it is when the friend has no money of his own that his need/desire will be the greatest and, of course, that he will most appreciate the gift. Thus, exchange relationships like these always turn on the notion of difference and hierarchy.[13] As we shall see in later chapters, the importance of difference figures not only in the exchange context but in others as well.

Finally, we can discern in Karabu's narrative a conception of personhood that is decidedly nonindividualistic. Not only are Kabre persons perpetually entangled with one another through the exchange of things; there is also a strong sense in which exchange such as this extends the boundaries, and redefines the agency, of persons. The individual self here is composed as much, or more, through its relationships with others as through anything intrinsic to itself. Indeed, we might say that the self *is* those relationships. If the hat a man wears, the field he cultivates, the crops he grows to feed his family (and, as we shall see in chapter 4, his body itself) are all from another, what then is he apart from that other? It is these others who fill and inhabit him.

It is not simply the other-as-debt that fills a person but also the other as living and sensuous memory. Witness, for instance, the comments of a man who described the field he was borrowing from a friend: "Whenever I go to that field, I think immediately of my friend. I remember how he 'saved' me by giving me this field. I think of his personality, and this pleases me. And, I come to know his field—its soil, its terraces, its rocks—and I feel that I am coming to know him as well."

But to establish such a view of the self entails also a reframing of the question of agency. For here it is not so much the self as the other, and multiple others, that become the source of one's actions. A gift from an other elicits my response, just as my gift elicits his. Such a process clearly locates one's agency outside oneself as much as within. I take the Kabre injunction that "if someone wants to exchange with you, you are obligated to accept" as an apt illustration of this point. "Elicitation" (Wagner 1981, 1986a, 1986b; Strathern 1988) would appear to be a better way of thinking about personal agency here than, say, "interest" or "self-interest."

Of Theories and the Individual

We might stop here and ask why Kabre do all this exchanging. To provide a safety net against environmental uncertainty? To level wealth differences? To help create social solidarity? These are the standard social science answers. However, such functionalist explanations are not only plagued by tautology and indeterminacy; they also betray an individualist bias. They assume that somehow it is more natural not to exchange—to keep to oneself what one has—than to exchange, and that when we see individuals exchanging, this fact needs to be explained.

However, Kabre begin with the opposite assumption—that being in relationship (exchanging), and all that connotes (hierarchy, etc.), is the more natural state of affairs. Systemic needs—whether ecological, social, or whatever—may draw on such relationships but they are not their *raison d'être* and cannot possibly be called on to explain the existence and complexity of the relationships themselves. For social theory, then, the task should be not so much to account for why people like Kabre exchange, as if it were some "problem" that needed explaining, as to try to understand the cultural logic that informs their exchange practices.

Indeed, if one wanted to find a problem Kabre set for themselves, it would be the inverse of the one social science poses: what needs explaining and commenting upon, from the Kabre perspective, is not why (most) people exchange but rather why some do not. The general view is that such individuals—the person who stands apart, the isolated individual—are abnormal. Thus, a Kabre person who dies of dropsy (*kʊtɔŋ sʊsɔɣʊ*, literally "bigness disease"), a horrifying swelling of the body said to be produced by a person's refusal of his/her spouse's food after they have quarrelled, is buried not in the family tomb but apart in a separate tomb. And one who dies of leprosy (*kʊtɔŋ kʊsɛmʊɣʊ*, literally "redness disease"), evidence that the deceased had stolen food from someone else's field, or that he or she was a witch, is similarly buried apart. As well, the ancestral stones of such individuals are not placed next to those of the house's other ancestors in the center of the homestead's courtyard but instead are set off to the side. Alone in life, the judgment seems to be, such individuals will remain alone in death as well.

A woman I knew had neither of these diseases when she died but nevertheless received a similarly ignominious burial. At her death, many of the community's elders refused to accompany her body to the tomb as is the norm, and Tamouka, the community's interrer, refused to bury her, so her family had to seek out an interrer from a neighboring community. Both were extraordinary steps, and when I encountered Tamouka going to one of his fields as the cadaver was being escorted to the tomb (thus violating a major taboo) I asked him why she was receiving this treatment. He stated simply that it was because of her lack of generosity and because she gossiped openly and maliciously about others. "For this reason," he said, "she can bury herself."

This general point—that those who stand apart (refuse relationship) are abominations—is evidenced even more clearly in Kabre beliefs about witches. It is the witch who is the prototype of the nonrelational person, the individual who has turned his or her back on others (cf. Apter 1993: 118; Auslander 1993: 178; Bastien 1993: 138–39). Kabre witches are said to "eat" others for their own selfish reasons, typically in order to acquire wealth objects (animals and/or money) from the spirits who participate with them in the consumption of their victims. The logic of this exchange is precisely the inverse of the prestational logic I have been describing in this chapter: instead of producing persons with things, witches produce things with persons. Thus, confessed witches are despised and dealt with cruelly—through beatings and/or through exile from the community.

A recognition of the inversion of values that witchcraft entails accounts, I think, not only for the moral repugnance of the witch but also for the way Kabre witchcraft beliefs, like similar beliefs in other areas of the world (Taussig 1980; Geschiere 1988, 1997; Shipton 1989; Shaw 1997), have become associated with a particular moment in Kabre historical consciousness: the advent of capitalist wage relations during the colonial period. Elders told me, for example, that certain changes occurred in Kabre witchcraft beliefs and practices at the time—the 1910s and 1920s—when they began doing wage labor in the mines and plantations of southern Togo and Ghana. Until that time, they said, witches were few in number and didn't kill people; they just ate little holes in their arms. Since then, and especially today, witches have become numerous and deadly. This association, and its implied commentary, should come as no surprise, for there is a striking similarity between the economy of the witch and that of the capitalist: both involve the conversion of persons into things—the "consumption" of persons by things—a process Gregory (1982), following Marx ([1857] 1973), refers to as productive consumption. Both represent an inversion of the logic and aims of gift exchange.

A Tale of Two Cultures

The value of giving is instilled in Kabre children at an early age. Walk into any homestead where a child is eating something—a yam, an ear of corn—and the mother will immediately tell the child to offer it to you. (The polite response is for you to accept it, thank the child, perhaps taste it, and then return it.) The rule to give is in a very real sense the first one children learn, for it is taught to them when they are a year old or less— that is, before they learn to walk and before they can speak the language. When in 1989 we returned to Kuwdé with our three-year-old daughter, she was repeatedly put to the test by strangers who entered our homestead. If she was eating or drinking something, they immediately demanded that she give them some (*ha-m*). At first she didn't, fearing— like a good middle-class American child—that if she gave it up she probably wouldn't see it again. After several failed attempts to get her to try to give (by suggesting, for example, that she might want to do it because everyone else did it), I gave in to the logic of self-interest and told her that if she gave it up, she would get it right back. This tactic worked: she hesitantly offered a cookie she was eating to the next stranger who came by and was delighted when he gave it back to her, patting her on the head appreciatively. Thereafter, she willingly offered any food she was eating to anyone who walked into our homestead and came to see it all as rather like a fun game. For awhile, she even became the hit of the community, with people joking about how she had "become Kabre." One day, however, when I told a young Kabre mother who had observed Kalina's initial reticence what I had done to convince her to begin giving, this woman said that a Kabre would never teach a child like that. "You give, and that's it. Sometimes you get back and sometimes you don't. But in either case, you give. That is what we teach our children."

Let me reemphasize that I am not intending here to reify the old orientalist (us/them) binaries. Kabre also embrace certain types of individualism—and, as the next section illustrates, commodity exchange— and Euroamericans like my daughter are in many ways and at many times motivated by relational concerns rather than self-interest. Rather, my point is to unsettle certain modes of analysis that are rooted in individualistic assumptions in order to enable a more complicated understanding of certain domains of Kabre economic and cultural practice.

◄○►

I stated earlier that it was my sense that the flood of gifts given us when we arrived in Kuwdé was an initial attempt not only to communicate and establish a relationship but also to contain and appropriate us. The meaning of such appropriation should now be more apparent. Any gift

Children at work and play, with Kalina; Kuwdé, July 1989

given establishes a relationship—of difference and of hierarchy—between two persons. As such, giving is always tied up with control, power, and the appropriation of an other. The other is in your debt and must "respect" you. "Every time he (the chief) saw me all year," Tikenawé said, "he had to let me know that he had not forgotten his debt with me."

We were no different from any other in this respect. Kabre immediately responded to our presence in the community by doing what they do with one another. They were enmeshing and appropriating us, trying to make a relationship on their model of hierarchy and difference. They were also, of course, attempting to appropriate the gifts we might return, the "powers"—mystical and mundane—we might possess, and the particularities of identity and difference we might project.

To foreshadow a point I return to in later chapters, when Kabre responded to colonial intervention through engagement—through the exchange of gifts, through swapping labor for access to roads and lands in the south, through forms of mimesis (see chapter 4), through appropriating rather than rejecting things Western—they were doing so not out of weakness, or out of an inability to forcefully resist. Rather, these were acts of enhancement—attempts to control, indebt, tame, tap into, and usurp the potency of a powerful other.

Commodities

In the 1970s and 1980s, the analytic category of the "gift economy" came for many anthropologists to define a prototype non-Western, noncapitalist economy: person-centered, governed by principles of inalienability, underwritten by qualitative rather than quantitative values, such economies seemed everything that capitalism was not (and all that it had lost). Located on the fringes of the capitalist world system, in societies that appeared still not fully colonized by capital, such economies also seemed to represent pockets of resistance to a globalizing, homogenizing capitalism: capitalism's alter, and its resistant "outside." But, as various scholars (Appadurai 1986; Thomas 1991; Miller 1995; Weiss 1996) have recently suggested, this view needs revising. Not only is it suspect and orientalizing to gloss whole economies (and regions of the world) in stark either/ or terms—the West as commodified, the non-West as gift-ed—especially when they have shared a common history over the last four hundred years and seem in most cases to manifest a plurality of transaction types, but also—an even greater provocation—it may be that gift exchange in the capitalist peripheries is a product of modernity itself rather than a residue of temporally prior or spatially exterior social formations. There is evidence, I would like to argue, that such is the case for Kabre.

On purely formal grounds, such a possibility should not be surprising. After all, gift exchange and barter are present at capitalism's core, not only within families and (increasingly) between craftspeople—the plumber who exchanges services with the painter and the electrician— but also in the commodity markets and international trade (Humphrey and Hugh-Jones 1992; Matison and Mack 1984). Further, as Marx ([1867] 1977) suggested long ago, capitalism is more plausibly depicted as an economy of exchange spheres (C-M-C, M-C-M, M-M')—rather like a gift economy (Bohannan 1955, 1959; Gregory 1982)—than one given to unfettered, promiscuous conversions and commensurabilities. Thus, if commodities and gifts/barter are functionally related to one another at capitalism's center, surely the same could be true of global capitalism as well.

In the Kabre case, it is useful to begin by noting that commodity exchange is not at all alien to Kabre, nor has it been for many centuries.[14] In markets that date at least to the time of the slave trade (c. 1700), Kabre have bought and sold products for money (today the CFA, formerly cowrie shells) with members of other communities, both local and beyond. These are the famous periodic markets described in Bohannan and Dalton (1962) that rotate from one community to the next on different days of the week. Most adult members of Kuwdé today go to two or three such markets a week. There, in well-worn clearings under large shade trees, women buy and sell small quantities of foodstuffs (palm oil, locust bean paste, pots, grain, and so on), while the men purchase hoe blades and animals before retiring to small kiosks on the market's periphery to drink beer and eat dogmeat. While the popularity of the markets is due in no small part to the expanded sociality they offer—the opportunity to visit with friends (especially ɪkpantʋna) and stay abreast of local politics—it is also owed to the fact that people often prefer buying and selling to barter exchange (kʋlʋɣʋsʋɣʋ) because, as they put it, in the market they can avoid the often burdensome demands—the indebtedness and hierarchy—that accompany ɪkpantʋrɛ.[15] They like to pick and choose, going to market when they want to avoid indebtedness, and bartering when pursuing ɪkpantʋrɛ, and they find having the option of being able to do either an attractive one.

In some domains Kabre have carried commoditization to extremes unacceptable even in the capitalist core. As mentioned in the last chapter, during the era of the slave trade, Kabre sold their own kin as slaves in return for cowrie shells (see Piot 1996). And today, in another example of commoditization at the heart of kinship, when a woman makes market beer, she requires her husband to pay for it as if he were not a family member. It is also strictly within the domestic sphere that witches—those neocapitalist accumulators—operate, exchanging family members for wealth and money.[16]

However, despite the longstanding centrality of commodity exchange and markets among Kabre—a centrality evidenced in the fact that the word for market (kɪyakʋw) is the same as that for day of the week—and despite the increasing penetration of capitalist wage relations over the past century, Kabre gift exchange persists and, indeed, as in certain other areas of the world, appears to have intensified during the colonial and postcolonial periods.[17] Kabre I spoke to said that there is much more ɪkpantʋrɛ today than in the past—that while their fathers and grandfathers had just one or two ɪkpantʋna, today many people have as many as a dozen. The social field from which ɪkpantʋna are drawn has also expanded. While earlier generations drew theirs almost exclusively from within the village, today's draws from beyond the village as much as within, a change everyone dated to the time of forced labor. Moreover, the Kabre ritual system—the domain of gift exchange *par excellence*—

is larger and more prolific today than in the past. Thus, as northern Kabre have migrated into the diaspora and as the northern communities have become increasingly enmeshed in the nationalist project of a Kabre president, ritual—the mediator of these translocal relationships—has come to assume an even greater role.

But Kabre gift and commodity spheres of circulation do more than just peacefully coexist; they also cross-fertilize one another. Not only does having money allow one to have more *ikpantʋna;* it is also money, and largely southern money earned in the wage sector, that finances the ritual system, enabling the purchasing of animals whose sacrifice is the gift of all gifts (because doubly so: offered first to the spirits, they are then distributed to humans). Another culturally salient conversion of money to gift is represented in the tin roofs—again purchased by southerners—that adorn certain houses in northern homesteads. The prestige value of these roofs, and especially their value as symbol of the enduring relationship between those who have departed for the south and those who remain behind, far outweighs their utility. Indeed, I was always struck by how empty most of these houses were, often used for little more than storing hoe blades, machetes, and baskets (a glorified tool shed). But the traffic between commodity and gift spheres is two-way: not only has increased involvement in wage labor produced expanded gift exchange, but also the gift system has generated increased involvement in the wage and commodity sector, for making money allows one to participate more fully in the gift-giving that leads to expanded social relations.

It is perhaps for this reason that Kabre—unlike the Colombian and Bolivian peasants and miners Taussig (1980) writes about—see money-making as positive and life-enhancing, and that money/cowrie shells appear as energizing symbols of potency in various ritual contexts. Thus, at key public moments, male initiates adorn themselves with cowrie shells and are given money to symbolize and celebrate their maturation, and bereaved widows and widowers are offered money to help them heal their grief. Similarly, virtuoso dancers are rewarded for particularly impressive performances with money—25-and 100-CFA coins—which they (or others) stick to their foreheads. Giving visible expression to the animating, alchemical powers of money, these gifts jolt the dancer like an electric shock, sending her or him to new heights of frenzied movement. Divination is also intimately tied up with money and its symbolism. Not only does it take place in the markets, but the diviner uses money—cowrie shells—to divine, throwing the shells on the ground and then "reading" them to decipher the intentions of the spirits and ancestors. Finally, money and its symbolism are central to gift exchange itself. Not only is money a highly valued "gift," as Tikénawé's response to my money gift indicates; the act that lies at the heart of *ıkpantʋrɛ*—the gift that "saves" a friend in time of need—is described as "buying [with money] that person's head" (*oyapa ma-nyuɣu*).[18]

In summer 1996, when I was pressed for time and unable to thank a man I had just interviewed by buying him beer as I usually do, I asked if I could instead give him the money I would have spent on beer. This went against all my better instincts, however. I had done hundreds of interviews over the years, always exchanging words for beer, a practice that not only seemed less tainted by commoditization but also fit the local system of thanking people with beer for work in their fields or with help in building their houses. However, this man not only accepted my money without hesitation but also delivered a short speech about how this was a much better way to thank him. Buying someone beer, he said, may or may not come at a time of "need," but giving him money meant that he could wait to cash in the gift until a truly needy occasion arose. "This makes money a much stronger gift," he said.

It is important to note here that this view of money is not at odds with Kabre views about witches and the capitalist economy in the south. There it is the *illegitimate* production and consumption of money and wealth that is at issue—money used to enhance the self at the expense of others. But when money-making is put to use producing and enhancing social relations, it is regarded as something of great value.

If Kabre gift exchange today operates inside and feeds off of capitalist modernity, what about the history of this relation? Unfortunately, little is known about the prehistory of Kabre exchange modes, but what we do know suggests that in this case the standard origin myth of classical and neoclassical economics—that barter precedes money but eventually gives way to the latter (and to the market) because money solves the problems of barter—is in need of revision. The earliest record of exchange among Kabre, for instance, is not of gift but of commodity exchange: the sale of people into the slave trade (an era, as discussed in the last chapter, associated with the "origin" of Kabre culture itself). Moreover, we also know that during this time period cowries by the millions flowed like water through the markets and societies of the area, suggesting an era of pervasive, if not profligate, commodity exchange. (Jane Guyer [1993, 1995a and b] has argued the same for Central Africa, suggesting that African societies there were accustomed to buying and selling everything from items of utility to ritual knowledge to political office long before the arrival of the first Europeans.) I am not suggesting that gift exchange did not also exist during this time period. But the evidence indicates that its sphere of operation was more restricted than it is today, and that it was only with the advent of colonialism and capitalist wage relations in the south that it began to grow and came to occupy its current more dominant position.

Four

PERSONS

Engendering Subjects, Spectacular Rituals

I suggested in chapter 3 that a structure of reciprocal desire drives the Kabre economy. The same is true of houses (*ɖɛsɪ*), sites *par excellence* of Kabre material and social reproduction. Here it is male and female persons, defined through their differences—and thus through their reciprocal "need/desire" for one another—that combine to produce livelihoods and families. In this chapter I examine the processes through which such gendered persons are produced. Since Kabre do not conceive of gender as given in nature, and since they see children as gender undifferentiated, they must work to achieve the differences that constitute gendered subjects. This task is accomplished largely through ritual—through the initiation ceremonies children undergo during the course of their maturation.

The work of these ceremonies is not confined to the household alone, however. They also play a salient role within the diaspora, annually drawing tens of thousands of people back to the north and thus providing an important point of articulation in relations between those who have left the north and those who remain behind. On a larger scale yet, Kabre initiation ceremonies have recently come to play a role in national politics. Each year the president brings government business to a halt for two weeks while he returns to the north to attend the wrestling matches of southern massif male initiates (*afalaa*), an event that is broadcast on state TV.

Here the cultural apparatus of the postcolonial state—a state that constitutes itself through spectacle (Toulabour 1986; Mbembe 1992)—and a local commitment to the power and efficacy of public ritual converge. Ritual is necessary, Kabre claim, because it is through ritual that identities

76

and relationships are made known, "visible," and thus real, to others. "Without funeral rituals," I was told, "how would others know that a person is dead? And without initiation ceremonies, how would they know that a child has become an adult? Whose words would we trust to make these things known to us?" The president is similarly attempting to draw power from public images. He is not only making himself and the state "visible," and visibly concerned with the local; he is also attempting to center Kabre within the representational space of the nation-state.

The Histories of Children

At birth, and when speaking of the newborn, Kabre say that a "stranger" (*ɪkɔm/akɔmaa,* literally "who has come?") has arrived. The baby is a "stranger" because its prior history (in the unseen world) is unknown, as are its motives for coming into this world: Did it come in search of its twin? Is it an ancestor who has come to plague someone? Is it a mother's daughter returned—the one who died suddenly and who people later discovered was a spirit that had come back to afflict her? Or are its motives more benign? Only time will tell. The newborn is also a stranger—and here Kabre manifest a certain anthropological sensibility—in the sense that coming from a place where social practices and conventions are different, it will have to learn the habits of its parents (and vice versa) and to develop the everyday understandings that constitute a relationship of familiarity.

Far from a *tabula rasa,* the Kabre newborn is thought of as already having a history, a personality, desires, relationships, and so on; further, it is up to the living to decipher this history and to accommodate themselves to it (cf. Gottlieb 1998). Indeed, Kabre adults feel they must adapt to their children, rather than the other way around.

Much attention is thus devoted to attempting to discover the hidden histories and ulterior motives of newborns. A week after birth, elders from the father's and the mother's brother's houses come to inspect the infant to see, as they put it, "what it was that the mother gave birth to"— a child, an animal from the bush, or a nefarious spirit. During the early months, diviners are consulted to interpret various signs—a baby's prolonged crying, the call of a certain bird at night—that might indicate something about its relationships with those in the unseen world, and therefore something about its present desires: is its twin calling it to return to the other world? Does it want to go or stay? Is it the reincarnation of a dead ancestor? Such divining is complemented by the placing of small charms on children—a wooden flute around the neck of boys, a bracelet on the right arm of girls—to deflect the interest and attention of spirits. A full-blown hermeneutics is thus brought to bear on a child's prebirth history: it is read, pondered, discussed. The hope is that with time and through careful coddling—appeasing those forces that would pull the child back to the other world (cf. Gottlieb 1998) while simultaneously whetting the child's appetite for the things of this world—this "stranger" will begin to forget about its previous ties and its powers of clairvoyance (*kınaʋ*)—an ability many children are said to possess that allows them to "see" into the other world and so perpetuates their connection to that world—will become attenuated.

The Sex of Children

Kabre parents must also attend to another type of separation. As already mentioned, children are not yet gender differentiated, and indeed are considered androgynous.[1] As they mature, however, and in order to get married, they must become sexually single, for households are composed of the labors of two opposite, gendered single-sex beings. Children must therefore be separated from androgyny and "divided" from one another.

To say that they consider children androgynous is not to imply that Kabre see little boys and girls as totally indistinguishable. Their sex *is* taken notice of—symbolically marked—from the beginning: the day after birth, for instance, a young child is sent to the house of the newborn's mother's brother carrying a bow on its head if the child was a boy and a sorghum stalk if it was a girl (symbols that refer to the work of each gender—hunting and cooking). As they grow up, little girls spend more time doing "female" work—taking care of their younger siblings, helping their mothers with cooking and marketing—while little boys do more "male" work—accompanying their fathers to the fields and, eventually (around puberty), beginning to cultivate in small work groups of their own.

Still, much of children's behavior blurs the boundaries between the sexes: little boys fetch water for their mothers and help them with cooking; little girls consume dogmeat, a male food, with their fathers; and, more generally, both eat without regard to the sexualized taboos normally associated with adult consumption.

The sexual ambiguity of children also derives from their proximity to the spirit world—where gender identities are more fluid and ambiguous—and from the fact that children are identified with, and considered the reincarnations of, their deceased grandparents. The association with the latter collapses many of the distinctions between the two sexes, for old people generally are considered bisexual—old people cook *and* cultivate, need not follow gendered eating and dancing taboos, and so on.

Finally, the androgyny of children resides in the fact that they are seen as embodying and conjoining that which produced them: male and female bloods (at conception), male and female labors and foods (after birth), and, more generally, the productive energies of the two ("male" and "female") families that nurtured and produced the child's parents and, by extension, the child.

We get a very clear image of the androgynous self in the meat divisions after Kabre sacrifices conducted during life cycle ceremonies. As is true elsewhere in Africa (see for example Evans-Pritchard 1956; Heusch 1985), the animal sacrificed represents, and stands in for, the person. After the blood of this surrogate has been spilled on the ground, the animal is dismembered and distributed to the relatives of the child being initiated: the hind legs belong to the child's father, the front legs to the mother's brother; father and mother's brother, in turn, send parts of their legs to *their* fathers and mother's brothers. Other, lesser shares are given to more distant relatives and friends. The most important shares, the front and back legs, are gendered—female and male, respectively. These belong to those "female" (mother's brother's) and "male" (father's) families that are seen as having produced the child. The animal thus embodies the dual nature of the productions that went into creating the child and symbolizes the fact that children are conceptualized as the product of the difference between their parents.[2]

If Kabre children are sexually ambiguous and, as it were, symbolically complete, they must nevertheless become sexually single and "incomplete" as they mature. The task of creating incomplete, gendered persons—of deconstituting androgynous persons—is the aim of a child's initiation ceremonies.[3]

Dividing Persons

While my focus will be on the role initiation ceremonies play in the differentiation of male and female gender, the ceremonies accomplish much else as well. Indeed, to say that their content is overdetermined would understate the case. In addition to addressing issues of gender identity, the initiations also vitally influence household and community-wide productive activities, establish relations with the ancestor and spirit world, play an important role in selecting the next generation of community diviners, and activate relations between homesteads, clans, and communities. As indicated above, they also engender a type of north-south reunification, for those Kabre who have migrated into the diaspora return to the north at the time of these ceremonies to initiate their children. And, over the last two decades, the ceremonies have come to play a role in national politics. Thus, in focusing on a single theme for analysis, we must nevertheless be wary of looking for the essence of these ceremonies in that theme alone.[4]

I should also note that the ceremonies of the two sexes are not simply analogues of one another. For one thing, boys have more ceremonies than girls; for another, while the ceremonies of both are concerned with "extracting" (Strathern 1988) them from androgyny, those of girls are also concerned with achieving a different sort of separation—dividing a girl from her parents and resituating her productive energies in the homestead of her husband.

Male Separations

When a boy begins to develop the muscled physique of a man and to hold his own in cultivating, his father will start him on his round of initiations. The first occurs around age fifteen, and the fifth (and last) almost ten years later. Each initiation ushers a boy into a new grade—*ɪfalʋ, sɪŋkarɪɣʋ, ɪsɔkʋ, kɛŋtʋ, ɪkʋlʋ*—and confers on him a new status. Differences in dress, personality and temperament, productive activity, food consumption, and spatial identification accompany each new grade. The changing identifications these differences engender are instrumental in effecting an initiate's gradual separation from the world of his mother and from his androgynous self, and his increasing identification with the world of males: as he identifies with male domains, foods, animals, and so on, he "becomes" male and is thus divided from the world of females. Simultaneously, his "need" and "desire" for a female other are created.

Space. The space in and around Kabre homesteads is gendered in a very specific way. The interior of the homestead—the central courtyard—is "female," for this is where women do much of their work—preparing and cooking food, and birthing children. That which lies outside the homestead—both the shady lounging/meeting area immediately outside the entrance and the fields beyond where men work—is "male." There is also a third, symbolically significant, space—a courtyard that extends out from the side of the homestead where grain is dried after the harvest. This courtyard is associated with various transitions, both material and ritual: In addition to being the place where crops rest as they undergo the journey from field to fire, it is also that ritual space where a deceased person's "double" (*warıtʊ*) is brought and resides between the burial of the body in the fields (where the tombs are located) and the fixing of the ancestor stone at the center of the homestead's courtyard.

The ceremonies of initiates take place within the coordinates of this gendered spatial system and appropriate its symbolism in achieving their ends. Thus, the first ceremony for *afalaa,* conducted when a boy is around fifteen years old, begins with him seated on his mother's cooking stool—in the heart of the homestead's female space. Then, after a series of sacrifices, a period of confinement in his mother's hut, and a ritual refusal of beer offered him by a woman of the house, he exits the homestead—running—through the grain-drying area and disappears into the fields. This flight from female space is witnessed by community elders who gather to watch the initiate's coming out.

When he becomes a *sıŋkarıyʊ,* three and a half years later, the initiate appears with his cohort at night, singing and playing his flute in the male space outside the entrance of homesteads throughout the community. Were a *sıŋkarıyʊ* to try to enter the homestead to play his flute, he would be barred. When he joins the next grade and becomes an *ısɔkʊ,* he is symbolically pushed even farther from the homestead—into the fields— where he makes his only ritual appearances and where he is expected to show his prowess as a cultivator.[5] Three years later, he becomes a *kɛŋtʊ* and is formally "shown," and thus associated with, another male space: the sacred groves where all the major sacrifices to the spirits of the community are carried out.

At this point in his initiations, after years of symbolic exile from the homestead, the initiate begins his return. Invited by relatives from throughout the community, he reenters the space of the homestead, following the path taken by crops and ancestral spirits—through the grain-drying area where, at the time of the spectacular quinquennial ceremony called *waaɣa,* he and his cohort dance as antelopes. Having been associated exclusively with male spaces over the previous seven years, and having thus "become" male, the initiate now reenters the female domain of the homestead as a different being, as someone transformed. His metamorphosis is reflected in comments I heard over and over again at the time of *waaɣa*. When watching the initiates dance, people would say: "We don't know who they are," "Where is my child? I don't see him," "The *kɛŋnaa* [those who dance *waaɣa*] are unrecognizable."

Finally, two and a half years later, when he becomes an *ɪkʊlʊ* and goes through his last rite of passage, the initiate is again invited to dance at the homesteads of family members, but this time in the central court-yard. This ritual return to the space where he began ten years previously stands in stark contrast to that earlier occasion, however: then he was a timid child identified with his mother, sitting on her cooking stool; now he stands tall and confident, draws attention to himself with his song and dance, and is in possession of those abilities—cultivation, strength, self-control—he will need to feed and care for a family.

Blood. If one of the modes through which a male initiate is divided from androgyny and the world of women is by identification with male spaces external to himself, another is through the internalization/con-sumption of various foods, and the changes those foods effect within his body. The sacrifices that occur throughout a boy's initiations are typically of "male" animals—rams, cocks, and dogs. While he himself does not consume all of each animal (much of which is divided and distributed to relatives), the initiate is expected to eat those body parts that are coded "male." Thus, he should eat the testicles of the ram and the head of the cock that is sacrificed when he becomes an *ɪfalʊ* and *sɪŋkarɪɣʊ*. He is also expected to eat the meat of those dogs sacrificed at each of his initiations and to consume the gravy made from the dog's blood.

The significance and symbolic role of dogs in the initiations is note-worthy. For Kabre, dogs are the most "male" of all domestic animals: they are forbidden as food to women between puberty and menopause (indeed, they are the only domestic animal women may not eat); they are cooked only by men, and in pots that are never used to cook food eaten by women; they are sold in markets that are set apart from the main marketplace (a female domain); and so on. Thus, in consuming dog, an initiate consumes the ultimate symbol of the nonfemale.

Even more than the meat, however, it is the dog's blood—which is cooked into a thick red-brown gravy—that carries special symbolic cur-rency. In consuming this substance (as well as its symbolic equivalent—*sɪlɪm*, the reddish sorghum beer that is a ubiquitous part of the initiation ceremonies), Kabre say that men make their blood "strong." Strong blood not only gives a man the strength to cultivate, and thus the ability to feed a family, but also produces his semen,[6] and thus enables him to have children. Through a type of symbolic blood transfusion, then, the ceremonies aim to fashion a certain embodied male potency.

The Head. While the entire outer body of the initiate becomes the focus or site of various markings, inscriptions, and identifications, it is his head in particular that receives the most attention. Among Kabre, the head is considered the seat of mystical power and knowledge, and therefore is the most important part of the body (cf. Swanson 1985: 214–16; Karp 1990: 86; Matory 1994: 130–38). It is also, of course, the highest part of the body, and is used metaphorically, as in English, to designate those at the top of hierarchies: the "head of the house" (*dɛɣa nyʊɣʊtʊ*), "the head of the initiation class" (*kɛŋnaa nyʊɣʊtʊ*), and so on. Thus, too, when sacrificing animals to spirits, it is the skull that is left behind at the spirit's shrine to show that a sacrifice has taken place there. Trading on this symbolism, the ceremonies pay special attention to the heads of initiates, which become metonyms of their changing identities.

The first grade (*ɪfalʊ*) is marked by the absence of anything on the head. Indeed, on the day of his initiation, an *ɪfalʊ*'s head is shaved clean. When he enters the second grade (*sɪŋkarɪɣʊ*), however, his head is adorned with a striking headpiece: a helmet of thick purple thread woven tightly into the hair, with a bright red cylinder, two inches in diameter and four inches long, protruding from the top. Attached perpendicularly to the cyclinder is a red wheel-like structure about eight inches in diameter. This headpiece, minus the wheel, is identical to the one the initiate will wear five years (and two initiations) later when, as a *kɛŋtʊ*, he will attach to it the horns of the antelope. The hornless headpiece of the *sɪŋkarɪɣʊ*, then, symbolizes that he is halfway along the journey to manhood: while potentially a man, he is not there yet. Or, as it was once described to me, a *sɪŋkarɪɣʊ* at once "looks back to the time when he was female and forward to when he will be fully male."[7]

When he becomes an *ɪsɔkʊ*, the initiate places the foot-long quills of the porcupine in his hair, and thus associates himself with an animal that is symbolically "male"—because, it is said, porcupines keep their distance from homesteads (a female domain) and promenade at night—as men (but not women) sometimes do.

When, three years later, the initiate becomes a *kɛŋtʊ*, he dons the enormous phallic horns of the antelope. These he wears for *waaɣa*, the ten-day dance that initiates see as the high point of their ten-year ritual passage into manhood. The antelope is regarded as the most male of all

Nnamnawé as *siŋkarɩɣʊ,* with child: androgyny doubled; Kuwdé, December 1982

wild animals, known for its strength and for its ability to gore other animals with its horns (as men do with their arrows when hunting and with their knives when sacrificing domestic animals).[8]

One of the striking things about the dress of initiates is its deployment of symbols of the "outside." This is true not only of the horns and furs of animals that are the centerpieces of an initiate's outfit, but also of the cowrie shells and iron implements (bangles, anklets, gongs) that adorn his arms and legs and dangle from his waist. (Cowries and iron, of course, are replete with associations of distant markets and the time of slaving, and, more generally, with Kabre connections to outside and distant others.) It is the outside's association with "power" and things powerful, and the Kabre desire to appropriate those powers (cf. Jackson 1982; Beidelman [1986] 1993; Werbner 1989; Jackson and Karp 1990; Karp 1990), that makes cowries, iron, and the horns of wild animals particularly apt symbols for these maturing males. Such appropriations also demonstrate the way the local is always also global, or, to use a different idiom, the way the inside is constituted through its outside.

A recent immensely popular addition to the headpiece of *kɛŋnaa* makes the same point. In the mid-1970s, a *kɛŋtʊ* from the south purchased a plastic, eighteen-inch doll of a baby and attached it to his horns when he returned to the north to dance *waaɣa*. The doll was widely ad-

Kuwdé *keŋnaa,* dolls on horns, returning home after a visit to a sacred forest in Faren; Boua, June 1985

mired, and by the mid-1980s plastic dolls on the horns had become all the rage, with dozens of initiates in each northern community imitating this southern innovator. (This, I was told, followed an earlier fad of tying plastic horses to the horns that was introduced by a Kuwdé initiate in 1970.) Thus, shortly before I returned to Kuwdé in 1985 to see *waaɣa*— and, I should add, much to my chagrin, for I was at that time under the grip of a romantic urge to experience the purity of a dance that many had told me would reveal the essence of Kabre culture—I received letters from Kouwènam and Nnamnawé, who were then dancing *waaɣa,* asking whether I would buy them each a doll. I did, of course, and they proudly attached these bright plastic babies to their horns for the duration of the ten-day ceremony.

My own sensibilities notwithstanding, the symbolism of these dolls is entirely consistent with that of other items *keŋnaa* place on their horns for the dance, as well as with Kabre appropriations of an outside domain associated with power. Thus, the dolls are attached to the horns next to just-harvested ears of corn and millet, small bottles of milk, and other symbols of fertility. Referred to as "white child" or "colonial child" (*ana-sara pɛɣa*), however, and thus unlike the other items, these dolls are coded European/colonial. Just as the dress of initiates draws from the outside, then, and just as certain of the ceremonies attempt to appropriate the outside powers of the bush, so too does this recent innovation appear to be an attempt to appropriate and subvert the fertility and "power" of the colonial/postcolonial other. I should add, however, that those initiates with whom I spoke about the dolls said simply that they were "just for beauty" and "nothing more than fun." A case, then, in which either the anthropologist's desire to impose meaning has overleapt its bounds or those I spoke to had their own sound reasons for remaining mute when questioned by the white outsider!

Comportment. The ceremonies also devote much attention to an initiate's inner bearing and attitude. As he approaches manhood, it is said that a boy must learn discipline and self-control: he must measure his speech and not speak or eat indiscriminately in public, like women and children are said to do; "he must learn," as one person put it, "how *not* to speak all the words that are in his heart." He must also learn how to treat people of rank—elders—and his in-laws with respect.

Afalaa are timid, quiet and reserved; *sıŋkarıŋ*—true to their sexually ambiguous, trickster-like nature—are loud and bawdy; *asɔkaa,* again, are quiet and reserved; *kɛŋnaa,* similarly, are very controlled, but they also—and this is even more true of *akʊlaa*—walk and speak with a measured confidence they lacked as *afalaa* and *asɔkaa.*

When I first arrived in Kuwdé and was just getting to know Nnamnawé—who was then a *sıŋkarıɣʊ*—one of the things that attracted me to him was his fun-loving, mischievous nature. In public, he was often loud and bawdy, constantly flirting with the line between propriety and impropriety. It was all in good nature, however, and others, like myself, seemed to find him a pleasure to be around. I was surprised, then, six months later, when his personality seemed to undergo a dramatic shift. In public, he became sober, quiet, and withdrawn. The prankster in him was entirely gone. Not yet aware of how heavy was the imprint of the initiation system on the identities and personalities of initiates, I imagined the worst: that he had family problems or had discovered a blight in one of his fields. When I asked someone one day what had happened to him, however, they simply said that he was now an *ısɔkʊ* and that if he were to behave as he had when he was a *sıŋkarıɣʊ,* he would be severely chastised. "Being the head of a family is a heavy responsibility," he continued. "Initiates need to develop the discipline not only to work hard so that they can feed their families but also to control their emotions and words in public. If they do not learn restraint, they will get into trouble with others and then later when they need help, they will find

Asɔkaa in the market: Togolese soldiers in the making; Farendé, June 1984

themselves all alone." (In poaching on these ceremonies to recruit initiates into the military [see below], Eyadéma has also appropriated the ethos of discipline and self-control associated with *asɔkaa* in particular and male initiates in general. Thus, I frequently heard Kabre compare the military to an initiation grade, and soldiers—and the discipline they must exercise—to *asɔkaa*.)

Work. As an initiate moves from female to male spaces, attire, foods, and comportment, so too does he move from female to male productive activities (and from productive dependence on his father to relative autonomy). As a child, and as befits his androgynous nature, a little boy engages in the work of both sexes—going to the fields with his father, while also helping his mother with chores around the homestead (cooking, fetching water from the spring, and so on). When he becomes an *ɪfalʊ* all this changes. He stops doing women's work and joins an adult male work group (*ɪkparɪ*) for the first time. This is an important step, for these four- to six-person work groups are the mainstay of the Kabre agricultural system, convening each morning throughout the crop cycle and mobilizing more labor than any other type of work group. Having established his place in the small work group as an *ɪfalʊ,* he then comes to assume a prominent place in the large (20–30 person) communitywide work group (*haɖaa*) as an *ɪsɔkʊ*. These groups convene in the after-

Kouwènam after a cultivating session; Kuwdé, April 1983

noons at bottleneck periods during the crop cycle—especially during the second sorghum weeding in June, and at the time when yam mounds are made in August. Indeed, *asɔkaa* are expected to lead the *haɖaa*—not only finishing first but also doing more of the work. Thus, if you are in attendance at one of these sessions, you will see a line of quilled heads, bobbing up and down, at the front of all the other cultivators. An *ɪsɔkʊ* must show, Kabre say, that he is ready to feed a family with his hoe.[9]

A *kɛŋtʊ* continues to demonstrate his prowess as a cultivator in special work sessions. As well, his work habits are subjected to public scrutiny and discussion. If he is a slackard—or otherwise not focused on cultivating—he will be openly criticized by others. When Kouwènam was in this grade, he spent some (and clearly in the eyes of others, too much) of the money I paid him drinking beer and fraternizing with friends in the market. After several months, people began to gossip about him—criticizing him for spending his energy on drink and talk, rather than conserving it and channelling it into cultivation.

It is often at this point in his development, between the ages of twenty and twenty-five, that a young man gets married and begins to acquire some independence from his father. To this point all of his work has been carried out on his father's fields, and all of the food he has produced has gone into his father's granary. When he becomes a *kɛŋtʊ,* however, he is given fields and allowed to build a granary of his own for the first time. He will still continue to work some in his father's fields, but from now on his energies will be more focused on feeding his own nascent family.

Two and a half years later, when he goes through his last ceremony—called "finishing" (*ntɩsɩrɩ*)—and becomes an *ɩkʊlʊ,* his independence becomes even more complete. At that time, he may build his own homestead in one of his father's outlying fields. When he does this, and begins to feed his family on his own, Kabre say the initiate has "arrived."[10]

◄○►

If this is the symbolic template that guides male initiates through their passage to adulthood, it is nevertheless amazingly malleable. Indeed, much of the strength of this set of ceremonies lies in its plasticity, in its ability to adapt to changing historical circumstances and to accommodate varying individual histories.

The French anthropologist Raymond Verdier (1982) has suggested, and he is doubtless correct, that this system of initiation had its origins in the time of the slave trade (and thus, I might add, within modernity—Gilroy 1993a) and served to recruit young men to the defense of the communities of the massifs. (The aggressive, warlike symbolism of some of the ceremonies today would tend to support such a claim.[11]) Whether or not it also served to organize Kabre resistance during the colonial era I was unable to determine. Kuwdé elders I spoke to said initiation classes were not sites of armed opposition to the Germans in the communities of the northern massif, though they may have been in the southern massif. They were quick to point out, however, that Mahate, the Kuwdé man who shot and killed the first German invader, was a *kɛŋtʊ,* and thus a member of the initiation class that is also thought of as a "warrior" class.

Certain of the ceremonies did engage colonialism in a different way, however. The French missionary Jacques Delord, for instance, was present at initiation rituals during the 1950s that mimetically incorporated colonial-era work projects:

> In one village, Kiriwude, a new and unexpected rite has been added [to the initiation of *kɛŋnaa*]: as the mound [the initiates were building] requires several rocks to strengthen it, the sponsors take the initiates to a

place about a half hour away, near a stream, and taking advantage of the fact that the elders did not follow, they imitate for the initiates the famous construction of the road from Sokodé to Lama-Kara, including the installation of the telephone lines, the building of the bridges, and those who deliver messages attached at the end of their sticks, as well as the gardeners who water the flowers of Madame, the wife of the administrator! (Delord 1961: 135, my translation)

Was this parody? Symbolic subversion? Mimetic appropriation? "Initiation" into colonial road work? Unfortunately, I was unable to find anyone who had been present on such occasions. Nevertheless, if such symbolic action is at all consistent with the logic and symbolism of the ceremonies generally, my guess would be that it was an attempt both to empower initiates faced with the privations of the colonial labor system and to magically appropriate and subvert the technology and power of the colonial Other.

It was also during the colonial era that the ceremonies of the initiation system were harnessed to the dynamics of the emerging Kabre diaspora. Thus, the return of southern initiates, especially *afalaa* and *kɛŋnaa,* to the north to undergo initiation came to be used, as it still is today, as an index of the nature of north-south relations. The expectation is that those who have departed for the south will return again and again— "that they will not forget those they have left behind"—and these ceremonies have come to assume much of the weight of that obligation. Thus, at the time of the initiations of *afalaa* every July and of *kɛŋnaa* in June of every fifth year, the roads are jammed with thousands of southerners returning to the north to initiate their children ("to show them their houses of origin"), and homesteads and communities in the north swell to many times their normal size. Those southerners who fail to return inevitably arouse the wrath of house ancestors and spirits who, like the rain spirit, will almost certainly repay their neglect with hardship.

Another way the spread of Kabre into the diaspora has affected the initiation system has been to skew it toward those ceremonies for which southerners choose to return. Thus, even for those who permanently reside in the northern communities, the ceremonies of *afalaa* and *kɛŋnaa* are today considered the most "necessary" to perform, while many of the others have become dispensable. When I asked Kuwdé elders about this change, and the resulting compression of the ceremonial system, they seemed untroubled and gave responses similar to those Karabu offered when discussing *ɩkpantʋrɛ* exchange: "It is not the quantity or size of the ceremonies that matters, so much as the intent of those engaging

Initiation and state spectacle; Lassa, July 1996

in them. Thus, if southerners can only make it back for *afalaa* and *waaɣa,*
it is because they are unable to return more often, and if northerners
can only find the means to do those two ceremonies, it is because of
hardship rather than unwillingness."[12]

Finally, as mentioned at the beginning of this chapter, the last two
decades have seen the dramatic intervention of the national government
into the ceremonies. Thus, the July wrestling matches of southern massif
afalaa[13] have become state spectacles, annually attended by Eyadéma
and his cabinet, and broadcast on state television. Although the osten-
sible focus of the event is the wrestling—the initiates appearing two at
a time, stripped to the waist, muscles abulge and glistening, to duel before the president—the occasion is striking for the way Eyadéma's presence displaces that focus. Arriving by helicopter, like a giant bird out of
the sky, moving briskly in suit and tie alongside a phalanx of soldiers to
a reception line to greet visiting dignitaries and local chiefs, seating himself front and center before the wrestlers, Eyadéma clearly becomes the
event. Indeed, when I attended in 1996 in the village of Lassa, the wrestling came to an abrupt end, even though many wrestlers had not yet
fought, when Eyadéma decided after an hour that it was time to move
on to the next village.

Needless to say, Eyadéma's participation in this single ceremony has

affected the entire initiation complex. Today, for many Kabre, and especially those from the south, *afalaa* has become the ceremony of choice,
and wrestling, an otherwise relatively minor part of the initiation of *afalaa,* its central focus. So, too, for non-Kabre, the wrestling matches have
come to stand not only for *afalaa* but also for Kabre initiation as a
whole—and indeed, through the martial image they project, for Kabre
and northerners generally.

But what is the state's interest in such rituals? Eyadéma himself
claims a charmingly personal reason. He is reputed to have been a great
wrestler during his youth and says that it is his nostalgia for that time
that brings him back to the north each year to witness the ceremonies
and ensure their continued survival. But clearly there are more instrumental reasons as well. Eyadéma uses the occasion to recruit new soldiers into the army, hand-picking those wrestlers he deems most able at
a closed gathering at his house in his natal village on the day after the
last matches.[14] Eyadéma also uses the event to show members of his
home region that he, like other Kabre who have departed into the diaspora, has not forgotten his ties to the north. Finally, and perhaps most
importantly, he aims to project a Mobutuist image to the entire country
of state support for local culture and also, by identifying himself with
wrestling, to further enhance the martial image that lies at the base of
his power. This latter is not without risk, however: his identification with
wrestling has been appropriated by his adversaries in the south, who use
such representations as evidence of the "savage," "uncivilized" nature
of the north, and therefore of Eyadéma's/the Kabre's unfitness to rule
the country.

◄○►

This ceremonial system's adaptability in the face of historical change
is matched by its ability to accommodate divergent personal histories
(Jackson and Karp 1990). As Nnamnawé put it when I asked him to
describe how different initiates went through the system,

> The ceremonies stay more or less the same but no two people go through
> the same way. Each has his own way. I didn't dance *konkoriŋ* [a dry season
> ceremony that directly precedes *waaɣa*], for instance, because I was in the
> south making money so that I could buy the animals I needed to sacrifice
> for *waaɣa*. And Kouwènam didn't do any of the ceremonies before *konk-
> oriŋ* and *waaɣa* because his father was old and had nothing. In such a case,
> instead of doing the whole ceremony, you just kill a dog and distribute the

meat. I think that's what Kouwènam did. But if you can't even do that—like Awurakum whose lazy father was never able to find the money to purchase the animals at the time of his initiations—you can kill a dog for each of the ceremonies you missed at the time of *waaya*. And, in Awurakum's case, since his father died before he danced *waaya*, he had to do this on his own. Another path is to do a ceremony for someone who isn't here—an initiate who couldn't make it back from the south. If he sends money to buy the animals, members from his house here in the north will do the sacrifices and tell the ancestors that it's for him. . . .

Initiates also show their differences when they are dancing. Each has his own song, his own way of fluting, his own style of dancing. And these distinctions are highly valued. It is the differences between initiates which are remembered when the old people talk about their initiations. "Atakpai won all the cultivations." "Tcheki came out with a flute melody that no one had ever heard before." "The words that Kundoukou sang were so beautiful because their meanings were hidden but very intelligent." You should have seen the pride on my father's face when I won the big race at *waaya*—when I showed that I was the best of my class. . . .

Another, and for many the most important, way [male] initiates divide themselves is by whether or not they have *hama* (power). As you know, someone who has *hama*—someone who can do extraordinary things like jump over buildings or, like the president, survive a plane crash—doesn't come out and admit that he has it. *Hama* is not something you talk about. It remains hidden. But at the time of certain dances, and *waaya* is one of these, you can reveal to others whether you have it or not. One way you do this is through the color of the animal sack you wear around your neck. A red skin [from a fox or a goat] indicates that you have *hama*. Another way is by attaching a second, smaller set of horns between the large horns on your head. . . .

Finally, each initiate has his own history—my mother's brother is different from Kouwènam's, I have *ɪkpantʊna* that he doesn't have, I am in a different work group. All of these differences come out in the sacrifices because I send meat to *my* relatives and friends, and he sends to *his*. The personal histories we tell through these sacrifices are in each case different.

Nnamnawé's commentary here indicates the general value Kabre place on a certain type of personal distinctiveness. The initiate who distinguishes him/herself, the dancer who improvises, the diviner with special powers, the person who makes others laugh, someone who is good at playing with words or who is quick with the biting insult, the best (male) cultivator or (female) sauce maker or marketeer—all these are personal traits that are highly valued (and it is these attributes of the person, among others, that are celebrated when someone dies). It should be noted, however, that such forms of self-realization are not opposed to the types of relational personhood to which Kabre are also committed. Always mindful of a set of relational commitments and constraints, they seek to author a self that is at once distinctive *and* relational. Thus, in the world of exchange, the most individual of Kabre—and the most esteemed—is also the one who is the most relational: he/she who has risen to the top of the system of exchange spheres. And in the world of music and dance, the highest praise is reserved for the drummer or dancer who improvises—but within parameters set by, and in relationship to, the other drummers or dancers (cf. Chernoff 1979).

◄○►

If one of the aims of Kabre ritual is to make identities known to a public, and thus more real to those (initiates) undergoing the ritual, another is to cater to various desires in that public. One such desire is strictly aesthetic—the longing, expressed by many with whom I spoke, to experience the beauty of the ritual, the grace of the dance, the elegance of a dancer who has mastered proper form and is willing to innovate upon that form. In Kuwdé, this aesthetic sensibility is steeped in a highly developed culture of criticism: a dancer's movements, an initiate's dress, the improvised words of a song are all subjected to ongoing critical evaluation and commentary. Such scrutiny, of course, not only deepens the experience for the aesthete but also spurs the competitive and creative juices of the performers themselves.

Another desire elicited by the ceremonies is more gendered. It consists in the longing of female spectators to witness and evaluate the maturation of their male counterparts, and vice versa. Thus, as *keŋnaa* move majestically beneath their horns in the homesteads and sacred forests, clusters of young women stand and watch attentively, gazing upon the dancers, judging their performances and their powers, and commenting on their beauty. Conversely, as *akpema* (female initiates) make their market appearances, young men gather to watch the female dancers and similarly discuss their strengths and weaknesses, their readiness for marriage, their appearance, their character. Here public spectacle situates a gendered gaze that fixes the other as object of desire—and thus powerfully furthers the process of division that is a central aim of these ceremonies.

Female Separations

As mentioned above, the ceremonies a girl undergoes are fewer in number than those of boys—there are only two, and they take place in the course of a single year. And while one of the aims of these ceremonies is to make a girl into a woman (to make her unambiguously female), an even greater concern is to separate her from her parents and relocate her at the homestead of—and in a complementary productive relationship with—her future partner.

As with boys, the timing of a girl's initiation—somewhere between the ages of fifteen and eighteen—depends upon her physical maturity and her productive development. "When a girl is small," a mother told me, "she learns how to work—she carries compost to the fields, she finds leaves for the animals, she gets water at the spring, and she helps her mother with cooking. Then one day, when we see that she is strong and has learned to work well, we know it is time for her to be initiated and get married."

Work. In the three to five years immediately preceding her initiation, a young woman takes over much of her mother's workload: she goes to market in her mother's place, does most of the household chores, and routinely cooks the evening meal. While the work a daughter performs considerably lightens the mother's workload, and therefore is a special—and eagerly anticipated—moment in the life cycle of every woman, its overt purpose is to give a girl practice in developing the work skills she will need when she marries.

The rituals associated with a girl's initiation repeatedly inscribe and articulate this theme of household work. Thus, at the beginning of her dry season ceremonies, the initiate makes a special trip one evening to her fiancé's homestead, where she grinds flour, fetches water from the spring, and cooks the evening meal for her future in-laws. In performing these acts, Kabre say, the initiate shows her in-laws that she can do women's work. Later, during the wet season, the initiate makes beer for her future spouse—again, to show that she will be able to do so when he needs beer for a ceremony or work group. On the same occasion, she is expected to collect firewood for her mother-in-law. In addition to demonstrating that she can perform domestic chores, she must also show that she can successfully engage in market commerce. Thus, at various times during the wet season, she makes "market beer" (under the supervision of her mother) and takes it to sell in the local markets.

Food/Bodies. There is a Kabre phrase I heard repeatedly, especially when people were trying to instruct me in the differences between men and women. "Men should drink a lot of *sɩlɩm* (beer) and eat only a little *mʊtʊ* (sorghum porridge)," they would say, "while women should eat a lot of *mʊtʊ* and drink only a little *sɩlɩm*." While this expression confers on men the undeniable privilege of consuming more beer, it also points to a contrast Kabre see between consumption practices and differently gendered bodies. Thus, if boys' bodies, and their blood/semen, is produced by consuming beer (and dog blood), girls' bodies, and their wombs, are produced by consuming sorghum porridge, for eating a lot of porridge, Kabre say, enlargens the stomach/womb (*lotu*) and prepares it for giving birth to a child.

Filling a girl up with food is thus a major preoccupation of the time leading up to her initiation, and both the girl's fiancé and her parents devote their energies to ensuring that she eats well. The fiancé does his part with the harvest prestations he makes—initially small, then gradually increasing quantities of sorghum, yams, and corn, each year for ten years leading up to the marriage. He also works the fields of his father-in-law two to three times a year over the same ten-year period. These gifts of food and labor are thought of not so much as an exchange between houses of property for a woman (as in certain bridewealth systems) as a direct gift of food to the woman herself. Their purpose, Kabre say, is to "feed" the man's future spouse so that when she goes to live with him she will be strong and capable of bearing children.[15] Significantly, the noun used to refer to these gifts, *kusuɣu,* means "filling up," and its verb form, *masuu-i*—used by a fiancé when referring to the gifts he makes—translates "I fill her up." Thus, in making prestations to the girl's family, a fiancé is thought to be "feeding" and "filling" his future wife with food—and thus helping to produce her body/womb. This practice, of course, is the complement to her role in making his blood—through the beer gifts she gives him at the time of the harvest.

The image of the full/fat wife, and of the role of the groom in the womb-making process, is strikingly represented on the occasion when a female initiate goes to her in-laws' to work and cook dinner for them. When she arrives, she is presented with a very large hen, which should have the appearance that "it is about to lay eggs." If she accepts it (if it is not big enough, she may ask for a larger one), it is killed, cooked whole, and then stuffed with salt. Later, when it is time for her to return to her parents' homestead, this stuffed hen is placed in a bowl filled with

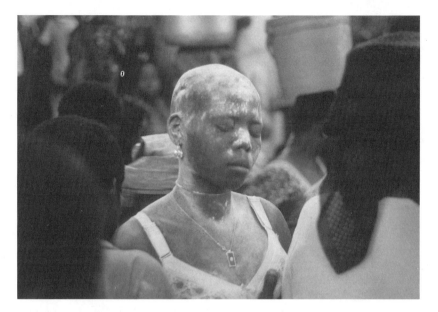

A Kouméa female initiate in the market; June 1983

red palm oil for her to take back to her parents—so that they can see that "she has been well fed."

A girl's parents, too, contribute to the feeding/fattening process. Especially during the year of her initiation, they make sure that she eats a lot so that when she "comes out" in the market—on a special day in September when her period of initiation is nearing its completion—people will remark of her that she is ready for marriage.

Separation. If ensuring that a female initiate is prepared to do women's work and to bear children are two of the major aims of her initiation, another is relocating her from her parents' homestead to her husband's.

This task is not easy, however, for it involves separating her from a situation that is known—from the family with which she has grown up—and assimilating her into a situation and a homestead that is unknown and about which most girls have enormous ambivalence: will she and her husband get along? Will he give her enough food? Will he buy her cloth to wear? How will he treat her if he takes a second wife? Will she and her co-wife get along? And, especially, how will she and her mother-in-law—for whom she must work during the early years of the marriage—make out? All of these questions in a girl's mind are informed by the knowledge that these relationships—husband/wife, co-wife/co-wife, mother-in-law/daughter-in-law—are among the most difficult and conflict-ridden in Kabre society. The girl's parents, too, have their reasons for hesitating to let her go. Not only are they concerned with how she will be treated; they are also loath to lose her labors and her children.[16]

In order to win over his in-laws—and thus to "extract" his future spouse from her homestead—a young man must convince her and her family that she will be treated well. Indeed, many of the activities of the initiation period have this sort of subtle persuasion as their aim. For instance, Kabre say that the purpose of the marriage gifts a boy makes—the ten years of harvest gifts and field labor he gives his parents-in-law—is not only to "fill" his future wife with food but also to show what type of character he has and what type of worker he is. Thus, much attention is paid to whether he works hard in his father-in-law's fields, whether the food gifts are on time, whether he merely gives the minimum required or more, and so on. By being successful, a young man hopes to slowly build his future wife's desire for him, and thus to prod her into eventually leaving her parents to live with him. Seeing marriage gifts in such terms, of course, is consistent with that which Kabre deem important in other exchange contexts: qualities matter more than quantities, and people's intentions matter as much as their actions. As well, to the extent that these gifts represent a type of "request"—a manifestation of a groom's "need/desire"—they create a hierarchical relationship between the groom and his in-laws and, it is hoped, initiate a process that will eventually lead to a return marriage between the families—and a reversal of the hierarchy. Recall that for Karabu, such a marriage (FZD) was the desired outcome of ıkpanturɛ.

The submissiveness of a boy toward his future in-laws is vividly illustrated in the following ritual scene. The occasion is the first day of his future wife's initiation ceremonies in February. At this time, the community's elders are "called" to her homestead to drink beer and witness the opening sacrifices. At one point during the festivities, a surrogate for the girl's fiancé (his family's ritual helper, ceu/ıkpantʋ) enters the courtyard crouching and clutching a chicken in his hand—a gift for the initiate's parents. When the fiancé gets to the middle of the courtyard, he lies face down next to the pot of beer. He is then asked by one of the elders to explain the purpose of his visit. "I'm looking for a sʋnʋɣʋ (a small gourd used in cooking)," he says. "There aren't any here," the elder replies. As the disappointed fiancé turns to leave, the elder hedges and asks him whether, if they can find such an implement, the fiancé would be willing to bring his hoe and replace the soiled dirt behind the homestead, where the bath water and urine drain out, with clean dirt. The fiancé agrees to perform this task and the elders express their pleasure. They then accept his gift of a chicken and offer him beer.

On the one hand, this ritual moment is about work and the complementarity of labors that constitutes a marriage: a husband-to-be, someone who works with his hoe, is in search of a cook, someone who works with a *sʊnʊɣʊ*. In this sense, the ritual reiterates one of the central themes of the initiation process. On the other hand, however, this spectacle is also about hierarchy and submissiveness: the initiate enters the compound low to the ground, in a position of submission, and, when addressing the elders, lowers himself even more by actually lying on the ground. He also agrees to replace the soiled dirt behind the homestead's bathing area. Needless to say, there are few more unenviable tasks than this, and a fiancé's willingness to do it is a sign of his accepting his in-laws as his superiors.

But it is precisely by thus submitting himself—and this moment can stand as representative of the larger relationship between a boy and his parents-in-law—that he furthers the process of coaxing his future wife away from her parents. By "giving them respect" (*ʊha-wa nyamtʊ*), he hopes to win them over, and hopes that they will eventually allow him to marry their daughter.

However, the success of these various seductions—timely and generous gifts, acts of submission[17]—is never total. The doubts and the ambivalence remain. Indeed, they are often exacerbated by the fiancé's behavior: if he skimps on the harvest gifts, fails to work energetically for his father-in-law, and so on, the girl's concerns linger on. (Understanding the manner in which a groom's behavior is surveilled helps make sense of a fact that puzzled me when I first heard it: that Kabre girls, but not boys, can refuse their future spouses (either at the time their marriages are first arranged by their parents, or later). This asymmetrical prerogative is consistent with the fact that it is the premarital behavior of boys, more than that of girls, that is subject to scrutiny and, indeed, may be found wanting.)

As if in recognition of the possibility that the marriage might never be consummated, a girl's initiation period ends—in a scene that graphically images what, following Strathern (1988), I have been referring to as a process of "extraction"—with her ritual abduction from her parents' homestead. On a Monday in October, she makes beer and invites her fiancé and his age-mates to her homestead. After several hours of talk, flirtation, and drink, they get up to leave and she accompanies them to the pathway outside the homestead to say goodbye. Suddenly, the boys seize her and forcibly take her to the fiancé's homestead. Once there, she accepts and spends the night. The next day she moves her belongings and cooking pots into her husband's homestead. From this day forward, they are considered married.

Thus it is that the initiation ceremonies of Kabre boys and girls fashion complementary single-sex persons, separating them from their pasts, and dividing them from one another in order to recombine them in new households. In chapter 5 I examine these processes of recombination; before proceeding to that analysis, however, I wish briefly to consider certain theoretical issues that are raised by these ceremonies.

The Power of Spectacle, Spectacles of Power

One question that has dogged theorists of ritual, and one which came back to me again and again as I viewed these ceremonies, is why they seem to do little more than the obvious. That is, why do Kabre initiation ceremonies spend so much time mimetically walking boys and girls through the paces of what they apparently already know—"teaching" them how to cook, cultivate, and so on? What is achieved with this type of redundancy?

There are, I think, several answers to this question. First, while certain actions may seem redundant, attitudes are not, and these ceremonies are as much about the display of an initiate's attitude as about his/her actions. This is true both of boys when they are working for, and making gifts to, their in-laws and of girls when they go to their in-laws' to cook the evening meal. Indeed, many a sour postmarital relationship has found its start in what were perceived as bad faith efforts at the time of initiation. There is, then, always uncertainty as to whether the ceremonies will succeed or not, with failure a distinct possibility.

Ritual outcomes are uncertain in other ways as well. Each initiate comes to the ceremonies with a different history, or rather, different histories—those from before birth, those of childhood, and so on. These histories and the relationships they embody (with both humans and nonhumans) all affect the timing (the age at which one starts, how quickly one proceeds through the various stages) and the outcome of each initiate's ceremonial journey. As mentioned above, the ceremonies can be delayed, or even skipped altogether, for any number of reasons—a father's inability to purchase the animals to be sacrificed, an ancestor's reluctance to give the go-ahead, and so on. Alternatively, an initiate's performance might be enhanced through the mystical power he has acquired from a bush spirit or a wild animal. Thus, the ceremonies become a template for the expression—the externalization—of an initiate's personal history. The point here is not just that someone's history has an effect on the rituals but also that the rituals are crucial to making known that history.

But there is another, equally important reason why the ceremonies achieve more than just the obvious. Much of the ceremonial action has to do with making visible actions and statuses that are not considered achieved until they are "seen" by others. Throughout their initiations—and especially so for boys, for among Kabre boys more than girls are objects of the gaze—there is an emphasis on display and spectacle. Thus, boys are required to dance and sing in public—in front of others. And as they enter each new stage, the initiates are expected to go into the markets, so that others will "see that their time has arrived." The sacrifices that accompany each initiation are similarly concerned with making actions visible: after slitting the animal's throat, the sacrificer rubs the victim's blood (and, in the case of a chicken, its feathers) all over the sacrificial site (the ancestral stones, the shrine of a spirit) so that others may see what actions took place there. What we have here is an everyday epistemology that relies on making things known by making them visible.[18] In this way, too, the ceremonies' performance is far from redundant.

Moreover, what is true at the local level is also true of the state. The reason Eyadéma attends so assiduously to ritual is that he understands the power and importance of spectacle—that his power will not be "real" to his subjects until it is made manifest and visible (in ritual). When he attends the ceremonies of *afalaa* (or insists that localities perform "animation" for visiting state functionaries), he centers himself and the state in a representational nexus that constructs the nation as his and himself as the nation, while also positioning spectators as witnesses to—and, of course, potential critics of—such representations. But consider here the traffic in meanings between local and state: is this not an example of the reverse colonization alluded to by Bassari when he commented that the nation is the village writ large? Has not Eyadéma here appropriated the (village) culture of the spectacle to enhance the power of the state, in the process also transforming the power of spectacle into a spectacle of power?

Theories of Initiation

Finally, a point about anthropological theory and initiation. This ritual system "divides" boys from girls, creating each as the object of "desire" for the other. As such it fashions gendered subjects who are partial/incomplete, configured through difference, saturated with hierarchy, and forever connected to others through embodied webs of affiliation. This is not the autonomous, self-authoring, propertied individual of the Western liberal tradition; so, accounts of this person, and/or of Kabre gender, that are derived from the individualistic assumptions of this tradition have difficulty engaging those processes at work here.

Consider two such theories. In examining ritual complexes such as this, descent theorists have focused on the ties initiation grades create between individuals and groups—in other words, on the problem of social cohesion (Fortes 1958; Gluckman 1962; La Fontaine 1985). Initiation ceremonies are said, on the one hand, to socialize individuals into groups, and on the other, to create ties of solidarity between members of different lineages (through the bonding initiates experience as they undergo their ceremonies together). Such an explanation not only assumes that "individuals" as such exist and that solidarity might be a problem for them,[19] but also misses the tremendous complexity of these rituals and the amount of energy Kabre commit to them. If the system of initiation were about cohesion, that could be achieved in a much simpler way—through, say, an annual barbecue or some such event.

Another theoretical approach, also rooted in the liberal tradition, is to see such ritual complexes as produced by, and serving the interests of, male power. It is argued that since they have more power than do women, men reserve the most spectacular and the largest number of ceremonies for their male children, and in so doing reproduce the greater prestige of men in everyday life (Nadelson 1981; Herdt 1981; La Fontaine 1985). (Here "power" has replaced "cohesion" as the functional explanation of social practice, and "groups" appear as "individuals."[20]) It is not necessary to rehearse once again the numerous analytical problems to which such a theory opens itself (see chapter 1; see also Strathern 1988: 43–97). Assuming, nevertheless, that men do have more power (and this is a complex issue I take up in detail in chapter 5), such a fact could hardly serve as an "explanation" of why Kabre expend such enormous amounts of wealth in this manner, on a series of such intricately detailed ceremonies, extending over so many years.

I asked many men and women in Kuwdé about this point, and invariably received answers such as the following from Atcham, an assertive, articulate middle-aged woman who has raised and initiated three boys and three girls.

> Yes, men are superior to women, but that is not why they have more ceremonies. Boys have more ceremonies because they have farther to go and more to learn than girls. Girls are close to their mothers from the beginning, while boys don't take up the hoe until many years later. As well, a boy must become head of a house and is responsible for feeding his family, and sacrificing to the spirits and ancestors. Being able to do all this depends not only on his skill with the hoe but also on his ability to save money, to drink in moderation, and to temper his words in public. Also, to find a wife, a boy must spend many years showing respect to his in-laws to show that he is worthy.
>
> For a girl, it is much easier. She learns her work from an earlier age by following her mother around the homestead. By the time she is ten, she already knows how to cook and care for children. Marketing will come later but the essentials are not difficult to learn. And, while her in-laws are certainly interested in whether she is a good worker or not, and whether or not she will bring trouble to the house, her behavior is not watched and judged in the way that a boy's is. It is *her* family that has the upper hand in this one.

I do not mean to say here that these spectacles do not also exhibit and even enhance male power, much as state spectacles enhance the power of Eyadéma. But that is not their aim, nor is it why Kabre expend enormous amounts of energy in this system.

Another problem with both theories—and with the type of anthropology that generated such theoretical problematics—is that they assume a bounded totality. Thus, they assume that there is a society ("Kabre") that has a set of cultural practices (initiation ceremonies) that can be accounted for through social dynamics (cohesion, power) internal to that society. But Kabre are not now, nor have they ever been, bounded in this sense. The gendered desires and complementarities that find expression in these ceremonies bleed into other desires and complementarities, both regional and national, thus complicating any simple reduction of the ceremonies to a function of locally systemic dynamics.

There is a Strathernian point here as well. Kabre person/gender-making is informed by a qualitative logic—by operations through which persons are differentiated from more encompassing states. Such a logic contrasts with the quantitative, "augmentative" (and indeed commodity) logic of liberal theory that searches for comparisons within and between genders. The assumption of such theory is that one can have, or be, more or less of one's gender, and thus that one gender can be compared to—and can be found to be more or less than—the other (Strathern 1995). Kabre seem to be engaged in processes that are at odds with such assumptions. The cultural aim here is precisely to make qualitatively different types of persons that are incommensurable—and thus, through their incommensurability, their difference, to bring into being certain relational possibilities.

HOUSES

Collapsing Binaries, Ruling Strangers

In this chapter I examine how Kabre houses are produced—both mate-
rially and symbolically. Houses/homesteads are where the end products
of the initiation system—gendered (incomplete), and thus marriageable,
boys and girls—come together to combine their labors and capacities in
order to produce food and people. It is in and around the space of the
house/homestead—and through the labors of its men and women—that
babies are born and children raised, that grain is stored after the harvest,
that food is cooked and consumed, that initiations and funerals for family members take place, and that the ancestors are venerated. Houses
also play a special role in the diaspora, for it is to their "houses" in the
north that departed Kabre return to sacrifice to ancestors and spirits, to
initiate their children, and, eventually, to be buried. I focus especially on
the logic that informs male-female relations in the house, for not only
are these the terms Kabre use when discussing the way houses are constituted but there is also found here a conception of sociality that is at odds
with the individualistic logic of the theories I reviewed earlier.

An Initial Description

Houses/homesteads in Kuwdé, and throughout the northern Kabre massifs, consist of a circular complex of mud huts arranged around a central
clearing.[1] Tall, carefully built stone walls connect the huts and close the
space of the inner courtyard to the outside world. Entry is made through
a single large hut in the homestead's exterior or, in its place—as in some
of the older homesteads and those of clan heads—through a pair of large

A Kuwdé homestead; January 1983

upright stones that are said to "catch" enemies (slave raiders?) who may try to enter. These erect stones are associated with the antelope horns *kɛɲnaa* wear on their heads (the entrance to the homestead is called its "mouth" and is metonymically associated with the head) at the time of *waaɣa*.

Descending into the belly of the homestead—its central courtyard—you enter the main place of work and worship. This is where much of the homestead's food is prepared (and consumed), for here is located a woman's hearth. It is also here that the ancestral stones—round pebbles cemented into the base of a wall close to the hearth—are found. These stones are periodically spattered with the dried blood and feathers of chickens—the remains of sacrificial requests for protection, and visible expressions of a house's ongoing connection to, and acknowledgment of, its past. A large, platter-sized hole, called "house breathing" (and thus resembling the head's fontanelle—the soft spot on newborns through which Kabre infants are said to breathe), is located near the center of the courtyard. This is the place of sacrifices to spirits who also watch over the homestead. The clean surface of the courtyard—swept out twice daily—is often streaked with a star-like pattern of dried white swatches of sorghum beer, the grainy dregs that workers, or those invited to ceremonies at the house, toss onto the ground with a sweep of the hand at the end of a drinking session.

Around the periphery of the central courtyard are the huts where people sleep, the circle of thatch roofs occasionally broken by tin, the metal monuments I spoke of earlier that are purchased by southern family members to show that they have not forgotten those they have left behind. The smooth mud finish of hut walls is sometimes scarred with the same patterns Kabre used to adorn the bodies of initiates, until the 1970s when the postcolonial government, in a nod to "development," outlawed scarification. Also etched onto the skin of one of these huts— colonial modernity's signature at the heart of the homestead—is an indelible four-digit census number, a visible reminder of the system of numeration that enabled the imperial state to track native peoples and extract taxes.[2] On the walls, too, scripted graffiti-like, are the slogans of "lycée" students: pronouncements of support for Eyadema—"Vive RPT,"[3] "Puissance!"; proverbs—"Celui qui est seul ne peut rien faire"; remarks upon life's inscrutability—"C'est Dieu seul qui sait." At the base of the huts, sunken into the courtyard, are small inverted pots where house members sacrifice to their "doubles." Also accessible from the central courtyard is the bathing/urinating/birthing area—a narrow alley-way, hidden from view, that slopes down to allow drainage out of the homestead. It was the soiled dirt outside this area that the submissive groom described in chapter 4 vowed to keep clean. The central courtyard also gives entry to the grain-drying patio—the space that serves to mediate the passage of crops, ancestral spirits, and initiates from field to central courtyard.

This anthropomorphic house (cf. Griaule 1965; Fernandez 1982; Blier 1987)—with its "head," its "fontanelle," its "scars," and so on—provides a degree of refuge from the outside world: the inside of the house is where one can "share secrets" with family. Also, as that anchored place to which one constantly returns—not only while alive but also after death—the homestead lends some fixity to an otherwise fluid world.

If the interior of the homestead is conceptually closed off from the outside world, however, the tree-shaded area outside it is not. This is where public meetings are held, and where people from different home-steads gather to chat and work during the heat of the day—men fashioning their hoe handles and weaving baskets, women shelling baobab nuts and pounding sprouted grain into the pulp that becomes beer. It is also here—beside the pathways that fan out to other homesteads—that one

Inscriptions, traditional and modern; Kuwdé, March 1984

finds the small shrines of stacked rocks where a house's in-married women sacrifice to their doubles, on the path that leads to their natal homesteads. Among other things, these shrines acknowledge the ties between issue and source—between household members and those houses from which their mothers originated. And, like the tin roofs in the homestead's interior, they stand as concrete expressions and reminders of the fact that, however enclosed and unto itself, the house is still always also connected to others, and indeed owes its very existence to those others.

Producing Food

One of the major preoccupations of the household is, of course, the production of food. Indeed, the relationship between husband and wife is explicitly conceptualized as based on food production. When asked why they marry—marriage being the act that establishes a new household— Kuwdé men and women not only mention the need to produce offspring but also, and especially, they invoke the complementarities that inform their division of labor, through which men cultivate and women cook and do the marketing. Thus, the men respond that they marry in order to have someone (a woman) to cook the food they produce as cultivators, while the women say that they need someone (a man) to cultivate food for them to cook.

In cultivating, a man is aided by his sons (and their work groups); in cooking and marketing, a woman is helped by her daughters (and daughters-in-law). Until a son marries, all of his labor is expended on his father's fields. Similarly, until she marries, a daughter's labor is spent in helping her mother cook and in preparing her mother's products for sale in the markets.[4]

The products of these male and female activities are used to feed the family, with the husband in principle contributing grain for the entire year and his wife contributing sauce ingredients. In fact, a husband's grain often does not last until the next harvest, and he will then ask his wife to help feed the family by purchasing grain with the surplus money she has obtained from her commerce or by selling off some of her animals.

In addition to field crops, men own and grow various tree crops (especially the fruit of palm, baobab, shea, and locust bean trees). Unlike the field crops, these tree crops are destined for sale in the local markets. Such sales provide a man with a steady, though small, cash income that

A male work group in a field overrun by weeds; Kuwdé, July 1989

he uses to buy his hoe, sorghum to make into beer for work groups, beer for personal consumption, and animals.

Animals—sheep, goats, dogs, and fowl—are considered a person's "wealth" (*nyɪm*) and are used, by men at least, strictly for sacrifices— both to the ancestors at the homestead and to the spirits whose shrines are located in the sacred forests. Sacrifice thus represents an important end point in the process of male production, for it constitutes the ultimate destination of most male wealth—and, of course, also represents the conversion of wealth back into relationships.

The marketing of male-owned tree products also provides women with the raw materials for their commerce, since much of that commerce involves the processing of tree products into sauce ingredients. For instance, in Kuwdé the women process raw baobab seeds into the white, macaroni-shaped nuts used in Kabre sauces. Kuwdé women go to a distant market each Sunday to buy the seeds from the men of Asiri. After returning to Kuwdé, they spend the better part of three days boiling and shelling the seeds and then drying the nuts, before taking them to sell in the Saturday market. With part of the cash proceeds from this sale, each woman buys the food she needs for feeding her family (sauce ingredients and grain), recycling the rest into the next round of commerce. (As I have described in more detail elsewhere [Piot 1992], the division of labor that organizes the productions of the women of the different communities—Kuwdé women specializing in baobab nuts, Wazilao women in pots, Kawa women in red palm oil, and so on—creates a complex set of dependencies and hierarchies among the women of the various communities.)

While women also own animals and can thus also convert small surpluses from their commerce into animal wealth—indeed, the largest herds of goats and sheep in Kuwdé were owned by women—they themselves do not perform sacrifices. Consequently, unlike those of men, women's animals are often converted back into the cycle of domestic consumption. During bad crop years, for example, it is often a wife's animals that will be sold at market so that a family can buy grain to eat.

A striking example of the threads that connect the global to the local may be seen in a change that occurred within this system of production in the mid-1990s. For the first time, women began cultivating, and even formed *ıkparı* work groups in order to do so. Thus, when I returned to Kuwdé in 1996 and 1998, most married women were spending part of each morning farming small fields of sorghum and yams in three- to four-person work groups. This innovation was clearly tied to events in Lomé and Paris: the recession that accompanied the political turmoil of the early 1990s when many expatriates and much development capital fled Togo, and the French devaluation of the CFA in 1994. Together these two events cut deeply into the life of the rural markets, drying up much of the margin that had previously flowed into them from the cities. As one woman put it to me: "In 1994–95 the markets just didn't come alive. We would take food to market and it wouldn't sell. Then we'd try again the next week, and the same thing would happen. Finally, we had no choice but to take up the hoe and begin cultivating our own grain."

It is too early to tell what the long-term effects of this innovation will be. Some women I spoke to said it was simply temporary—a stopgap measure until the markets pick up again. They also pointed out that the fields they cultivate are small compared to those of men, and that, unlike men, they only cultivate so that they can sell grain to buy sauce ingredients. "We are still cooks and marketeers, not people of the hoe," they insisted. Others, however, seemed to relish their new dual identity and the added income farming afforded them, and insisted they would continue to cultivate whether the markets returned to their prior levels or not.

A female work group drinking beer; Kuwdé, June 1984

The Meaning of Food

The food a house produces, however, is not simply a form of nourishment. It is also a vehicle for establishing social relationships. While Kabre use several other idioms as well for talking about relatedness among the members of a house—those who come from a single "womb" (*lotu*) or those who share "blood" (*calɪm*)—the most common is those who feed (*tɔɣɔnaɣa*) one another.[5] Thus, "parents" are those who not only give birth to children but also—and even more so—those who give them food. For this reason, children who are not born into a homestead but nevertheless grow up there will regard those who feed them as their parents, and vice versa.[6] The ties between living and deceased family members are also maintained and articulated through the idiom of food. Thus, when sacrificing animals to the ancestors, Kabre claim to be "feeding" their dead parents and grandparents.

The importance for Kabre of food over other factors (such as blood) in establishing connection was clearly brought home to me one day when

I was present at a dispute over a case of adultery. A man in the community who was impotent had become extremely upset when he learned that his wife had taken another lover and become pregnant. The man went to Palabéi—who, as chief, is the local arbiter of disputes—to request compensation for the wrong. His case, however, was almost immediately dismissed as groundless. As Palabéi argued, since the complainant had properly paid harvest gifts for (had "fed") his wife, the paternity of any children she gave birth to could not be in question (that is, it would be impossible for the lover/genitor to make any claims to a child of hers). Besides, Palabéi added, the complainant should be pleased that his wife had taken up with another man, for otherwise he would be childless! Another example similarly illustrates how food trumps blood in Kabre thought. I was told that if an already pregnant woman remarries and her new husband sleeps with her throughout her pregnancy—thus "feeding" the fetus with his blood/semen—the second husband, and not the first (the genitor), would be considered the newborn's father.

Food-related terms and expressions proliferate in many other kinship contexts as well. Thus, as shown in chapter 4, the term used for bridewealth/harvest gifts, *kusuɣu*, means "filling up [with food]," and the ideal Kabre marriage, FZD, is referred to as "she has returned to her cooking stool" (*ʋmɩla ʋ-kpeɗirɔɔ*). As well, the name used to designate a two- to three-generation cluster of dispersed households, *cacayuri,* means "the father's thigh-bone," and refers to the leg of the animal that is sent to the senior male of the homestead cluster at the time of a sacrifice.[7] Significantly, the figure of the witch inverts the association between food-giving and relatedness: this antisocial destroyer of families is described as someone who "eats" his/her victims (rather than feeding them).

If sharing food establishes and articulates relationships within the family—between parents and children and between the living and the dead—it also creates hierarchies between these groups, for feeding engenders dependence and debt. Thus, children are dependent on, and beholden to, their parents because they were fed by them. This debt, I was told, is so large that even when the feeding role is reversed later in life—when children care for and feed their elderly parents (and beyond, when they sacrifice to/feed them as ancestors)—it can never be entirely repaid. This debt carries into, and indeed is constitutive of, relations in the diaspora, for those who have gone south are forever regarded as the "children" of those who remain behind, and as such are considered perpetually in debt to their "parents" in the north.

"Census"

During an early stage of fieldwork, I set out to conduct a census of households in Kuwdé. My aim was to gather standard demographic, social, and economic data—genealogies, marital and migration histories, ritual duties, and animal and land holdings—and thus to begin to put together a social and economic profile of the community. From its inception, however, this project encountered obstacle after obstacle and became an object lesson in both the micropolitics of conducting fieldwork in a small community and the fraught nature of anthropology in a postcolonial world (cf. Stoller 1987: 8–11; Gottlieb and Graham 1993: 65–68).

Initially, there was a run-in with Palabéi, the chief of Kuwdé, that delayed the start of the census for three months. Before embarking on the census proper, I had decided to do a dry run with Kouwènam's father, a man named Tcheki. But I had not consulted Palabéi before doing so, and when word reached him that I had spoken with Tcheki, he called me to his homestead. Palabéi said he had heard "whispers" that I had interviewed someone without his permission, and he wanted to know what we had spoken about. I explained that I had talked to Tcheki and described the types of questions we had discussed. I told Palabéi that it was just a trial run, and—sensing that I'd committed a major blunder—told him that I would of course interview him before anyone else when I began the real census, and would make sure that he found acceptable the types of questions I wanted to pursue. Palabéi nodded approvingly and assured me that what I had done was fine, but that before I could proceed he would have to seek the approval of Halatakpendi, the "chef du village." After a week went by, I asked Palabéi if he yet had word from Halatakpendi. He told me that he had made a special trip to Halatakpendi's house at the bottom of the mountain a few days previously but that the chief had been away on business, and that he would try again in a few days. This went on for a month, until Palabéi told me one day that he had finally seen Halatakpendi and that the latter had approved the project. Nevertheless, Palabéi added, Halatakpendi needed to get the consent of the government's prefect before I could proceed. Week upon week went by—as I sat virtually immobilized—before, three months later, I finally received permission to proceed. Clearly, I was being taught a lesson in etiquette, hierarchy, and power.

Once I began the census—going each day for two months from homestead to homestead for a two-hour interview with the homestead's head—I encountered numerous other obstacles. Some of these were standard, though frustrating and inordinately time-consuming, problems of translation. After three weeks of interviews with almost two dozen family heads, for instance, I discovered that the family genealogies I had been collecting were missing half the family members—because I didn't know at the time that Kabre differentiate terminologically between older and younger siblings and use the French *frère* and *sœur* (French was the language I was then speaking through) to refer only to "older brother" (*ɖalʊ*) and "older sister" (*kɔyɔ*). Thus, in asking for a person's "brothers" and "sisters," I was getting only the individual's older siblings; for the complete information I was seeking I ought to have been asking for *petits frères* and *petites sœurs* (*neu*). Of course, once I discovered what I had been doing, I had to spend days reinterviewing all those I had visited previously.[8]

Other obstacles had more to do with politics and with what I later learned were deep suspicions people had as to my motives for living and conducting research in their midst. Again, unbeknownst to me at the time, my census came to be called *kʊkalʊɣʊ* (literally, "counting"). This, it turned out, was also the term Kabre had used for the census the colonial government had employed to help them administer their system of taxation and forced labor! Not surprisingly, some people responded to me as they had to the colonial census—with various forms of evasion. Thus, a widow who was living alone fled across the border to Benin "to visit family" on the day I was to interview her, and didn't return for a month. Several men simply lied about their animal and land holdings, one claiming, for example, to have no animals or fields when in fact, I later found out, he had many of each. Another man insisted I buy a sheep and several chickens to sacrifice to his ancestors before he would speak to me about the history of his house. Although these tactics frustrated my attempts to document more fully the social and economic life of the community, they nevertheless seemed entirely reasonable ways of responding to what many perceived to be the invasiveness of my work. They also revealed some of the ingenuity Kabre had employed during the colonial era in devising strategies of evasion—and of course call into question the findings of colonial-era census work in this area (Bezon 1955; Froelich 1963: 65–68; Marquiessac 1932).

In summer 1996, after an interview with a man who had always seemed a bit aloof around me and mildly suspicious of my work, I asked Nnamnawé what people had thought of me and my work when I first arrived in Kuwdé (I had told them that I was a university student and wanted to write a history of Kuwdé). He said that there had been many theories. Some thought, because I wrote everything down and had begun by doing a census, that I was an undercover agent for a foreign government and that some harm would soon befall them: planes would drop bombs from the sky, they would be subjected to a new regime of forced labor, or some such. Others thought I might be there to steal spirit power from the sacred forests. Still others thought I was a development worker and would bring some form of material aid to the community—a well, a hospital, a better school.

"And now?" I asked. "Do they think differently?" He hesitated, smiled, and said, "Yes, we know now that you mean no harm. But, of course," he added, "we also know that this is your 'commerce' and that 'merchants' are nevertheless in business for themselves."

Constitutive Combinations

A house's gendered division of labor (whereby men cultivate and women cook) is part of a larger set of symbolic oppositions that organize household activity. Thus, men's cultivating is seen as providing the raw products that women process into food for consumption. The same gendered contrast between the raw and the processed is carried into the domain of reproduction as well. A husband's blood or sperm, Kabre say, is "cooked" inside his wife's womb to produce children. In both domains, men's (raw) products—crops and sperm—are processed in (female) containers—cooking pots and wombs. Illustrating the parallel between the two types of containers, a woman who has miscarried is said to have spilled her pot of water on the way back from the spring and is told that she must return to "refill it."

The homestead space metonymically associated with these various activities is also gendered. The inside of the homestead—where women do much of their work preparing and cooking food, and where they give birth—is "female." By contrast, the outside of the homestead—where men farm the fields, sacrifice in sacred groves to the spirits that govern the seasons and the community's welfare, and conduct the politics of the community such as resolving disputes (this latter takes place under the shade trees immediately outside the homestead)—is "male." Because of these spatial associations, during the dry season, the male season, the beer of ceremonies and work groups is served outside the homestead, while during the wet season, which is female, it is served inside.

Houses are also gender-divided as to processes of life and death. While women give birth, and are thus associated with life-giving, men bury bodies (handling cadavers, peering into the tomb after the deceased has been placed into position by the interrer,[9] organizing funeral ceremonies, and so on) and are associated with death. For this reason, it is men, never women, who slit the throats and spill the blood of animals that are being sacrificed.

The Kabre house or homestead is thus the site of the realization and conjunction of a series of gendered oppositions—cultivating/cooking, raw/processed, contained/container, outside/inside, and death/life.[10] If these oppositions collapse, infertility follows. Thus, if a wife goes into the fields of her husband while the crops are growing, the crops are said to "flee"; if a husband talks to his wife while she is cooking, the porridge will similarly "flee"; if a man sleeps with his wife before he goes hunting, the hunt will fail; if a woman walks over sacrificial blood in the courtyard or looks inside the tomb of a deceased person, she will be unable to give birth. The powers and identities of men and women—men as producers (in the fields) and women as cooks and processors (in the homestead); the death-dealing powers of men (on the hunt, in sacrifice, in burying cadavers) and the life-giving powers of women (in birth)—must be kept separate (cf. Sapir 1970; Gottlieb 1988; Schloss 1988): their differences must be observed in order for the house to remain fertile.

There are many other examples of the importance Kabre attach to the idea that social action must proceed from a set of differences. As described in chapter 3, exchanges between persons create difference: the difference of giver from receiver, and the hierarchy that difference entails. Exchanges between ritual moieties within a community, and between communities within the larger region, as I elaborate on in chapters 6 and 7, also aim to create differences between groups and communities—differences which then serve as the basis for social interaction. Kabre beliefs about twins provide another example of their attachment to the idea of difference. Ideally, they say, twins should be opposite sex. When they are not, they are nevertheless so categorized: the firstborn is referred to as the "male" twin and the second as the "female." (In fact, since Kabre twins are defined not only as those children born simultaneously to a single woman but also, and indeed more frequently, as those born consecutively to a single woman or to co-wives, it is easier to ensure that they are opposite-sex. Indeed, I knew of no same-sex twins in Kuwdé, and in the dozen or so twins-naming ceremonies I attended, the twins were always opposite sex.) The point here is that, when faced with a relationship between paradigmatically similar persons, Kabre convert it to one of difference.[11]

Worlds of Difference

This cluster of associations—between difference and fertility—appears to be widespread throughout the cultures of the Volta basin, and beyond. In the origin myth of the Batammaliba (Blier 1987: 65–66), close neighbors of the Kabre, the creator god (Kuiye) is said to have initially descended to earth with the first people—two men and their wives. However, the myth recounts that this was a time of infertility (the trees bore no fruit and the women were childless). It was also a time of "undifference": there was no separation between sky and earth (the sky god lived on earth), no division of labor (humans were fed by Kuiye without having to hunt, cultivate, and cook), no distinction between the seasons, between night and day, or between life and death. It was only when Kuiye decided to return to the sky (and to take the two men with him) that the differences that order Batammaliba life—and the fertility that results therefrom—appeared. With Kuiye's departure (which not only separated sky and earth but also gendered them—for the men were above and the women below), death appeared (creating the distinction between life and death), the rains came (producing the two seasons— i.e., the difference between wet and dry), women learned how to cook and men to hunt (creating the division of labor), and the two women became pregnant. Here fertility is directly related to the appearance/ generation of those (gendered) differences that organize and sustain Batammaliba social and cultural life.

A similar set of associations is found among the Dogon.[12] The Dogon myth corpus, for instance, recounts how, after the creation, Amma, the sky god, descended to have sex with the earth but was unable to: he first had to excise the female earth's maleness—a termite hill located on its surface (Griaule and Dieterlen 1965: 17). That is, he had to create the earth's difference from him before they could have a relationship. Later, when Amma created the first two humans (the eventual progenitors of the eight ancestors of the Dogon), they were unable to have sex because they were androgynous, each possessing a male and a female soul. They had first to be made single-sex—by circumcising the man (which eliminated the female soul located in his foreskin) and excising the woman (which removed the male soul in her clitoris) (Griaule 1965: 22). This set of operations became a model for human agency and society, for Dogon children are believed to have dual souls ("spiritual androgyny," Griaule called it) and need to be made sexually single—through circumcision/excision at the time of initiation—in order to get married and procreate (Griaule and Dieterlen 1965: 155–61). There are echoes here of what Kabre initiation aims to achieve as well.

It should be apparent that, in coming to terms with a Voltaic theory of society, and of social action, social theory should be attending to concerns with difference and fertility. Social actors in this area are far less concerned with cohesion, or with which group is controlling resources (either material or symbolic), than with attending to the differences that move people to act (cf. Wagner 1977) and, thus, sustain life itself.[13]

Mutual Entanglements; or, Agency Reconsidered

The Kabre conception of the differences that organize household activity, however, is more complicated still. Consider again the exchanges that initiate a marriage (and thus constitute a house). On the one hand, these exchanges—a boy's gift of food to his future wife, and her gift of beer to him—create a set of reciprocal, mutually dependent differences: in giving beer to her future husband, a girl is making a boy's blood and semen, and so producing that which makes him different from, but also dependent on, her; conversely, when a boy gives food and labor gifts to his in-laws, he is making his future wife's womb, thus similarly producing her difference from, and dependence on, him. But also, through this process, each incorporates and contains the other, for a man's blood is the product of female labor/food and a woman's womb the product of male labor/food.

This incorporation, and presence, of the other in the self extends also to the domain of homestead space. A man's granary (which most typifies his productivity and identity) is located at the very heart of the homestead's female space—the center of the courtyard; conversely, a woman's grinding hut (grinding being that activity by which a woman transforms [male] raw products into [female] food, and therefore an activity that typifies her work and identity) is located in that most male of spaces—the area immediately outside the homestead. This oppositional logic is developed further, for Kabre also say that what each gender produces—in cultivating and giving birth—belongs to the other. Thus, the food husbands produce is said to be "owned" by their wives, and the children a woman produces are "owned" by her husband. And (anticipating the discussion in chapter 6) gendered opposites incorporate one another at the level of the community as well. Each community has two ritual groups—gendered moieties—which are responsible for sacrifices to community spirits. While each moiety largely owns and sacrifices to same-sex spirits, each also possesses (and thus incorporates) an opposite-sex spirit. As well, while each moiety is primarily responsible for the rituals of its own season—the male moiety for the rituals of the (male) dry season and the female for those of the (female) wet season— each also inserts itself into its counterpart's season at a single point dur- ing the ceremonial cycle. Thus, the male moiety performs a ritual during the female wet season and the female moiety performs one during the male dry season. Here, too, opposites incorporate one another.

Notice, then, how this set of insights about the relationship between spouses affects our understanding of the person and of agency. Not only is an other established as the source of the self—each is the product of the other's nurture, and of the other's difference—but also the value of one sex is its value for the other. Thus, the action of a self is meaningful only in terms of its relation to an other, and to a difference: cultivating has meaning only as the complement of cooking. As with gift exchange, then, it is an other who elicits—who is the cause of—the action of the self: cooking is the cause of a man's cultivating, and vice versa. Agency thus resides not within a singular identity (*within* the person) but in the relations people have with one another—and in the relations differ- ences construct.

Complementarity and Hierarchy

The complementarity implied in this vision of the house is aptly con- veyed by a verbal game Kabre men and women repeatedly played with me. Often, when engaged in light chatter with people—whether sitting in a courtyard drinking beer with a work group or in a market with a total stranger—I was asked, in the bantering manner Kabre so enjoy, who I thought was more important—men or women? If I responded that it was men—because, say, it is they who cultivate—my inquisitor would say, "Fine, but who does the cooking?" If I tried a different tack and suggested that it was still men because it is they who own all the land, or because it is they who perform rituals to the spirits and ancestors, he/she would respond by asking me who gave birth to the men who performed these rituals. If, on the other hand, I took the side of women, suggesting that they were more important because they gave birth, she/he would respond that it was men who owned the houses where women give birth, or that it was men who conducted the rituals that allowed birth to occur in the first place. Soon, of course, I discovered that there was no "right" answer: if I argued the side of women, my interlocutor would take the male side; if I argued the side of men, he/she would take the female side. The house, I was being instructed, is constituted through its complementarities.

Still, if relations between men and women in the house are complementary, they are also—like all Kabre relationships—hierarchical. Thus, Kabre men and women assert that men are superior to women, because it is they who own the houses. (Women are only "strangers" in their husbands' houses and can thus claim no ownership.) Therefore, it is men who possess the children born into a house (and with whom the children will remain in the event of divorce) and men who have ultimate say over a house's daily operation. It is also men alone who are responsible for the ritual well-being of the house, making sacrifices to the ancestors and spirits, visiting diviners when house members are sick, initiating its children, and burying its dead. (These latter responsibilities, however, are seen by many men more as burdensome obligation than as patriarchal privilege.)

But this model of male privilege and unilateral authority is offset by another set of understandings. As one man put it to me, while the man owns the house and for this reason is superior to his wife, the day-to-day relationship between spouses is more like the relationship between ɪkpantʊna (exchange partners). "You have a 'need' and ask your wife for help, and then she has a need and asks you. Ideally, this is what a marriage relationship is—an ɪkpantʊrɛ." A woman also compared the relationship between men and women in the house to the alternating hierarchy between exchange partners. "Men's cultivating, and the food they give to feed the family, places them above their wives—we are in their debt. But this doesn't last. When a woman puts her labor into cooking the food a man has cultivated, the husband is in debt to her." This alternating hierarchy, she added, is seen to work on a seasonal, rather than a daily, basis. Thus, after the harvest, and during the male dry season when grain is abundant, men are said to be in a superior position, while during the female rainy season, associated with female transformative activities (like cooking), women are superior.

While these models—one complementary and asymmetrical, the other complementary and symmetrical—help to organize gender relations within the house, it should nevertheless be kept in mind that hierarchy among Kabre is seen to lie less in categorical relations (between, for example, "male" and "female," or "senior" and "junior") than in personal relations, and that hierarchies in general are much more fluid than those to which many Westerners are accustomed. Thus, while Palabéi was a male chief, the fact that he was indebted to Tikénawé (his junior and a woman) for beer was in many ways as important as the fact that he occupied a categorically superior position. And whatever the categorical imperatives at work between spouses, these are cross-cut and displaced by myriad everyday interactions and reciprocal debts that are in many ways more significant than the others. It is also important to note that the model of gender hierarchy that operates in the house does not necessarily hold elsewhere. Thus, in the market—a female domain—women are considered superior to men, and, as I describe in chapter 6, in certain ritual domains women and female principles reign supreme.

For all these reasons, I found it difficult, and ultimately unproductive, to arrive at a single characterization of gender relations among Kabre—as, for example, unequivocally "patriarchal." Not only are there multiple models at work, and different models operating in different domains (Bloch 1987; Meigs 1990; Sanday 1990), but also, despite assertions that men are superior, Kabre women struck me as also possessing significant social power (and, frankly, seemed in many ways better off than women elsewhere). They run the markets, keep their own purses, in many cases have more wealth than men, and are generally afforded respect as spokespersons and political actors. And, as the high (60 percent) divorce rate indicates (for it is invariably women rather than men who leave a marriage), they are also fully supported in their right to leave a man who doesn't treat them well—who doesn't work hard and produce enough food, who plays favorites among his co-wives, who unjustly beats a wife.

I should add here, however, that issues of gender hierarchy among Kabre were for me among the most difficult to come to terms with. Given the unequal and contested nature of gender relations in my own society, I was keenly interested in Kabre gender politics. But I found it difficult to escape my own culture's epistemological commitments to thinking about gender in terms that are individualistic, universalizing, aggregative, and comparative (Strathern 1988). Thus, I found myself repeatedly adding up and comparing male and female resources, both material and symbolic. As Strathern (1988) reminds us, however, this way of thinking about gender has emerged within a society rooted in the commodity form—gender, as it were, on the model of commodities. At least in the Kabre case, such a conception is at odds with local constructions of personhood. For these reasons, I still do not feel that I can claim with certainty to have gotten to the bottom of this matter.

A Note on the Kabre Binary

In light of poststructuralist critiques of binaries (Butler 1990, 1993), it is worth considering at greater length the nature of Kabre dualisms and the way in which they differ from those gendered oppositions with which many Euroamericans are familiar.[14]

First, as noted above, there is a recursiveness in Kabre oppositions that is quite different from that to which many Euroamericans are accustomed—opposites produce and incorporate one another, male incorporating female and vice versa. For Kabre, the "other" is both cause and register of the "self": male a product of female, and female of male. As well, as shown in chapter 4, the terms of the binary have histories—they are actively, processually produced. Thus, single-sex (male and female) adults are produced from androgynous children through the process of initiation.

Second, while cultural categories in the West often present gendered differences as rooted in natural, unchangeable essences (in biology), and therefore as irreconcilably opposed, Kabre imagine them quite differently. Indeed, they conceive of opposed terms (such as genders) as analogues (Wagner 1977) of one another (and as internally connected). Take, for instance, the opposition between cultivating (men's work) and cooking (women's work). The verb used by men when they are making the ridges in their fields where they plant sorghum—*pʊwasɪɣɪ*—also means "to boil (water)." The affinity between ridged fields and boiling water, I was told, lies in the fact that both have "bubbly" surfaces. Further, the first sorghum weeding is called "cooking weeds"—*pasaa casɪ*— the only time the verb "to cook" is applied to an activity that takes place outside the homestead. As it was explained to me, in the same way that women cook food for people, men pull weeds from the earth and leave them by the sides of the sorghum plants—to "cook" in the sun and become "food" for the sorghum. One of the other sorghum weedings is called "removing from the heat"—*pakuriɣi ntalaʊ*—employing a verb otherwise used only when removing food (especially meat) from the cooking pot. This weeding, among the most important, involves snatching the weeds from the ground—as meat is pulled from the fire—and heaping them around the base of the sorghum plants where they become "food" for the plants. Thus, for Kabre, cultivating fields is a type of cooking, and vice versa.

If the terms of the opposition cultivating/cooking conceptually collapse into one another, the same is true of the opposition death/birth. Thus, in spite of the apparent difference between the male act of burying bodies and the female act of giving birth, Kabre see continuities—both metaphorical and metonymical—between the two. On the one hand, tombs and wombs are said to be alike in that they are both "containers" that house people. On the other hand, burial and birth are thought to be part of a continuous process, with birth leading to burial and burial back to birth (for Kabre believe in the rebirth of a deceased person in a subsequent generation). Thus, at the time of burial, the body of the deceased is inserted into the tomb—a cave in the ground—in breech position (bottom first, with legs folded up to the head) through a hole that is birth-canal tight. (Indeed, it is so tight that it often causes abrasions on the sides of the cadaver.[15]) This position ensures "that the person will be reborn [emerge from the birth canal] head first."[16] Symbolically, then, tombs are wombs, and the activities associated with the two merge together.

It is because of the fluidity of categories and the ambiguity of symbols—a tomb that is a womb, a field that is a home, a male space that is a female space, or, indeed, a man that is a woman—that Kabre attend so assiduously to the processes of difference-creation (cf. Wagner 1977) and to the boundaries between them. Without those boundaries, differences collapse, and social action becomes unthinkable.

But because opposites are analogues of one another and because gendered differences are not naturalized, the identities of (individual) persons can reverse themselves—with men becoming "women," and women "men." This is true not only of persons in the developmental cycle (where "female" boys are made into men, and where post-menopausal women become "men"), or indeed of women who take up farming, but also—as I discuss in chapters 6 and 7—of the identities of persons in various ritual contexts. Thus, women in the male moiety behave as—and indeed *are*—"men" and men in the female moiety behave as and become "women." Since Kabre gender is not naturalized, men and women can thus exchange identities with relative ease. What matters to Kabre is preserving a dualistic framework for action rather than maintaining the essential identity of those who occupy the two poles of the system. We are faced, then, with a world that is assertively organized by gender difference, but in which the specific identity of gendered persons is fluid and reversible. This is the opposite of the dominant Western model, which only ambivalently (if at all) endorses the idea that social life should be organized around gender difference, while simultaneously holding to the idea that individuals have an essential, nonreversible, gendered identity.

A House of Strangers

I have focused thus far on the internal organization of the house—on the way it produces food and persons through a system of gendered differences. But the house is not a kingdom unto itself. It is connected to other houses—through labor and ritual exchanges, and, most importantly, through the women who marry into it. Indeed, these women remain inalienably tied to their natal houses and are buried in those houses' tombs at death. Women are simply "borrowed" as wives, Kabre say, to help produce food and children for the husband's house. However, it is not only these women but also their children who retain ties to their (mother's) natal houses. Indeed, children are said to be "owned" by their mother's brothers' houses, in spite of the fact that they are born, raised, and initiated in their fathers' houses.

This maternal/avuncular ownership of children is manifest in myriad ritual and everyday practices. At birth, for instance, a baby's placenta (a maternal "container") is sent from the father's house (where the birth occurs) to the mother's brother's house, where it is buried in a terrace near the homestead; at initiation, the mother's brother receives a front leg of all sacrificed animals, and must be present at the father's house for the most important ceremonies; at death, it is only the mother's brother who may open his deceased sister's child's money box.[17] In addition—a fact always cited by Kabre as the ultimate index of a mother's brother's ownership of his sister's children—during the time of the slave trade, the mother's brother (but not the father) could sell children into slavery.[18]

For their part, sisters' children are entitled to take ("snatch," as it is referred to in the classic literature—Radcliffe-Brown 1952; Goody 1959) food—especially beer and chickens—from their mother's brother's homestead; more generally, they have license to behave there as a child of the house.[19] Indeed, the kinship term used to refer to the mother's brother, *ekpele,* comes from the verb *kpem,* "to go home." Thus, sisters' children are constantly visiting their mothers' brothers, asking for advice, enlisting their help in various work projects, cajoling and joking with their wives and children, and, sometimes, seeking refuge there from their fathers. The avuncular relationship is unquestionably the most affectionate and supportive of all Kabre intergenerational relationships, and stands in marked contrast to a boy's relationship with his father—a relationship that is fraught with all the tension that results when one (a son) works for and inherits from the other (the father).[20]

When asked why the mother's family retains such strong claims on her children, those I spoke to said it is because they "fed" and nurtured the mother when she was growing up. Thus, it was they who indirectly made her children. As many people pointed out to me, the principle is similar to that applied to the offspring of borrowed animals: the person who loans a dog, a sheep, or a goat to a friend, for example, is entitled to a share of any offspring born to that animal while it is in the friend's custody—because he raised and fed (put "sweat" into) it, and thus produced its ability to give birth before it was loaned out.

While children are owned by their mothers' families, their fathers nevertheless begin to appropriate them—to pull them into their own house—as they feed and care for them. A father's providing food and shelter for his children (not only after, but also before, birth),[21] purchasing clothes for them and books for their schooling, and organizing and subsidizing their initiation ceremonies are all seen as contributing to this process of appropriation. Indeed, with time, a father's work in producing his children is seen as surpassing that of the mother's family. Thus, at the time of *waaŋa,* a ceremony is held at the mother's brother's house that is said to "finish" the relationship between sister's son and mother's brother. While the relationship is, of course, never entirely terminated, this moment nevertheless signals an important shift—a separation—in the relationship between mother's brother and sister's son,[22] and marks the long-awaited arrival of sons in their father's homestead.

Each Kabre person, then, straddles two houses (and each house is thus linked, chainlike, with houses from all over the community): born into one house, a child is nevertheless "owned" by—and owes its very existence to—another.[23] Houses are thus made up of strangers who are present, and members who are absent. It is only through time—and through their father's labor—that "stranger" children are converted into members and eventual owners (and, by the same token, that member children are lost to them). Houses, as Kabre conceive them, are not natural entities, containing members whose identities are given by the fact of birth or genealogy; rather, they are made and transacted through and through.

Return Marriage

Karabu, the man whose long meditation on *ɩkpantʋrɛ* exchange was presented in chapter 3, stated that people in Kuwdé have a preference for FZD marriage—and this because it reverses the one-way hierarchy of a single marriage between two houses. Thus, when a woman marries, the hope is that her daughter will marry back into her natal house, as evidenced by the moniker for such a marriage—"she [her daughter] has returned to her cooking stool" (*ʋmɩla ʋ-kpeɖɩrɔɔ*). Of course, for any number of reasons, either personal or demographic, such a marriage may be unworkable. But, as with gift exchange and sacrifice, when one object or person is unavailable, another will do just as well. Thus, any return marriage between two houses—for example, a son's marriage to any other same-generation woman from the FZD's larger house cluster, or a grandson's marriage to a woman from that house cluster in the ensuing generation (FFZSD, FFZDD)—is considered equivalent to FZD, for it achieves the aim of renewing the tie and reversing the hierarchy between two houses. Indeed, while only a handful of houses in Kuwdé have managed marriages with the actual FZD, every house has engaged in return marriage of the more expanded variety over the last two generations with at least one, and often with several, other houses, and thus sees itself as conforming to the ideal. Once again, then, those theoreticians who have been concerned with the way a society's "real" practices deviate from its "ideal" model—here applied to the realm of marriage preferences—miss the point of this marriage system, for this is a society in which many "reals" conform to the ideal.

House Histories

If houses produce themselves according to a pervasive and uniform set of principles, each house nevertheless has a distinct history—itself a product of the histories and relationships of its members. Thus, the achievements of members of the house—someone who is chief, someone with great wealth, the winner of an initiation race—attach themselves to a house and serve to distinguish it from others. Such achievements are remembered for generations and sung about by male initiates during their ceremonies. So, too, there may be a darker side to a house's history. Houses where there is much conflict, and much coming and going, or houses where many people die of witchcraft, acquire more tainted histories—histories that are also subtly referred to by initiates from other houses when they sing in public.[24]

Another often-cited aspect of a house's history has to do with how it came to its present location, for many houses have a history of movement. This history is written into the landscape, for the remains of old homestead sites are visible, like scars on the skin, all over the rocky terrain. One common relocation account is that the members of a particular house were afflicted by ancestors or spirits and moved from site to site—an arresting thought considering the enormous amount of labor and energy that go into building a new homestead—until settling where they currently reside. "In that other location, I didn't sleep well," I heard repeatedly when inquiring about why a homestead had changed location. "Not sleeping well" is a euphemism for spirit or ancestral affliction, affliction often made known to a person in his dreams at night. There are, of course, other reasons for why people move—poor drainage, conflict between brothers, and so on. But the most frequently mentioned reason was the uneasy relationship between the members of the house and the beings of the unseen world.

One such history: the father of a man I knew had moved from one site to another, and then to another—in each case building anew on land that he himself owned. But each time, the untimely death of animals at the homestead indicated that the ancestors were unhappy with the location (for reasons that were never explicitly revealed to me; if the reasons were spoken, the ancestors might feel they were being gossiped about and become angry). So, this man decided to build on borrowed land. This apparently worked, for he lived out the rest of his life on the land of a friend. However, while he himself did not mind the position of indebtedness this placed him into with the owner of the land, his son—who was living there in 1996—did. The son resented having occasionally to work for the owner of the land, to send him a pot of beer each year, to side with him in disputes, and so on. Thus, during my visit in summer 1996, this son was busy visiting diviners to find out whether the ancestors would permit him now to return to his own (and their) land.

Houses are also connected, and in complex ways that serve to distinguish one from the next, to those who have departed for the south. Indeed, houses are the pivotal nodes in the networks of the diaspora, for it is to their "houses" in the north that those who have left for the south return while alive (to visit with family and to be initiated), and that they return at death (to be buried and to become ancestors). Much of a house's north-south traffic is of course tied to labor, commodity, and money flows. In principle, labor flows south—the sons and daughters who depart the north to live and work with family in the south—are replaced by commodity flows north: the expectation is that those who have left will send annual remittances back to the north to compensate for their lost labor. In reality, however, the flows of grain and money back to the north are small and irregular—rarely enough, I was repeatedly told, to make much of a difference. (One of my roles in the community was as intermediary—scribe—in communications between households in the north and those in the south. I was repeatedly struck by how few requests for help met with success and by the ingenuity of those denying the requests in coming up with new reasons for why they were unable to help—but would "next year.")

Different northern houses are, of course, affected in different ways by these north-south flows. While some houses have been virtually emptied of members (nevertheless ensuring that someone remains behind to carry out house sacrifices), others have been able to stem the tide of emigration, retaining many of their members in the north. And during the 1990s, as the economy and political situation in the south worsened, triggering a small reverse migration, some households have even begun to experience an increase in membership.

The translocality of houses—one half in the northern homeland, the other scattered across a southern frontier hundreds of miles away—and the never-ending traffic in persons and things between the two are features as central to the culture and life of the house as any other. Most houses are thus deeply drawn into the contradictory dynamics of this diaspora, dynamics that pull its members in opposite directions, and all are affected by the cultural imaginings that such a diaspora engenders.

—◄o►—

If there is any space that Western ideology has imagined as pristine, as untouched, as unpolluted by the state and all it signifies, it is the domain of the domestic. All the more so, one might imagine, of the domestic in the heart of Africa, that supposedly most natural of places. But Kabre imagine it quite differently. Not only is the Kabre house a place that has been repeatedly touched and remade by history and the state, and a place characterized by the perpetual transactability of things and persons; but also its every constitutive act engages it with the outside. Thus, it is peopled with "stranger" children and "stranger" wives, and through sacrifice it opens itself to and attempts to appropriate spirits of the wild. It also bears the weight and preserves the presence of those who have departed into the diaspora and of its long engagement with modernity and the slave trade. This point was eloquently captured in a conversation I had one day with Palabéi. He was talking about what Kabre refer to as the "big houses" (ɖɛsɪ sɪsɔsɪ), the oldest houses in Kuwdé where rituals for the entire community are performed.

> These houses are heavy with history, the history of the first people who settled here and cut the forest, the history of fighting Samasi and later the Germans, the history of children sold into slavery, the history of witches, the history of those who left for the south. These houses meet all this history with their rituals, and tame it for us. That [a history with the outside] is where we find our power and why they are the big houses.

Six

COMMUNITY

Spirits, Mimesis, Modernity

This chapter addresses a question that preoccupied British anthropology at mid-century, and especially those ethnographers—Meyer Fortes, Jack Goody, David Tait—who worked among the savanna peoples of northern Ghana and Togo: what is the nature of community, and what are its forms of solidarity? Of course, it is now a commonplace to remark that there was a certain complicity between an anthropology preoccupied with such questions—and more broadly with African political processes—and colonialism. Thus, not only were these anthropologists working on subjects of keen interest to colonial governments (and presumably exchanging their knowledge for research access and funding); there also seemed to be a tidy fit between the objects of knowledge they were constructing—static, bounded, self-contained societies—and the colonial need to name, fix, and control colonial subjects.

While there is certainly much truth to this view, it is also the case, as with functionalist arguments generally, that things are more complicated—that the work of individual anthropologists didn't correspond so neatly to colonial interest (Asad 1991; S. Moore 1994; Goody 1995) and that colonial need was more varied and contradictory than such a view suggested (Comaroff and Comaroff 1991, 1997; Thomas 1994; Cooper and Stoler 1997). Indeed, while Fortes did construct a static picture of Tallensi society, and took little account of the colonial presence, his books are nevertheless filled with descriptions and analyses that also suggest a more fluid Tallensi reality. And while in many places throughout Africa colonialism sought fixity and stasis, here in the coastal hinterland of West Africa it was more interested in mobility and in societies that were able to accommodate such mobility. (Recall that colonial inter-

est in this savanna area was in its capacity to serve as a labor reserve
supplying workers to the coast.) Ironically, then, in the Volta basin, anthropological depictions and colonial need were at cross purposes.

My focus in this chapter is on Kabre conceptions of community, conceptions that seem on the one hand significantly at odds with those of
descent theorists, and on the other remarkably in concert with colonial
(and postcolonial) agendas in the Volta basin. I will suggest that there
is a fluidity to social relations that enabled Kabre to intersect almost
seamlessly with and adapt to the new ruptures and circulations of the
colonial era, while nevertheless engaging it on terms that were more or
less of their own choosing. The fluidity I refer to derives not only from
the mobility of people into and out of houses and communities but also
from a life centered around invisible spirits whose motives are inscruta-
ble and forever unpredictable. When I spoke in chapter 1 about the cosmopolitanism of life in these savanna societies, I had in mind this very
fluidity and the uncertainties that accompany daily life in a world governed by spirits.

Boundaries

It is no easy matter to decide where Kabre communities begin and end,
who their members are, what their sources of solidarity are. Kabre ethnographers have offered up a host of terms—*tɛtʊ* (earth), *haɖaa* (work
group), *dikoye* (the clearing where warriors gathered in time of attack)—as signifying the term "community."[1] While any of these might
be invoked on occasion, none was commonly used by those Kabre I
knew. Indeed, there was no single term they used to refer to the place
where they lived, other than the place name (Kuwdé, Faren, Wazilao).
If pressed to come up with a more generic term—"community," "village"—they would scratch their heads and offer up expressions such as
"our home" (*ɖa-tɛ*), or "in our place" (*ɖɪ-ɪcaɖɪ taa*). None of these, however, has fixed references; each can be used to refer to any place one
considers home—from one's homestead to the region more generally.
When, one day, I asked a group of elders about the terms cited by other
Kabre ethnographers, they chuckled and said that these ethnographers
had talked to children who, after all, know nothing.

If the community cannot be fixed terminologically, what about spa-
tially/geographically? This proves equally difficult. There is, for instance,
no line marking its boundaries nor any path tracing its circumference.

Paths connect homesteads to fields, and fields to fields, and homesteads to homesteads, but none marks the boundary of the community. Nor is there a break in homesteads at the limit of the community: homesteads are more or less evenly distributed across the hilly terrain, with those of one community flowing into those of the next. Indeed, certain Kuwdé members' homesteads are "in" other communities and vice versa. Nor is the cultivated land of community members isomorphic with the community. While many of the fields of same-community members are clustered together, not all of them are: the fields of members of other communities are mixed in with those of members of Kuwdé and vice versa (to say nothing of the complex borrowings of land—discussed in chapter 3—that go on between members of different communities). Moreover, I think this was not just a "boundary problem"—that is, a problem produced by the fact that otherwise discrete communities overlapped at their boundaries, creating a certain messiness. Rather, as with the person and the homestead, communities by definition intersect in complicated ways and, indeed, are defined in terms of one another. Communities are not "individuals" writ large.

Trying a different tack, one might ask whether the residents of a community are fixed. But again, one's desire for some pure definition—some bounded entity called a "community"—meets with frustration. Many of the people living in Kuwdé are from elsewhere—from Faren, Wazilao, Boua, and Kawa. Indeed, fully one quarter of its residents do not claim to be from Kuwdé (and can be dispatched back to where they came from if they make trouble). This is so despite the fact that they have built homesteads in Kuwdé, work in Kuwdé work groups, and perform rituals for Kuwdé. By the same token, many Kuwdé people live elsewhere—in other northern communities and scattered throughout the communities of the diaspora in the south.

It is interesting here to note—given the above-mentioned view that British social anthropology was responsible for constructing an image of African societies as static, bounded, and self-contained—that in the opening pages of one of this school's classic texts, *The Dynamics of Clanship Among the Tallensi,* Fortes (1945: 13–29) wrestles with the problem of community boundaries and reaches a conclusion similar to my own. He is completely at a loss to decide where one Tallensi community stops and another begins—spatially, linguistically, or politically. Sounding rather like a postcolonial theorist, Fortes describes Tallensi communities as "overlapping," "intermeshing," "merging" and "blending" into one another. He claims one can only have an "implicit" feeling that one settlement is different from another. The same is true of Tallensi clans—they overlap, chainlike, with other clans.

Jack Goody, Fortes's student, also worked among a Voltaic people of northern Ghana, the Lowiili. Goody claimed that Lowiili communities had even fewer distinct boundaries than Tallensi ([1956] 1967: iii). There is a continuum of settlements, he writes, which flow almost indistinguishably into one another. Further, he could find no names that identified the people of a particular place. Instead, the Lowiili employed shifting markers—directional terms—to refer to those who lived nearby, terms whose referents changed according to the context and position of the speaker. (Indeed, "Lowiili" is a name Goody invented for the purposes of his monograph.)

It is the challenge of coming to terms with such an unbounded—and, indeed, in this area widely known for its "acephalous" societies, a radically decentered—notion of community that I take up in what follows. I begin by discussing the elaborate set of calendrical rituals members of Kuwdé hold each year for the spirits they see as governing their world. For not only do Kabre accord a certain primacy to their relations with the spirits; it is through the rituals to these spirits that (a modicum of) community-wide activity is organized and some sense of collective identity is created. Still, we must be careful here not to impose, and falsely reify, a notion of community more "ours" (social science's) than theirs. As with Tallensi and Lowiili, Kabre "communities" are borderless, fluid entities—places in which people constantly come and go. Any fixity they possess comes less from people than from the spirits, which, unlike their human counterparts, stay put.[2]

Cosmic Mimesis

The spirits (*akɔlıma*), Kabre claim, were inhabiting their present-day locales—uncultivated groves scattered around the communities of the mountains—when the first people arrived. It was to these spirits that the first people turned for help, to secure protection from enemies and to help the crops grow. In return, the spirits—more commonly referred to as "trees" (*tıŋ*), after the places in which they live—demanded that the people make offerings to them. Thus, there came into being a series of sacrifices and ceremonies for these spirits—eight rituals in all, at different times throughout the year. Today, each of the ceremonies is performed in each northern massif community on consecutive weeks, starting with the highest-ranking (Faren) and proceeding to the lowest-ranking (Asiri).

Within each community, the ritual labor is divided among two sets of "houses" (ɖɛsɪ). Each is named and, not surprisingly, each is gendered, one "male" and the other "female." Thus, in Kuwdé, those homesteads in "Tɔʊtɛɛ" are symbolically male and are responsible for conducting the rituals of the (male) dry season. By contrast, the homesteads of "Komatɛ" are female and perform the rituals of the (female) wet season. There is also a third group of houses, called "Cacarɛɣa taa," that plays a minor role in ceremonies at the change of the seasons. As I show below, Cacarɛɣa taa's role is one of mediation, and its presence appears not to challenge the dualist understanding Kuwdé members have of their community.[3] When asked, for example, they categorically assert that there are only two (important) houses in Kuwdé. Indeed, it was not until I had witnessed the *cɪmʊɣʊ* ceremony, six months after my arrival in Kuwdé, that I even knew of Cacarɛɣa taa's existence—for its role is practically nonexistent and no one had mentioned it to me.[4]

While the principal aim of the ceremonies is to attend to the spirits, the ceremonies do much else as well. They provide the occasion for initiation and funeral ceremonies, mark important transitions in the work cycle, and articulate relations/hierarchies between different communities within the larger region. In addition, they have recently become a site of contestation with the state: as part of its plan to show support for local culture, the government intervened in some of the ceremonies in the late 1980s—demanding that they be performed on fixed days each year and at locations convenient for state officials to attend. For northern Kabre, this would have meant abandoning the flexibility they have in setting the dates of the ceremonies (which are tied to the growth of the crops) and having to move them from the mountains down into the plain. They thus refused to accommodate the state—arguing that such switches would offend the spirits and disrupt the agricultural cycle—but nevertheless agreed to participate in a separate state-sponsored version of one of the ceremonies in a nearby town in the plain.

In what follows, I first give a synchronic reading of the ceremonies, focusing on their role in ritually regulating the crops and the seasons. I then offer a historical reading, for these rituals also speak to and embody the long history of the Kabre encounter with modernity (cf. Comaroff and Comaroff 1993; Stoller 1995). Finally, following a brief reprise on chiefs and chiefship, I explore the social relations between houses that emerge from the ceremonies, thus returning to the question about the nature of "community" that so preoccupied descent theorists such as Fortes and Goody.

◄O►

The ritual cycle and the Kabre year in the communities of the northern massif where Kuwdé is located begins with a dry-season (early January) ceremony called ɗɔyɔntʊ, "throwing out." ɗɔyɔntʊ comes each year from the west, moving from community to community in the southern massif, before arriving in the communities of the northern massif. After each northern massif community has performed it on consecutive weeks, it crosses the border into Benin, where it is carried further by a group called Logba, who in turn send it farther to the east when they are finished with it. (These migrating ceremonies are a common feature of the West African landscape and add substance to the claim that the groups of this area are anything but neatly bounded.)

A feature of the ceremonies that was striking to me was the fact that they attempted to elicit the spirits' help largely through nonverbal means. Indeed, very few words were spoken to the spirits at the ceremonies. Instead, the officiants aimed to affect the spirits largely through display and mimesis—the display of ritual objects and sacrificed animals, and the (miniaturized) miming of cosmic events. In what follows I focus on this object-centered, nonlogocentric ritual language.

The aim of ɗɔyɔntʊ is to "throw" death, and things evil, out of the community. Performed during the season of death—the dry season when the harmattan dust hangs in the air above the bare, stubbled landscape, and when funeral ceremonies abound—it aims to purify the community by figuratively gathering up evil (death, witchcraft, infertility) and expelling it into the bush. Throughout the day of ɗɔyɔntʊ, the dried grasses in sacred groves are set afire (fire is cleansing) and forbidden reptiles (snakes, toads, and others who bring death) are hunted by the head of Tɔʊtɛɛ (the male moiety) and members of his house. These dead reptiles are placed into a disk of pottery—a sherd from a broken pot—with mud from a special spring—a "medicine" that is said to immobilize the reptiles' deadly effects. In the late afternoon, the men of the community gather for a dance around the broken pot.[5] (Pre-menopausal women are tabooed from participating, for fear that they will become infertile through contact with death.) Dressed as warriors, these men encircle and attack the pot as they dance, periodically firing arrows into the deadly mix. At the end of the dance, *kɛŋnaa* (the newest grade of warriors) run the pot down out of the mountains and jettison it, along with their dress from the dance, in the plain to the east.

Two weeks later, a small ceremony called *lɛlaɣa* is performed that closes the period of cleansing opened by *ɖɔɣɔntʊ*. A dome-shaped rock mound, six feet high, that had been dismantled by Faren elders on the day of *ɖɔɣɔntʊ* is rebuilt on *lɛlaɣa*. This act of (re)enclosure (of death) is accompanied by another type of metaphorical containment: the wind, released at the *kamʊɣʊ* ceremony (in October) to dry the sorghum and expedite dry-season hut-building,[6] is no longer needed after *lɛlaɣa,* and Kabre thus attempt to bottle it up. They do so by (re)inserting a stick into the tree of the spirit who controls the wind, the tree from which the wind had been released at the time of *kamʊɣʊ*. Also on this day, infertile women are "given earth"—earth from the ground of one of the spirit forests is rubbed on their chests—to make them fertile, and those who were so helped in the past—by my count, half of the women in the community—take beer and chickens as offerings to the spirit. In these various ways, then, the ceremonial actions of *lɛlaɣa* seek to contain/recontain that which had been set loose (death, the wind, and infertile wombs) throughout the previous year.

The five-month dry season, punctuated by these two ceremonies, is a season of ironic contrasts. Symbolically associated with death, and a time when the land is bone dry, and the temperature soars to near 100, the community is nevertheless full of life. With little obligatory work to be done until the rains begin again, and homesteads brimming with food from the harvest, the community takes on a festive atmosphere. Hut-building—the most collective of Kabre work activities—and funeral celebrations fill the days. The markets become more animated than at any other time during the year—pressing with people buying and selling, and drinking beer. Also at this time of year, emigrant Kabre suddenly reappear—returning to the north to see family and to make sacrifices to house spirits and ancestors. Their arrival sets the community abuzz with stories and gossip of life in the south, and with the heightened and often ambivalent emotions that accompany reunions with departed family and friends. Also during this period, many northerners go south to do piece-work in the sorghum fields of Ewe, or to help southern family members harvest cotton. Then, toward the middle of March, as the heat of the dry season becomes oppressive and the storm clouds begin to gather, people slowly return to their communities and ready themselves for the field

Hut building during the dry season harmattan; Kuwdé, January 1984

work that lies ahead, bringing to an end the fluid, festive atmosphere of the dry season.

As the first rains fall (in early April), Kabre mark the transition—the dramatic shift from the heat and dust of the dry season to the cool, verdant rainy season—with a ceremony called *cɪmʊɣʊ*. Kuwdé ritual leaders gather at the ancient homesteads of Tɔʊtɛɛ, Komatɛ, and Cacarɛya taa (the third "house"), located on the highest ridge in Kuwdé, where they kill a chicken and, with a member of Tɔʊtɛɛ holding the chicken's head (the head is said to be "male" and to represent the dry season) and a member of Komatɛ holding its tail (which is "female" and represents the wet), cut the bird in half with a knife. This act, they say, "cuts" the wet season from the dry. The elders then drink a pot of beer—first outside each homestead, and then inside. The movement from the outside (where all drinking occurs during the dry season) to the inside (where wet-season drinking takes place) also marks and, indeed, brings about the transition from the one season to the next: the rain will intensify, Tamouka, the head of Tɔʊtɛɛ told me, as it sees the elders move inside.[7]

The role of Cacarɛya taa in this ceremony, and again at the time of *sɪŋkarɪŋ* (which marks the reverse transition from wet season to dry), is symbolically straightforward: as an ambiguous, boundary-crossing house that straddles and confounds distinctions between male/female, adult/

child, and insider/outsider, it makes its appearance at a transitional time of year, and thus conceptually mediates the move from one gendered season (and moiety) to the next.

Once the rainy season is underway, Komatɛ, the female moiety, takes over the ritual cycle. (*Cimʊɣʊ*, like *siŋkariŋ* at the other end of the wet season, is "owned" by neither house.) The first of Komatɛ's ceremonies, *kucontuɣu*, takes place in early June, a time when the sorghum is waist-high and begins to fill the spaces between homesteads—tin roofs floating in a sea of green. On the days leading up to the ceremony, an elder from a house in Faren who has charge of the rain spirit promenades from community to community visiting the houses of important elders. In each, he places an empty calabash in the middle of the courtyard and fills it with beer until it overflows, spilling in puddles on the hard dirt floor. This action—which imitates the falling, splattering, abundant June rains (the early rains of April and May are light, but the June rains should be heavy to help the sorghum grow)—is said to bring that rain to the massif.

Kucontuɣu also marks the onset of the early stages of male and female initiations and lifts the ban on eating the new locust bean crop. In Kuwdé, the entire community gathers in the late afternoon in one of Komatɛ's spirit groves to do sacrifices and to eat locust beans. A joyous occasion attended by children, this first fruits ceremony celebrates a food (*cotu,* the sauce ingredient made from locust beans) that is a prototype of female tranformative powers, and thus appropriately stands for the many transformations—of both crops and people—that take place during the female wet season.[8] (Notice the thematic progression of ceremonies, from those of the dry season concerned with pre-birth—the expulsion of infertility and the successful insemination of women ["giving them earth"]—to those of the wet season concerned with the post-birth phases of the growth and initiation of children.)

Three ceremonies occur during the second half of the rainy season (late August, September, and October)—*saolaɣa, kʊyɛlina,* and *kamʊɣʊ*—which seek the aid of spirit powers in taming the elements (especially wind and rain) and in helping the crops through their final stages of growth. At the late-August *saolaɣa* ceremony, an elder from Faren seeks to ensure the continued growth of the sorghum by sacrificing in the forest where the sorghum spirit lives. Men and boys from throughout the various mountain communities further urge the sorghum skyward—it grows to twenty-five feet—with their flutes, taking them to the fields to play while they are cultivating. Such playing is audible all over the mountains at this time, and its sweet melodies are said to seduce the sorghum into achieving its maximum height—in the same way that workers are sometimes urged on by musicians to help them through a difficult field, to "sweeten" the work.[9] Another *saolaɣa* ritual attempts to equalize the rates at which the sorghum is growing in the different communities. Since the (June) ceremony of *kucontuɣu* was performed in the different communities on consecutive weeks (Faren, the highest-ranking, went first, followed by Boua-Kuwdé, Wazilao-Somdé, and Asiri), the sorghum in each community is said to be at different stages of growth (with that of Faren the tallest and that of Asiri the shortest). And yet, since the November harvest ceremony takes place in each community on the same day, the sorghum of the other communities must be allowed to catch up to Faren's. Thus, on the day of *saolaɣa,* an elder from Faren goes into one of the spirit forests and clears a patch of ground, leaving only four clumps of grass—a miniaturized representation of the sorghums of the four communities. He ties the top of each with a piece of twine—stopping the various communities' sorghums from growing. Then, on consecutive weeks, he unbinds one at a time—beginning with Asiri's and ending with Faren's—thus allowing the others to catch up with Faren before the harvest. This activity not only metonymically abolishes crop differences but also serves as a metaphor for the temporary elimination of the hierarchies among communities (which are reflected in the order in which the ceremonies are performed throughout the year).[10]

On *kʊyɛlɪna* (in mid-September), the day when female initiates come out in the markets, an elder in Faren does a forest sacrifice to stop the rain, for too much rain at this time of year will rot the roots of the sorghum plants and thus spoil the crop. The sacrifice is said to bring rainbows, which—since they materialize when both sun and rain appear together—are a sign for Kabre that the rain is letting up. Indeed, when I was in Kuwdé in 1984, rainbows abounded after *kʊyɛlɪna* and indicated to all that the ceremony had been successful.

A month later, at the *kamʊyʊ* ceremony, Kabre attend to the wind—this time bringing it "out," to dry the grains of the sorghum before it is cut at harvest. An elder from Boua goes to the forest of the wind spirit, where he makes a sacrifice and removes the stick from the hole in the tree where the spirit lives (and where the wind remains bottled up during the wet season). At the same time, farmers throughout the massif must toss away the leafy stems of the yam plants they harvest rather than—

as they have prior to this time—reinserting them into the holes in the ground vacated by the yams. This action, too, is said to let the wind out.[11] In addition to the wind, the *kamʊɣʊ* ceremonies attend to yams. In Kuwdé, which does the yam rituals for the whole northern massif, an elder sacrifices a chicken to the spirit of yams and digs up yams he had planted in a ceremonial mound the previous year. If these ritual yams have grown as expected, the year's crop will be good. The elder then buries newly harvested yams in the mound, which he will dig up the following year. *Kamʊɣʊ* is also associated with red palm oil, and is the first time the new oil may be consumed. The red oil—symbolically male and associated with the dry season—thus contrasts with the female salt of the wet season which appears at *cɪmʊɣʊ*. Note, then, the paired symbols at work here. The sherds and broken pots of the dry season are contrasted with the whole containers of the wet; the plugged-up holes and filled granaries of the dry with the unplugged holes and open granaries of the wet; and the red oil of the dry with the (white) salt of the wet. All of these are, of course, consistent with the gender contrasts that define the two seasons.

All of these late rainy season ritual actions—which regulate sorghum growth, stop the rain, bring the wind, and attend to the yams—lend to September and October an accelerated sense of time, and produce growing anticipation of the year's major event, the sorghum harvest, and its accompanying festival, *sɪŋkarɪŋ*. The timing of *sɪŋkarɪŋ* is set by an elder from Faren who in late October begins walking the fields of sorghum—their tall stalks now bowed beneath their weight—to determine when they should be cut. When he decides it is time (this depends on the color of the grains), he announces the date—two Saturdays later—when *sɪŋkarɪŋ* will be held.

The two weeks leading up to the ceremony are a period not only of intense work (bringing in the entire harvest, and making beer and food for the ceremony) but also of concerted ritual activity. Field owners make sacrifices to field spirits to thank them for the harvest; homestead heads move the ancestral spirits of any recently deceased family members from the grain-drying area of the homestead into the central courtyard; and initiates prepare for the final stages of their passage into adulthood and marriage. This is also the time of one of the year's most memorable visual transformations: in the two weeks preceding the ceremony, a time when the harmattan dust is beginning to drift across the savanna, the forests of tangled sorghum that have blanketed the community for months are felled to the ground, baring homesteads and sweeping views across hillsides, and giving the community a startling, clean-swept look.

On the morning of *sɪŋkarɪŋ,* as homesteads buzz with the activity of women cooking and men sacrificing to the ancestors and the doubles of house members, the heads of Kuwdé's two moieties go to their spirit groves to "sweep out the forest"—to make it tidy for the spirit—and to offer sacrifices. In one of these forests, the head of the female moiety visits a "granary"—a hole in the ground covered by a flat rock like that used to seal the entrances to homestead granaries—to see whether the grain he placed there the previous year has survived or not. If so, it is said that the harvested grain will resist spoiling in house granaries (where it is put a month after the harvest). By midday, a festive atmosphere has taken over the community and people begin to stroll from homestead to homestead, drinking the beer and eating the bean fritters made especially for the occasion and freely offered to all comers. An ambience of plenitude and celebration fills the community.

Late in the afternoon, Kuwdé's ritual leaders—often tipsy from their promenading—return to their ancient homesteads on the ridge to repeat their actions at the end of the dry season and to mark the transition of the seasons: they sever chickens and drink beer, though now reversing their actions of seven months before (at the time of *cɪmʊɣʊ*), by drinking first inside each homestead and then outside. These movements signal the passage from the "inside" (female) activities of the wet season to the "outside" (male) activities of the dry season and the wholesale shift in social and productive activities, and in sensibilities, that this passage entails. Moiety leaders also enter the ancient homesteads on this occasion and bring out a gourd, called a *tokuu,* which is the central emblem of each group, often attaching it to a wall of one of the huts where they leave it for several weeks. Gendered female, the *tokuu* is said to have brought fantastic powers with it from the bush (where, when it was cut from the vine, it is said to have bled human blood—the blood of menstruation/birth?). Among other things, the *tokuu*'s powers enabled it to give birth to all members of the moiety and allow it to protect them from harm. Here, then, is an instance of female power at the center of things.

At the time of *sɪŋkarɪŋ,* a stone instrument—a lithophone—is placed on a bed of leaves on the ground outside each Kuwdé homestead. A set of large flat rocks played by beating them with two hand-held stones, the lithophone is mostly played by children, though on occasion older men can be persuaded to take their turn and pridefully demonstrate their skills to all who have gathered. The lithophone's rhythms may be heard throughout the day and night—from a distance, a rapid, wind-chime tinkling—between *sıŋkarıŋ* and *ɖɔɣɔntʊ*. As elsewhere in this region (Chernoff 1979), Kabre employ an "instrument" of percussion to mark a time of transition.

It is thus largely through the visual and the nonverbal, through actions of display and mimesis—the display and jettisoning of broken pots, the plugging and unplugging of holes, the cutting of chickens, the movement in and out of homesteads, the filling of calabashes, the tying of tufts of grass, the insertion of yams into ritual mounds and sorghum into meta-phorical granaries—that Kabre coax their spirits and magically affect the world in which they live. In so doing, they employ a symbolic code that "speaks" not so much through words as through objects and actions.

◄○►

These rituals are also sedimented with history (cf. Fernandez 1982; Werb-ner 1989; Kelly and Kaplan 1990; Apter 1992; Matory 1994). They em-body the long history of Kabre encounters with modernity, thus provid-ing an apt illustration of Taussig's (1993) suggestion that the mimetic is also a modality of historical consciousness. As such, they constitute a type of historical memory and, through their periodic enactment, help to produce a present that forever stands in relation to its past, and to the struggles of those who came before.

The historical nature of these rituals is perhaps most apparent in the two dry-season ceremonies, *ɖɔɣɔntʊ* and *lɛlaɣa*. Here the symbolism of fighting and war predominates, refigured today as a fight against witches and evil, but clearly referring back to the time of the slave trade and the wars with Samasi. The shrines for these ceremonies are located on the eastern edge of the massif—the direction Samasi came from on horse-back—and both are associated with war. Moreover, at the end of *ɖɔɣɔntʊ*, *kɛŋnaa* armed with bows and arrows run into the plain to the east and there jettison the pot of death. As well, one of the central em-blems of the *lɛlaɣa* fertility ceremonies is a whisk made from hair that is said to have come from the horse of a Samara warrior. Here again is the association between fertility/potency and an outside domain/person/ enemy.

But these ritual connections to a warring past are not simply quaint throwbacks or "survivals." They represent periodic attempts to magically reappropriate the potency of the victory over Samasi and, in so doing, to revitalize the present. Moreover, this history and these rituals can be called on at a moment's notice to fight a new enemy, as they were when things heated up for Kabre in the south during the early 1990s. I was told that during this period the activities and sacrifices at the war shrines were intensified and that elders returned there for the first time in decades to make poison for their arrows.

Another moment in Kabre history is represented by the *kamʊɣʊ* ceremony in October. Recall that this is the time when yams are buried in a ceremonial mound in a Kuwdé forest called Laoda. This, it turns out, is precisely the location where the German interloper killed by Mahate was buried (and where Kuwdé youths went to dig up his bones a few years ago). Though no one ever told me as much, the annual burying of yams is almost certainly a reenactment of this historical event, a symbolic reburial, and indeed a type of human sacrifice[12] whose aim is not only to memorialize a victory over the enemy but also to appropriate that enemy's power.

Notice once again the way in which these ceremonies, like those of initiates, involve a constant interaction with and appropriation of that which is "outside." But it is not just the powers of enemies that the ceremonies attempt to capture. Many of the ritual objects used during the ceremonies, as well as the spirits that are called on, come from and retain an identification with various outside domains. When large animals are sacrificed (goats, sheep, cows), for instance, they have to be obtained from outside the community—either through exchange with a bush community or through the capture of an animal found wandering in the bush. Similarly, the yams planted in the ceremonial mound in Kuwdé at the time of *kamʊɣʊ* cannot be local yams: they must come from the fields of Kawa, Kuwdé's sister community in the bush. And the sacred gourd (*tokuu*) and central emblem of each moiety that is displayed on the day of *sɩŋkarɩŋ* (as well as on *cɩmʊɣʊ* and *kucontuɣu*) retains its identity as a product of the bush through the stories that are told of its origins and through the awesome powers it is said to possess and to have brought with it from the bush. Finally, the powers of the tree spirits, the "trees," that Kabre attempt to appease and control through the ceremonies and also, more positively, to appropriate, are those of the outside: these denizens of the wild, whose volatile natures Kabre liken to those of wild animals and creatures of the bush, reside in the community's only uncultivated spaces, its "forests."[13]

A spirit's "house" in a sacred forest: where powers are tamed and the diaspora finds its anchor; Kuwdé, July 1989

I could give many other examples, but the point would be the same: the ceremonies are constantly drawing in that which is outside—spirits, animals, crops, gourds, enemies—for the outside is where special (and dangerous) power is seen to lie, and its appropriation is believed to renew and regenerate life within (cf. Jackson 1982; Beidelman [1986] 1993, 1997; Werbner 1989; Jackson and Karp 1990; Karp 1990).

Another type of history is embodied in the August *saolaɣa* ceremony. At that time, elders from Faren descend into the plain to the location where Kumberito, the first Kabre, is said to have touched down after his descent from the sky. This return to the beginning of Kabre time—to a time of androgyny and formlessness—is thus also a return to the historical moment when Kabre fled slave-raiders into the massifs and there gave birth to the constellation of communities that today make up the larger region. The ceremonies reenact this origin through the movements of elders—from mountain to plain and back to mountain again—and through the mimetic abolition and recreation of the hierarchies among those communities.[14]

The calendrical ceremonies, then, are a highly condensed code, whose symbols and ritual actions not only attempt to affect the crops and seasons but also call up and reiterate the turbulent history of Kabre, and especially of their encounters with the outside. The aim throughout is to appropriate that history so that it might empower the present.

Separations and Innovations

Since it is a theme that has been central to my analysis, I should also draw attention to the way the ceremonies operate, and indeed inscribe, a system of differences. It should be clear from the acts of cutting central to the ceremonies of *cɪmʊɣʊ* and *sɪŋkarɪŋ* that Kabre strive to make clear breaks between—to separate—the seasons, and thus to keep apart the gendered activities, powers, and categories of the two: to separate wind from rain, dry from wet, red oil from salt, hunting from agriculture, funerals from initiations, and so on.[15] As in the homestead, violating these separations—hunting during the wet season, drinking inside during the dry, holding initiations out of season—is said to invite calamity: the rain disappears, crops fail, humans lose their fertility. It would be a mistake, however, to see these taboos/separations as simply restrictive. They are also formative—"productive" in the Foucauldian sense—for they bring into being the major conceptual oppositions—the differences—that organize the Kabre world.

The seriousness with which Kabre attend to the maintenance of these separations was clearly brought home to me one day in a market where I was drinking beer with some of Kuwdé's elders. The government prefect was due to arrive for a visit to make an announcement about the upcoming election of the Chef du Canton. Those from the community in which the market was being held had decided to honor the prefect's visit by having the drummers play. But as the music started, the elders I was sitting with noticed that they were playing rhythms that were out of season—they were playing music from the dry season ceremony of *ɗɔɣɔntʊ* in the middle of the wet season. One of the elders seated next to me, the head of Kuwdé's male moiety, immediately got up and ran across the market to chastise the drummers, and instructed them to play only the music of the wet season ceremony that had just passed. When I questioned him later about his actions, he said that playing dry season music during the wet season would "call out the spirits of the dry season"—thus stopping the rains and bringing the wind. In short, it would turn the wet into the dry. I witnessed another example of the same principle at the time of *ɗɔɣɔntʊ*. A woman whom most people thought was not yet past childbearing age caused a stir by joining the dance (in which

only men and post-menopausal women are permitted to participate).
The dance was stopped while elders argued with the woman about
whether or not she had gone through menopause. (If she was pre-
menopausal, they claimed, both her fertility and the ceremony would be
ruined.) As one might expect, the elders won the argument and the
woman retreated to the sidelines.

While these two incidents clearly show the exercise of power—of ritual leaders over drummers, and men over women—they were not, I
think, merely about power. Rather, the concern of the elders was also
categorical and cosmological—to maintain the set of differences pain-
stakingly put into place by the various ceremonies, and to avoid the natural and human calamity they believed would result from their collapse.

But it is important to add here that if the ceremonies aim to reinscribe
certain categories—and thus to enact what seem to be pre-scripted
codes—the outcome of such enactment is never certain. It is always, to
some extent, up for grabs. Not only does one not know whether the
ceremony will succeed (since both spirits and humans are forever unpredictable); ritual meanings also constantly get resignified as they are performed.

Take for example the ɖɔyɔntʊ ceremony. While women are forbidden
to dance in Kuwdé, they *do* dance in Kagninsi (the last northern massif
community to perform it before it goes to the Logba in Benin). But how
could it be that women are permitted to dance a dance in Kagninsi that
is elsewhere exclusively associated with men and that is said to produce
infertility in women who dance? Of course, one might see this as a
"transformation" in structuralist terms—as marking a "difference" between communities. But such an interpretation does not comport with
what people told me about why women participate in Kagninsi. They
said that women there had more mystical power than women elsewhere
and thus had insisted that they could dance without harm to themselves
or others. The men had initially resisted but, fearing the women's powers,
had eventually given in. Such "revision" (Gates 1988) of the ceremony's
meanings in this community, however, would come as no surprise to anyone who has attended Kabre ceremonies—where arguments between
the participants are more the norm than the exception, and where meanings are constantly challenged and played with (cf. Drewal 1992).[16]

My point, then, is that these ceremonies do not so much produce a set
of representations as they do a set of performances and practices (Bourdieu 1977; Sahlins 1981, 1985; Ortner 1984; Butler 1990, 1993). They
"constitute" as much as they "express." They do not simply enact the

values of a given cultural tradition, so much as they embody, to use Bhabha's (1994: 3) felicitous phrase, "the signs of the emergence of community envisaged as a product—at once a vision and a construction."

Chiefs

One of the principal ways colonialism touched African communities, and Kabre were no exception, was through "indirect rule"—through the appointing of local chiefs to carry out the unseemly business of collecting tax and recruiting labor for the colonial government. As mentioned earlier, in the Kabre case these chiefs were often brutally exploitative— "worse than the colonials," I was told—and, when colonialism ended, the huts of many of them were destroyed.

In Kuwdé, there was a special irony to the engagement with indirect rule. Because the first chief in the area, a man from Faren named Patapu, and his successor Patchao, showed little restraint in exercising power, in the 1930s Kuwdé sent a delegation to the colonial office in Sokodé (100 km by foot) to demand that they be allowed to have their own chief. Their request was granted and Palabéi's father, Kansoukou, the son of Mahate (who killed the first German), was appointed chief of Kuwdé and Boua. Thus Kuwdé-Boua came into colonial chiefship, as it were, to save themselves from colonial chiefs.

While Kansoukou and subsequent Kuwdé chiefs were more benign than their counterparts in Faren, they nevertheless found it hard to resist the seductions of power. There are many stories of these chiefs attempting to enrich themselves at the expense of their subjects and of their trying to exceed the powers defined for them by the colonial government. However, despite the fact that most colonial-era chiefs became wealthy and were able to translate their wealth into power, their subjects were successful in containing and even marginalizing them. Chiefs throughout the communities of the northern massif were allowed no special privilege in either of the two major venues of male power and prestige—farming and ritual. While they were occasionally given free work group labor, they were never able to accumulate land, nor were they given unfettered access to community labor pools. And no chief that I know of played any role whatsoever in the system of calendrical ceremonies (nor were chiefs ever selected from the houses that ran the rituals). Indeed, there is a rule in northern massif communities that while animals sacrificed to ancestors at the homestead may be purchased in the market, those that are sacrificed to the "trees" in the sacred forests cannot. Instead, they must be obtained through barter with a bush community. Among other things, this rule prevented wealthy chiefs from angling their way into the domain of community ritual.

The divided and ambivalent nature of chiefly power—powerful in some ways, powerless in others—continues into the present. Today, of course, a chief's role as tax collector and recruiter of labor has ended, as has the remuneration colonial chiefs received for these tasks. But chiefs continue to serve as intermediaries between the state and the local community—announcing the dates of elections, collecting monies for communal projects, disseminating state policy on development projects and schooling—and gain some standing in the process. They also hear disputes within the community, especially those that are not resolved within the house. This latter role is particularly important, not only giving chiefs some income[17] but also providing them with a source of everyday power, for everyone is at some point involved in a dispute, and many are involved often. Thus, only the foolhardy do not respect and stay on the good side of a chief. Palabéi, for instance—and this in spite of the fact that many had mixed feelings about his performance as chief—was sent beer whenever a *haḍaa* work group convened, whether he was present for the work or not.

Despite such "perks," however, today's chiefs, like their colonial predecessors, are permitted no special access to land or work groups, and thus have no base from which to build economic power. Nor do they have any say in the running of the community-wide ritual system. Indeed, I was repeatedly struck by how relatively powerless these chiefs seemed. Denied the spoils of colonial-era chiefs, they are left with little to subsist on but the spent symbolic capital of an institution whose power has always been inextricably associated with the mixed valences of its colonial past.

State-Sponsored Fetishism?

Understanding the ambivalence people feel toward chiefly power—as opposed to ritual power—helps explain, I think, something in the attitude of those Kabre I know toward Eyadéma, Togo's president from 1967 to the present. While certainly appreciating what he has brought to the north (paved roads, clean water), and proud that a native son has been able to hold national power for more than thirty years, many nevertheless speak about him in surprisingly irreverent terms. They are quick to criticize him, for instance, when he meddles in local affairs—and, as with the example mentioned above of the state's attempt to control the timing and location of certain local ceremonies, they usually get their way. They also openly point out that, with few exceptions, he has largely failed to deliver on his promise to enhance the material well-being of those in the north.

When I returned to Kuwdé in 1996, I was told about an event that typifies the often testy relationship between the president and his homeland. In 1995, in an attempt to show support for the northern communities, Eyadéma sent state money to buy animals to sacrifice at the shrines of the major spirits. While northern ritual leaders purchased the animals and carried out the sacrifices, they nevertheless found the gesture inappropriate. One of these leaders told me, for instance, that the monetary nature of the gift defeated the whole aim of such sacrifices—and that the spirits would simply ignore them. "The powerful spirits ("les grands fétiches") need to see an effort, a display of 'will/desire,' from the members of the community," he said. "This is why they insist that the animals cannot be purchased but must instead be obtained through barter for grain, and why each house must contribute grain for the cause. Where is the will/effort of the community in Eyadéma's gift? He simply doesn't know the rules."

My sense here, however, is that there was more at issue than simply Eyadéma's ignorance of local custom. The strong negative reaction of community members to this "gift" also seemed informed by the longstanding desire to keep chiefs—for in many ways Eyadéma is to them little more than a glorified chief—out of the domain of community ritual, and thus to maintain the separation between chiefly and ritual power.

What then of Eyadéma's intervention in the rituals—the wrestling matches—of the male initiation system? When I asked people, they responded that those rituals are different altogether. Initiation ceremonies, they said, are for "children" and are not "serious" in the way that ceremonies to the spirits are. Thus, Eyadéma's involvement there doesn't matter and won't offend the spirits. Consider the implication, however: the president of the country consigned to a domain identified as "child's play"!

Of Spirits and Social Relations

In addition to addressing relations between humans and spirits, the calendrical ceremonies described earlier enact and realize various social relations between humans—between adult and child, between houses/moieties, and between communities. It is the relationship between moieties I will focus on here, thus returning to the question of community structure discussed earlier. I want to argue that Kabre understandings about the nature of the relationships among groups/houses are somewhat different from those described by descent theorists such as Fortes (1945, 1949), Goody ([1956] 1967), and Tait (1961) for other Voltaic societies.[18]

Kabre communities, like those of the Tallensi, are organized around a dual system of "houses"[19] that perform the calendrical ceremonies. But the relationship Kuwdé houses have to one another is rather different from that described by Fortes for the Tallensi. Kabre characterize the relationship between Tɔutɛɛ and Komatɛ as like that between "husband" and "wife," and, following the household analogy, they see the relationship between this married couple and Cacarɛya taa as similar to that of parent to child. It is because of their gendered relationship that Tɔutɛɛ and Komatɛ (but not Cacarɛya taa—"children" don't perform rituals) divide the ritual calendar as they do.

These gendered identities encompass all members of each moiety—all men and women nominally born into the houses of the moiety (though see below)—and are carried by those members throughout their lives. Thus, not only when performing the calendrical rituals themselves but also at the time of initiation and death, both women *and* men in Komatɛ adopt female behaviors and traits—they sit on the western (female) side of spirit groves during ceremonies, cover their bodies with white (female) oil, assume the taboos of women, and so on. Similarly, all men *and* women in Tɔutɛɛ adopt male behaviors and symbols on these ceremonial occasions.

It is interesting to note, however—and it is consistent with the pattern of opposite-sex incorporation found in the homestead—that the gendered oppositions that organize the annual cycle also incorporate and contain one another. Thus, at one moment during each season, the season is ritually turned inside out, as it were. For instance, when a certain age-grade initiation occurs at *kucontuɣu,* during the wet (female) season, the male moiety performs a condensed version of *ɖɔyɔntʊ,* the most male of all dry season ceremonies. This performance "dries" out the wet season, temporarily turning the wet into the dry, and inserting a male ceremony into the cycle of wet season female ceremonies. Conversely, during the dry male season, the female fertility ceremony that accompanies *lɛlaɣa* is performed by the female moiety, the sole such ceremony performed during an otherwise consistently male ceremonial sequence.

While the relationship between moieties is complementary (and incorporative), the male (Tɔutɛɛ) nevertheless holds higher rank and has ritual priority in various contexts. This, too, comports with the hierarchy between spouses in the homestead. For example, when ceremonies are performed in the forests of both moieties on the same day, they take place in Tɔutɛɛ's forest first ("because they are males"). And when initiates from the two groups travel from homestead to homestead and community to community at the time of *waaɣa,* the head of the male moiety leads while the head of the female moiety brings up the rear.

While a single house stands at the head of each moiety,[20] the year's ritual labor is nevertheless also distributed among the other houses of the group. Thus, while the two head houses are responsible for the most important ceremonies during the year, many of the other ceremonies are performed by lower-ranking houses within each group. And even when the head house is performing its ceremonies, it is assisted by (often several) other houses—one house being responsible for "sweeping out" the forest early in the morning, another for contributing beer and calabashes for the ceremony, a third coming up with the chickens to sacrifice, and so on. In this way, every house in the community has certain ritual responsibilities and is incorporated into the ritual system.[21]

What we have here, then, is *not* a system of "mechanical" solidarity like that described by Fortes for the Tallensi. That is, it is not a system of segmentary lineages—"individuals" writ large, each having similar (and competing) interests and identities, all finding their solidarity through opposition to some outside other. Rather, these are organic communities in which each house plays a different, and complementary, role within the system of rituals, and in which each has a fundamentally *different* identity from every other house (just as each individual exists in relation to others and also has his/her unique identity). Moreover, the rituals performed by Kabre houses are not so much—as Fortes (1936, 1940, 1987) would have it—some solidarity-producing apparatus whose purpose is to cement social relations between groups. Rather, Kabre ceremonies aim to do the opposite—to divide and differentiate groups and seasons.

While I witnessed a good deal of conflict at a point in the system where Fortes would have expected to find it—between the heads of Tɔʊtɛɛ and Komatɛ—the etiology of that conflict seemed to me very different from what Fortes would have assigned it. These heads were constantly getting into fights at the time of rituals—arguing with one another over proper ceremonial procedure, disputing the contributions (of grain, animals, beer) each had made to the ceremonies, and so on. Although Fortes would have said that such conflicts are inherent within social relations between competing clans and that it is the aim of rituals to diminish such conflict, the opposite seemed to be the case here. That is, it seemed to me that it was the rituals that created the conflict, and that this was part of the necessary (and positive) process of differentiation on which social life depends. Far from threatening the Kabre community, conflict and difference create and constitute it.

Again, the model of exchange elaborated in chapter 3 provides an instructive parallel. Just as exchange *creates* differences (separating giver from receiver) rather than overcoming them, so the ritual "exchanges" between moieties separate rather than unite: Tɔʊtɛɛ's rituals set it off—define it as different—from, and create a debt with, Komatɛ, and vice versa. Or, to use a different, though still Voltaic, idiom: John Chernoff's (1979) classic account of northern Ghanaian Dagbamba drum music describes the way multiple rhythms ("polyrhythms") and apart-playing are the essence of the music. There, drummers unite—like the houses in a Kabre community—through their differences rather than through their similarities.

I would suggest that the organic logic I have described for Kabre may be true of the Tallensi as well. Fortes (1987: 44) notes, but never develops the point, that the two Tallensi clans—Namoos and Talis—are also said to be "husband" and "wife" to one another and play complementary roles in Tallensi calendrical rituals. However, while Fortes saw relationality as central to the lineage system—this was the core idea of the segmentary principle[22]—he nevertheless characterized all lineages and clans as equal and competing segments—"like units"—in a system of "mechanical" solidarity.[23] To reiterate the point made in the introduction, this I think is where Fortes's individualist bias got the better of him.[24]

It is important to emphasize, moreover, that to Kabre, social/structural concerns like those that have preoccupied British anthropologists working in this area—such as the house structure that realizes itself in the calendrical ceremonies—are secondary. It is first and foremost their relations with the spirits that preoccupy them and to which they refer when discussing these ceremonies. One might say that Kabre ceremonies use what is at hand—the structure of houses—to achieve their cosmological ends, rather than—the other way around—the house system generating these ceremonies in order to represent, concretize, and mediate relations between the houses. The ceremonies are not reducible to— are not a mere reflection of—the system of clanship, as Fortes argued for Tallensi. Here spirits precede—and exceed—social relations (cf. Schloss 1988).

Colonialism and Community

I said earlier that for Kabre it is the spirits who stay put while people come and go. I am not thinking here of the insight proffered by descent theorists that lineages/clans are "corporations," which endure through time while their members come and go (Fortes 1953)), though such is certainly the case. Rather, I mean by this that there is much circulation of people among houses and communities during their lifetimes. There are five houses in Kuwdé, for instance, that have switched moieties— moving from Komatε to Tɔutεε—during the last two generations. Thus, whereas these houses used to identify as "female" in all major ceremonial contexts, they now identify as "male" in all the same contexts and perform ceremonies for Tɔutεε. Further, as mentioned earlier, a quarter of the residents of Kuwdé are considered "strangers" who nevertheless permanently reside in Kuwdé and play a role in the ritual life of the community. In some cases, this role is a major one, for they have sole charge of important calendrical ceremonies. Similarly, there are members of Kuwdé spread across the landscape in other communities both north and south. The Kabre community, then, is perhaps best thought of as a ritual center, a place where spirits reside and are attended to by human communities whose constitution is fluid and ever-changing.

But what is the relationship between such fluid, spirit-centered communities—between the notion of community as ritual center—and colonialism? Is this not some sort of resistant "outside" to colonial modernity, a relic of premodern social relations and cosmology?

As with Kabre gift exchange, all of the evidence suggests otherwise. Not only do the rituals themselves contain the marks of modernity's articulation with Kabre—the slave trade, the arrival of the Germans, interactions with the postcolonial state; there also appears to have been a close fit between colonial interest in this area and the fluid nature of these societies. As mentioned previously, it was here that the Germans, French, and British sought their workers for the mines and plantations at the coast, and here that they recruited laborers to build the colonial infrastructure. Above all else, then, colonialism demanded of these societies a plentiful and mobile labor supply. Moreover, in addition to uprooting workers from their communities (sometimes at a moment's notice and for varying lengths of time), the colonizers also expected those communities to bear the costs of social reproduction. (Similar pressures were exerted on the northern communities by the diaspora.) Accommodating such needs, however, required household and community structures of inordinate flexibility, and this is precisely what these communities possessed. Indeed, one of the most striking things to me when I lived in Kuwdé—during the postcolonial period when the mobility of labor was every bit as important as it had been during the colonial era—was the way households and communities were able to shuffle people around to meet variable labor requirements. (These movements, it goes without saying, often involved making adjustments for family members who had departed for the south.) If colonial modernity hadn't found fluid social structures when they encountered the societies of the northern territories, it surely would have had to create them.[25]

Further, the spirits may be seen as also playing a central role in the shuttling of people/laborers between north and south. For it was the spirits and their ceremonies that anchored the movement of people from north to south and back again. And it was the spirits who insisted on the perpetual "return" to the north of those who had departed for the south. Such an injunction is clearly convergent with the colonial interest in continually returning workers to the north to have their home communities bear the burdens of lifelong social reproduction. It is as if the spirits had here been recruited to the colonial cause.

I do not want to suggest, of course, that the features of these communities—their fluid nature, the salience of spirits—were/are nothing but a reflex of an encompassing colonial/postcolonial system. Clearly, these aspects of community life both predated the arrival of the Germans and manifest/ed a complexity that is not reducible to social need and colonial interest alone. Indeed, it is also through the spirits, these denizens of the wild, that Kabre were able to combat colonial conquest (Lan 1985), as well as to contest the postcolonial state, and through the spirits that they have fashioned a sense of empowerment and a distinctive identity that has allowed them to engage modernity on terms that are largely their own.

Seven

DIASPORA

Reciprocal Desires, Circulating Stories, Supernatural Contestations

Chapters 4–6 have moved from the level of the person, to that of the house, to that of the community, exploring the way each is constituted as structure and practice. In this chapter I move to an even more encompassing context, that of relations between north and south within the Kabre diaspora. Since the early colonial period, this larger context has affected, and in many ways conditioned, all others. The south is a constant presence within the life of northern Kabre, influencing gender relations, cultivation and marketing, rituals to the ancestors and spirits, initiation ceremonies, and so on. So, too, is the north an ongoing presence in the life of southerners. To reiterate one of my major points throughout: if exchange, gender, and ritual in the north are forever inflected with the experience of the diaspora, so too are they "inside" modernity, for this diaspora is colonial modernity's creation through and through.

A Modern Landscape

When you leave the Kabre north, the hilly homeland, with its gardenlike terraces and rock paths and spirit groves, you board a bush taxi in one of the major markets—Saturday in Farendé, Tuesday in Kara, Wednesday in Kétao. The road south threads its way through the Atakora mountain range, fighting tough terrain, across bridges and tunnels built by Kabre under the German and French whip. Today, many of the road's sharp turns are littered with the rusted carcasses of 18-wheel trucks which, under heavy load, were unable to negotiate the mountain's steep grades. These graveyard spectacles add fuel to the popular perception that travel on the national highway is fraught with danger, both mundane and mystical.[1]

As the road reaches the southern edge of the mountains, it enters a sprawling market town, Sokodé, an important stop on the ancient trade route from Hausa to Ashanti. Home to Kotokoli, a Muslim merchant people whose men, kola-nut-in-cheek, drive many of the long-distance taxis in Togo, Sokodé was the seat of colonial power in the north (and the place where Kuwdé members went to demand their own chief). Old German and French buildings, run-down and peeling, ring the market and taxi station in the center of town—and seem an apt *fin-de-siècle* emblem of crumbled colonial power. For Kabre, Sokodé is an unwelcome stop, for there is a long history of enmity between the two groups. Kotokoli were intermediaries in the slave trade, selling Kabre to the south, and Kotokoli assisted the Germans during the period of "pacification." More recently, during the early 1990s when things were hot in Lomé, Kotokoli sided with Ewe and allowed only Kabre women to pass to the north.

An aside here: in 1993, word reached Palabéi in the north that his civil servant son, Kokou, had been killed by a mob in Lomé. Since Kotokoli were blocking north-south traffic, Palabéi was unable to confirm the report. He nevertheless initiated funeral ceremonies, for fear that if his son's soul were not properly cared for, it would become angry and cause trouble. Just at that time, however, Kokou's wife—who had planned a trip to the north to visit her parents—successfully passed through the blockade in Sokodé and arrived in Kuwdé just as the husband she had left in Lomé the day before was being symbolically "buried." Stories like this—today told with equal parts humor, irony, and pathos—filled the air when I returned to Kuwdé in 1996 and 1998, and mark the culture of the 1990s as distinct from that of the 1980s.

Fifty kilometers south of Sokodé, as you enter a flat plain that stretches all the way to the coast, the first Kabre settlements appear: clusters of mud huts that begin at roadside and extend deep into the tall grass of the savanna. This was one of the early resettled zones whose inhabitants—grandparents of contemporary Kabre—initially resisted relocation but then were won over by the rich soils they found. "Yams grow to twice the size of those in Kuwdé," I repeatedly heard when asking about the advantages of cultivating in this central zone, "and the soils are not filled with rocks like they are in the north."

The bush taxis make frequent stops here, in roadside hamlets that often bear the names of Kabre communities in the north: Soutouboua,

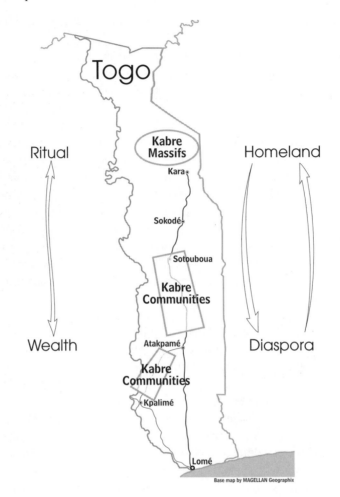

The Kabre Diaspora

Lama-Tessi, Landa. Each stop generates a flurry of activity—the driver climbing atop the roof to dig for bags, people scurrying from huts to greet those they know and get news from the north—before a passenger descends and disappears into the tall grass beside the road. Interspersed amidst these smaller settlements are larger towns with daily markets, entrepots that feed satellite villages spread for miles into the bush. The stops in these centers are animated by the presence of food vendors, drawn to the bus as to a magnet, peddling fruit, bread, and skewers of grilled meat to the empty-bellied passengers.

Continuing south, the savanna slowly turns to rain forest and the dry

Kuwdé goes south: northern teens cultivating in southern Togo during the summer holidays; Goudevé-Kpéledji, August 1998

northern climate is replaced by sticky, tropical air. Tall teak trees, originally planted by the Germans, their pancake leaves covered in dust, line the road. The rains come frequently here, downpours that pound the road and drench the straw roofs of the hamlets. It is to this zone, with its rich soils and cash farming, that Kuwdé schoolchildren come during summers to help their brothers cultivate and to earn money for school. It is also in this southernmost tip of the diaspora that Kabre settlements intermingle with those of Ewe. Here there is a long history of cultural cross-fertilization and ritual collaboration; tragically, however, this tradition was largely forgotten when Ewe opposition to Eyadéma emerged in the early 1990s, and lives on both sides were threatened and houses sacked.

The ceaseless circulation of people, goods, and information along the national highway that connects north and south, and along the lattice-like paths that connect villages in the two zones, is one of this diaspora's defining traits. On my trips to the south I was repeatedly surprised to discover people I had just a day or two previously seen in a market or a homestead in the north, and to find that the latest news from the north—of a death, about the rains or the harvest—was already common knowledge. When sending mail between the zones, as friends would instruct me whenever I was tempted to use the postal service, it is always quicker, and saves the cost of postage, to find someone making the voyage. That way, you are virtually assured of next-day delivery.

Needless to say, this dispersed yet dense network of communities and kin is thoroughly imbricated with the modalities of modernity. Not only are roads and cars its lifeblood; crucial information about recent deaths circulates between the zones as much by radio as by word of mouth. Each day at 7 P.M., people throughout the country, in bush and city alike, tune in state radio to listen to the latest funeral announcements. (While the aim of these broadcasts is, of course, the speedy dissemination of information, they also enable the state to insert itself into local culture. In that it has become a mark of distinction to have a deceased family member's name announced on the radio, this practice has also come to play a role in the production and reproduction of local prestige hierarchies.) Another artifact of modernity also figures prominently in the culture of far-flung Kabre: the tin roofs in the northern homesteads that sparkle like cut gems amidst the browns, yellows, and grays of mud and straw. Purchased by those who have left, they convey connection to those who remain behind. Moreover, as a measure of this commitment, in the southern zone of cash crops and money, tin is much scarcer: there homestead roofs are typically made of straw.

Needless to say, none of this landscape—the teak trees, the road with its bridges and tunnels, the web of southern hamlets and market towns that line the national highway, the tin-hatted northern homesteads—existed before the colonial era began. This is a landscape that owes its distinctive features to modernity. For all that, however, it is no less "Kabre."

Constituting a Translocality

For Kabre, migrating to open up new communities is not strictly a recent phenomenon. Long before the colonial era began, Kabre were leaving the mountains to establish offshoot communities in the plain surrounding the two massifs. Each of the first communities in the northern massif where Kuwdé is located—Faren, Boua, Kuwdé, Wazilao, Somdé, Asiri—has one or more offshoot communities in the plain—Tchi-Kawa, Kawa, Kaningada, Ayangtoro, Kagninsi. The same pattern—originary communities located in the mountains and offshoots in the plain—is true of the southern massif as well.

The relationship between the communities of origin and their offshoots is seen as that of "parent" to "child," and, as with the filial relationship generally, the latter are expected to "respect" the former. Such respect is especially evident on ritual occasions, when offshoot communities are expected to defer to their "parents" in the mountains. Thus, it is to the mountains that initiates from plains communities must return to participate in the big dances, and in the mountains that deceased men of important houses in the plain are buried. If these respect relations break down—if the hierarchy is flaunted—hardship and calamity invariably follow. When a mini-drought gripped the area in June 1989, for instance, a diviner suggested that the rain's absence was caused by the failure of a house in Kawa, one of Kuwdé's offshoots, to bury an important elder in the mountains. When, at the diviner's suggestion, the burial was reenacted, the rains returned.

The hierarchy between "mountain" (*pʊɣʊ taa,* in the mountain) and plain or "bush" (*nyɪtʊ taa,* in the grass) communities is also conceptualized as the difference between "male" and "female," and, as in the domains of the house and the community, these gendered differences are seen as mutually constitutive (the "female" bush is both complement to and productive of the "male" mountain, and vice versa) and reciprocally dependent. So, too, is the bush, like women and children in the house, seen as possessing an essential source of vitality without which the larger whole could not exist.

It is at the time of important community-wide rituals to the spirits that these dependencies and reciprocal potencies are made visible. When Kuwdé sacrifices a cow to a major food spirit (it is mountain communities alone who perform such sacrifices for the region as a whole), it obtains the cow through barter with a bush community—Kagninsi in 1982, Kawa in 1989, Tchi-Kawa in 1996.[2] This transaction makes manifest not only the (ritual) dependence of bush to mountain but also—the inverse—mountain communities' dependence on (the wealth of) the bush. Indeed, in this case, and again on the model of exchange discussed earlier, since it is the mountain that has the greater "need" and thus initiates the exchange, here is an example of a center that is in debt to its periphery. Note, too, that it is the *differences* between mountain and bush (a mountain identified with ritual, a plain with wealth) that matter in this scheme, and that it is rituals such as this that are responsible for producing (rather than—the classical view—overcoming) them.[3]

The origin stories of bush communities define a further set of complementarities, as well as competing claims and ambivalences, in the relationship between mountain and bush. These stories often refer to acts

Ritual exchange: Kuwdé women carrying sorghum to the plains community of Kagninsi, in exchange for a cow demanded by a spirit in the mountains; January 1983

of transgression that led to the founding of bush communities. Both Tchi-Kawa and Kawa (offshoots of Boua and Kuwdé respectively), for instance, are said to have been established by a brother and sister from the mountains who were sent to chase birds from a field in the distant plain, and there had sex. As punishment for their transgression, they were ostracized from the mountain and made to live in the plain—at the site of their misdeed. Of course, such accounts position mountain and bush within a hierarchy that defines mountain communities as upholders of norms and bush communities as violators, valuing the former and devaluing the latter. At the same time, however, these stories portray norm violation (incest) as dictated by necessity, associating it with food production and, by extension, the pursuit of wealth. Moreover, food/wealth is something that all desire and on which all rely. As such, these origin accounts capture something of the mix of affirmation and ambivalence, dependence and disavowal, that characterizes not only the relationship between mountain and bush communities but also the culture of Kabre regionalism more generally.

It was almost certainly during the colonial era that the tension between ritual and wealth, and its constitutive role in defining relations between mountain and bush communities, became salient. During the nineteenth century, not only was the mountain ritually superior, but those from the mountains were also said to have possessed greater wealth—manifest in large herds of cattle. With the advent of colonial rule, however, the wealth of plains communities came to surpass that of the mountains. At the insistence of colonial administrators, some of the major markets were relocated from the mountains to the plain, centering commerce in these communities and giving their members greater access to sources of wealth.[4] It was also in communities of the plain that colonial administrators conducted cash-cropping experiments, and while many of these failed, some, like cotton, succeeded and contributed to the growing wealth of plains communities—and thus of the Kabre periphery.

This new relationship between the two zones revalued ritual and re-signified the relationship between "ritual" and "wealth." To wit, as bush communities gained greater access to wealth, mountain communities came more and more to assert the importance of their rituals, and, through their ceremonies, several of which involve the symbolic appropriation of peripheral wealth, to assert that ritual still trumped wealth. By the same token, peripheral communities came to challenge such privilege, if not in a direct and absolute way (for they still acknowledged that spirits reigned supreme in the hierarchy of values), then in a less direct but nevertheless inordinately powerful manner: through the display of that which they purchased with their newfound wealth—radios, clothes, bicycles, and occasionally cars. Through mere visibility—and, ironically, by drawing on local cultural principles: achieving effects and making things real by making them visible (see chapter 4)—this emergent colonial culture of wealth staked claim to a power that captured the imagination of many. Even if unspoken, wealth's allure became hegemonic, in the Comaroffian sense (1991, 1997),[5] unconsciously shaping desires and identities, and engendering antagonisms, that remain at the heart of Kabre culture today.[6]

Reprise on Identity

Before returning to the larger landscape of the diaspora, I would like to note the way personal identities in this system are transformed by more encompassing affiliations—and, thus, the way identity is mutable and nonessential (cf. Drewal 1992; Matory 1994). Consider, for instance, the identity of a man who comes from a house in Kuwdé's female moiety as opposed to a man from its male moiety. The former, the man in a house from the female moiety, becomes "female" in various contexts. Thus, when participating in calendrical ceremonies in the sacred groves, he sits on the west (female) side of the forest, is associated with the right (female) hand and with white (a female color). He also eats female portions of sacrificed meat and is associated with the wet season and wetness generally. And, since the male moiety is superior (as men are in the homestead), he must follow rather than lead during various ritual activities. This man's female identity is one he carries with him not just at the time of calendrical ceremonies but also when he is initiated and at death. At these crucial junctures in his life, he is associated with all of the symbols of femaleness and becomes "female."

Conversely, this man's wife may undergo the opposite transformation. If she is a member of the male moiety (often, though not always, the case), she eats male portions of sacrificed animals, is associated in various contexts with the symbols of maleness (the color red, the east, the left, dryness), and will be buried in a tomb of the male clan at death. Whereas her husband is "female," she is "male."

At the level of the region, a similar transformation occurs, for here a person's identity is also governed by membership in a particular gendered zone of the larger region. For example, for a man of the female moiety in the male zone of the mountains, his male identity is reasserted when interacting with members of the bush. And while all members of the female zone of the bush are inferior to their mountain counterparts, the bush's identity as female serves to transform the relations between bush moieties, resulting in a system different from that which operates in the mountains. In the bush, the female moiety is superior to the male moiety, because of the bush's location in the regional system's female zone. Thus, houses of the female moiety have ritual priority, and men in the male moiety are inferior. A man in the male moiety in the bush, therefore, is ranked below all other men throughout the entire system.

A man thus has multiple identities—male in one context, female in another, and male again in yet another. A woman, too, has multiple identities—as a woman, as a man, and so on. Only the male identities of men in the male moiety in mountain communities remain untransformed. However, for such men, there is an intensification of what it means to be male, for they are triply male, as it were—an intensification that has its own obviational logic.

These identity switches are not trivial. A person's moiety and regional identities are every bit as important as his or her household identity. While household identities govern the everyday, moiety and regional identities govern the two most important moments in a person's life— initiation and death. So, too, do moiety and regional affiliations define a person's role in the calendrical ceremonies that govern the annual cycle.

It is important to note, however, that such identity switching is not so much a type of "play" (Drewal 1992) as it is a type of politics, for the relationship between different Kabre domains is a political one. Hierarchies structure the domains and impose themselves on lower-level domains. Thus, moieties dominate houses, setting up hierarchies among them; and regional identities dominate moieties, similarly establishing hierarchies between the moieties. It makes a difference in terms of the hierarchies of the system, then, whether one belongs to one moiety or the other and to one region or the other. Moreover, to claim that the relationship between domains is about politics is also to claim that it is about history, for the long history of Kabre migration and regional expansion lies behind the identity politics—a politics of priority and privilege—that characterizes this regional culture.

Attractions and Antagonisms

When, during the 1920s and 1930s, the French began relocating Kabre to southern Togo, these emigrants carried with them northern models of, and sensibilities about, intercommunity relationships. Thus, southern Kabre were regarded by northerners (and regarded themselves) as "children," and they deferred ritual privilege to those who remained in the north. It has always been in the north that major initiations are held, that a person is buried and enshrined as an ancestor, and that the major spirits reside. Consequently, southerners (and, indeed, family members as far away as France and the United States) flock back to the northern villages at the time of these ceremonies. And, in what for me has always represented an extraordinary example of commitment to the principle of inalienability in a truly Marxian sense, the soul (*warɪtʊ*, behind-person) of every Kabre, even those who are second and third generation southerners, is returned to that person's natal and/or family homestead in the north at death—there to become an ancestor. The south, by contrast, is the land of cash-cropping and wealth, wealth that is used to support not only those who reside there but also those they have left behind

The terraced terrain and tin roofs of the northern homeland; Kuwdé, January 1984

in the north. It is also to this southern zone that northerners journey (mainly during the dry season) in search of money to feed their families and to help finance upcoming ceremonies.

As with mountain and bush communities in the north, it is these two values and identities—ritual and wealth—that define north and south, homeland and frontier, as distinct yet dependent, and it is the reciprocal pulls—of ritual responsibility to family and homeland on the one hand, and the need/desire for wealth on the other—that keep Kabre constantly on the move back and forth along the national highway. Indeed, I find it useful to think of the diaspora as constituted by these reciprocal desires (of northerners for southern wealth and of southerners for northern ritual). Note, moreover, the way ritual and wealth interact and cycle into one another—for it is southern wealth that feeds northern ritual and northern ritual, as producer of people, that generates wealth. And, in one of modernity's ironies, and evidence of Appadurai's (1990, 1991, 1997) point that globalization generates difference as well as homogeneity, this colonial diaspora has produced an expansion of the ritual sphere. "Today," I heard repeatedly, "we do more rituals than in the past." Such expansion—as if parrying capitalism's commodity proliferation—follows from the fact that it is ritual that has become a mediator of the translocal and a signifier of attachment.

Here I want to draw attention to two additional features of this diaspora, features that contribute to maintaining a sense of identity among far-flung Kabre (Marguerat 1994: 206–11)—and to preserving the north as homeland and moral center. One is its reliance on forms of mimesis, the other the way in which it is constituted and reconstituted through discourses/stories that circulate between north and south.[7]

The first, the mimetic, is manifest in the way the southern communities reproduce many features of their northern communities of origin. In addition to carrying the names of their home communities with them, southern Kabre tend to live with, and marry, those from their villages in the north (Marguerat 1994: 206–8). They also imitate many aspects of northern social and productive organization. The gendered division of labor within households—with men cultivating and women cooking and marketing—remains unchanged,[8] as does the way productive processes themselves are organized (e.g., southern men cultivate through the same work group structures—*ıkparı* and *haḍaa*—found in the north, women work with their daughters, daughters-in-law, and co-wives as northern women do, and so on). So, too, is the ritual organization of southern communities similar to that in the north—with each centered around two (similarly named, similarly gendered) moieties that organize spirit worship and initiations.[9] In many ways, then, southern communities are attempts to produce near-perfect copies of their northern communities of origin. (Recall, of course, that for Kabre mimesis is a form of power.)

I am not suggesting that there is cookie-cutter imitation going on here. As Derrida ([1972] 1982) has shown with language, and Gates (1988) with (African) diasporic narrative forms, mimesis always involves slippage—"repetition with a difference." If the southern communities are "copies," they are at best imperfect ones. Moreover, subtle changes in practice, such as replacing straw roofs with tin, are also conveyed back to the north and there transform village culture in significant ways. Indeed, it may be more accurate in this case to say that the "original" rather than the "copy" is the site of transformation, and that the copy preserves the original more faithfully than the original itself.

Even more striking to me was the fact that those Kabre I know in Lomé—civil servants of the state, researchers, petty entrepreneurs: people like Bassari and Kokou—seem every bit as committed to preserving northern practice in their everyday lives as are those in the farming communities of the central and southern zones. They, too, tend to marry those from their villages of origin in the north and to follow its gendered patterns of household labor. And although they are often unable to live in neighborhoods with their same-village compatriots from the north, many convene monthly in associations organized by northern village affiliation. Thus, members of Boua and Kuwdé gather on the first Sunday of each month (as do members of Faren, Wazilao, and Asiri) to share news from the north, to talk about upcoming northern elections and ceremonies, and to provide aid to members in need. With the press of events in the early 1990s, this latter activity became particularly salient, with members spending much time aiding others who were in trouble or in prison, providing shelter for those whose houses had been destroyed, helping one another send information back to the north, and so on. Here, then, was a conjunctural moment (Sahlins 1981, 1985; Apter 1992) that had both innovative and conservative effects, organizing southern Kabre around issues focused more on the nation than the north, but doing so on northern terms.

Perhaps even more important to the maintenance of a sense of Kabreness than mimetically reproducing northern organizational forms, however, is the continued participation of far-flung Kabre in the conversations and debates that spread like brush fire along the roads and pathways of this diasporic landscape. One such debate occurred at the time of the rain's disappearance in July 1996 (see chapter 2). As the drought stretched on, discussion as to its cause spread from the north into the farming villages of the south, and then into the neighborhoods of Lomé. Once the cause became widely agreed upon—namely, that the southern sons of a deceased member of the house of rainmakers in the northern community of Faren had failed to bury him properly—attention shifted to deciding what should be done to rectify the situation and bring back the rain. Of course, such discursive events not only produce a sense of common identity but also continue to position the north as moral center and homeland—here, a homeland to which all deceased Kabre must return at death.

Another flap over a funeral drew in people from both north and south in summer 1996. When an elderly woman died—a woman born in Wazilao who married into Kuwdé—one of her sons, who runs an auto parts store in Lomé, refused to take her ceremonies back to the north. Among other things, these ceremonies make public the woman's passing, and, through the distribution of meat from the sacrifices, acknowledge those who fed and nurtured her as a child as well as those who similarly nurtured her parents. Without the ceremony, a deceased person remains "alive" and cannot enter the ranks of the ancestors; and, as several Kuwdé-ites pointed out to me, without the ceremony, there is no public acknowledgment of the role played by the community in feeding and nurturing her and her children. This acknowledgment, one woman told me, is the main purpose of these ceremonies.

News of the son's refusal carried quickly to the north, where he was roundly condemned. His decision was also discussed at meetings of the Boua-Kuwdé association in Lomé, where there was widespread consensus that he had erred in not taking his mother's ceremony back to Kuwdé. The son claimed penury—his business had never recovered from the events of the early 1990s—but everyone knew that his refusal really had more to do with his strained relationship with those in his natal village.[10] It was only when his younger brother intervened—a brother who, although living and teaching in France, had maintained strong ties with those in Kuwdé—that he agreed to hold the ceremony.

A similar translocal fracas occurred in the early 1990s, this one with a tragic outcome. Halitoké, the head of the house I lived in in Kuwdé, had for years had testy relations with a brother who lived in the south. The brother, who made good money as a cocoa farmer, repeatedly promised to help Halitoké in meeting family ritual obligations. (As senior male residing in the north, Halitoké was responsible for sacrificing to house spirits and ancestors, and for repeatedly hosting southern family members who returned for funerals or initiations.) But the brother rarely helped out, often claiming that the harvest had been bad or that obligations to near-kin had absorbed his surplus cash. And yet when this same brother made his annual visit to the north, he always wore new clothes, invariably showed off a recently purchased radio, and seemed able to spend limitless amounts of money on *sɪlɪm,* the local beer.

Halitoké returned the insult in the only way he knew how—through public humiliation on ritual occasions. Thus, Halitoké openly made fun of his brother when the latter had forgotten the particulars of a sacrifice—which types of animals were demanded by different spirits, which pieces of meat to distribute to whom—and relished jumping in and taking over. (I was caught in the crossfire between these brothers at one point, for, unbeknownst to me at the time, the tin-roofed house we rented from Halitoké belonged to the brother. But Halitoké kept all the rent money for himself, and indeed had never sent word to the brother that we were staying in his house. Thus, when the brother showed up in Kuwdé four months into our stay, he was, not surprisingly, astonished to find us living in his house. Moreover, when he discovered that we had been paying rent, and that his brother had, as he put it, "eaten" all the money, he became incensed—as much over the fact that he had not been informed that we were living there as that he had received no money. A row ensued between the brothers, and then a mediation session with Palabéi, before it was agreed that our future rent money would go to paying for a door for the house and cement for the floors.)

The tensions between the brothers carried into relations between their children as well. Thus, when Halitoké was doing a sacrifice for one of the brother's sons who had returned to Kuwdé for *waaɣa* (the quinquennial age-grade ceremony for *kɛŋnaa*) in 1990, he intentionally kept a piece of meat for himself that should have gone to the son. A month later, when Halitoké abruptly fell ill and died, the son was immediately blamed for the death and accused of witchcraft.

I am suggesting that discursive translocal events such as these—ironically, events typically touched off by conflict (and often triggered by the ritual/wealth divide)—provide a sense of common Kabre identity. For it is through the heated arguments and debates that course through the arteries of this diaspora—debates about rain and funerals and witches, but also always about the proper treatment of kin and community—that far-flung Kabre come to be participants in a single moral community.

The Value of a Relation

The prolific return of departed southerners to the north has always intrigued and amazed me: why do Kabre keep coming back by the tens of thousands—to cover the roofs of their parents' and siblings' houses with tin, to initiate their children, and to bury their dead? Why do these emigrants convert wealth into ceremonies and tin for relatives they have left behind, while often depriving themselves? Moreover, why does the president of the country, accompanied by his cabinet, return to the north each year—not only to further his nationalist project but also to show those in the north that he remains a good "son"?

If, for the capitalist, value and wealth reside in commodities—and lead in societies of the metropole to a proliferation of commodity production and consumption—for Kabre value is also measured by relations. Moreover, as I showed above, relationships are invariably mediated through exchange and embodied/externalized in, among other things, gifts and ceremonies. This, then, is what tin roofs and ceremonial return are all about. "When someone from the south brings a ceremony to us [in the north], or when a son buys tin for the house of his father," Tamouka once said in response to my probing, "they show us respect.

They show that they have not forgotten where they were born. This is all that we ask." Tin roofs and ceremonies are material—and highly visible/ public—expressions of relatedness and respect, of dependence and deference, between kin.[11] As such, they embody connection (as well as hierarchy) and constitute diaspora. In so doing, they call up a history of dispersal and return that is as intrinsically "Kabre" as anything else.

Of course, in thus suggesting that Kabre return—that they are diasporic—because they are committed to social relations—that they convert wealth to ceremonies and tin because they continue to value their commitments to persons—I risk tautology. Namely, the suggestion is that they attend to relationships because they value relationships. But this, as I have repeatedly stressed, is an irreducible premise of this social world (and, in any case, is no less self-referencing than the claim that the capitalist is a seeker of profit). Moreover, I see little gain in reducing such a premise to something other—to a "utility" or "function"—as social science would have us do. Not only are such functional reductions tautological in their own right; but also, in that they are rooted in the individualisms described earlier, to deploy them here would be to engage in a form of epistemic violence and colonization.

Eight

A KABRE MODERNITY

Modernity is a discourse in drag; it is always cross-dressed. It must always reach out to appropriate what is alien in order to perform itself, to establish its difference. In this attempted appropriation, dislocation occurs and points of weakness emerge. It is from these points that a post-Orientalist critique can begin. (Mitchell and Abu-Lughod 1993: 83)

The *Man with a Bicycle* [a Yoruba sculpture of a man on his way to market standing beside his bicycle] is produced by someone who does not care that the bicycle is the white man's invention—it is not there to be Other to the Yoruba self; it is there because someone cared for its solidity; it is there because it will take us further than our feet will take us; it is there because machines are now as African as novelists. . . . (Appiah 1992: 157)

One morning in July 1996, just after school had let out for the summer and Kuwdé (male) teens were preparing to depart for the south, Tikén-awé and I happened by Palabéi's homestead as he was sacrificing a chicken and a guinea hen for his sixteen-year-old son, Tetiyiki. Tetiyiki was preparing to leave to work on a brother's farm near Kpalimé, and Palabéi was enlisting the protection of house ancestors for the journey. As we stopped to greet them, Tikénawé noticed that Tetiyiki had a new haircut—shaved at the base, long on top—and she immediately burst out laughing, mocking him for having cut his hair "like a Fulani" (herders who live in the plain surrounding the Kabre massifs). Tetiyiki retorted that it wasn't Fulani he was imitating but the hairstyle of those (American Blacks) he had seen on MTV the last time he had visited his brother, Kokou, in Lomé. When, later that day, I saw Tetiyiki and a friend leaving Kuwdé, adidas bags looped over their shoulders, the friend was sporting the same haircut as Tetiyiki. Here, then, are voyaging teens equipping themselves for the journey south with both ancestral protection and the latest global coiffure.

As should be amply clear by now, the Kabre world is one of promiscuous mixing, in which sacrifice and MTV, rainmakers and civil servants, fetishists and catechists exist side by side and coauthor an uncontainably hybrid cultural landscape. If modernity is constantly trying to draw boundaries around itself by differentiating itself from that which is non-modern ("tradition") (Mitchell and Abu-Lughod 1993), Kabre refuse such boundaries and the distinctions that accompany them. They are as at home in the world of so-called tradition as in that of the modern, and see the mixture of the two not only as unproblematic but also as desirable.

Moreover, confounding another of modernity's presumptions, this is a world in which the so-called traditional—gift exchange, initiation ritual, spirit worship—has increased and intensified along with modernity's embrace. Indeed, I have suggested that this intensification is intimately related to the advance of colonial modernity—to the colonial and post-colonial preoccupation with and commodification of (primarily male) bodies, to the dispersal of Kabre by colonial-era migrations and resettlement schemes, and to a postcolonial culture in which ethnic politics has come to dominate Togo's public sphere. It is only in such an indisputably modern—colonial and postcolonial—context that the proliferation of the traditional is fully intelligible.

But if this tradition owes its present form to, and derives its meaning from, modernity as much as from anything local or "indigenous," it becomes analytically impossible to separate the two. Where does the "traditional" end and the "modern" begin? Where is there an "outside" to modernity's "inside"? Where is there a "local" that is not also "global"? As Jean and John Comaroff (1993: xii) suggest (see also Mitchell and Abu-Lughod 1993: 79), modernity should be seen as less a historical condition than a political project, whose aim has always been to center the West and marginalize the rest. An empty signifier whose content is forever shifting, modernity itself is not only intrinsically impure and hopelessly hybridized but also incorrigibly plural and forever incomplete.

If the Kabre world refuses orthodox understandings of the modern, it also troubles theories of the colonial encounter that look for acts of clear resistance to, and rejection of, things colonial.[1] Such theories—modernist in their assumptions of the boundedness and the autonomy of individuals, or of cultures-as-individuals—have difficulty coming to terms with the sorts of responses that characterize Kabre engagements with colonial modernity. While Kabre mounted resistances of the classical sort to German and French rule—they killed the first German, fled armed retaliation, evaded French censuses, reacted with outrage to the predations of the early chiefs—they also, like the Yoruba on his bicycle, welcomed things European: roads and cars, the opportunity to move south, the cash that wage labor brought, radios, tin roofs. They also embraced the opportunity to enhance their cultural repertoires by purchasing European cloth and making it standard dress, by adding plastic dolls to the headdress of male initiates, by decorating their houses with tin hats. And many Kabre welcomed the chance to add a Christian deity to their pantheon. But this appropriation of an Other was nothing new. Kabre have long drawn in and creatively absorbed the outside—whether spirits of the bush, products from the trans-Saharan trade, the cultural practices of neighboring groups, or the technologies and signs of the colonial.

Moreover, it would be a mistake to see such appropriations as disempowering—as a type of capitulation or surrender. Not only do those Kabre I know see culture as additive and labile, ever-changing and improvisational, but also—as scholars of the transnational have repeatedly found elsewhere (Thomas 1991; Hannerz 1996; Appadurai 1997; Comaroff and Comaroff 1997)—things appropriated from the outside are forever refigured and resignified in locally meaningful ways. Thus, the Dutch cloth that is a staple in Kabre markets is deployed in local prestige and fashion hierarchies in quite distinctive ways (cf. Hansen 1994; Hendrickson 1996; Comaroff and Comaroff 1997). And, as I suggested in chapter 7, the tin roofs on their houses are fed into and reauthored by local histories and values.[2] Rather than seeing local appetites for things Western as a type of colonization,[3] I prefer to see them as creative appropriations—as "cannibalizations" (Jewsiewicki 1997: 103) of the cultural inventory of the West.[4]

There is in the Kabre colonial and postcolonial encounter a more aggressively assertive dynamic as well, not unlike that described by Taussig (1993). Taussig suggested that interactions across the colonial divide might be understood as attempts to tap into, usurp, and steal the powers of the Other—Europeans/colonizers stealing the labor power and appropriating the exoticism of the colonized; those same colonized others appropriating the technologies and deities of Europeans. Something of this sort characterizes certain Kabre responses to the colonial encounter

Self-portrait: teen women dressed as men; Kuwdé, July 1989

Self-portrait: teen cultivators camping it up as school boys; Kuwdé, July 1985

as well (although of course Kabre, like other colonized peoples, responded to the colonial order in a multiplicity of ways). This is why the
Kabre buried the first German in a sacred forest; why age-grade initiates
mimed colonial officials; why colonial dolls adorn their horns; and, indeed, why some go to church and school. (This latter is a form of mimesis
whose aim is not so much to become like Europeans—"men of the
book," I often heard them called—as to discover and usurp the source
of their power and make it their own.)

Witness, for instance, the following story that was circulating in the
northern communities in the mid-1990s. One night a plane landed at the
Niamtougou airport—the airport just to the north of the Kabre massifs
that Eyadéma built in the 1970s, and a place known for its mystical
power. The man in charge of the airport—a European—had not expected any planes that night and went to investigate. He found only Africans on board, who, although he did not know it, were witches. They
surrounded him and took away his book—a book in which he'd been
writing. Then they let him go, and the plane disappeared. This is clearly
a story about power and its appropriation: Africans with magical powers,
in command of a technology that is coded as European, attempting to
appropriate another of the colonizer's powers (writing/books). Note,
moreover, that in this encounter tale, the European was not killed, nor

Young cultivators at play: impersonating European technology; Kuwdé, June 1989

was his technology disabled or rejected. To the contrary, these power-ful Africans were attempting to make his powers their own.[5]

To say as much, however, is not to deny the clear asymmetries in the colonial situation.[6] Nor is it to suggest that in appropriating the powers of others, Kabre cannot also be discriminating, even defiant. In 1995, for instance, a Catholic priest in Piya, the president's home village, transgressed local norms by asking some of the women who attended his services to carry the body of a deceased churchgoer to the family tomb on the mountain. As mentioned in chapter 5, women who come into contact with cadavers and peer into tombs risk infertility, so this request violated those norms that associate women with life and men with death and cadavers. There was an immediate outcry and, following Eyadéma's intervention, the priest was transferred to southern Togo. As with the episode of the drought described above, the problem was not the presence of a priest, or of a Kabre engaging in Christian worship, that provoked such a strong reaction—Kabre welcome the addition of other deities to their pantheon so long as they are permitted to mingle with diviners and spirits. Rather, it was the use of an exclusionary practice that was not also mindful of local practice and, crucially, one that threatened the fertility of persons.

As I have suggested throughout, these materials once again force us to pursue other (less modernist) genealogies of response and agency—genealogies and histories that take us beyond the simple binary of resistance or capitulation, into a world of proliferating and multivectored agency. Moreover, responses to the colonial and the modern such as these are consistent with the types of personhood dynamics I have been at pains to describe in the preceding chapters: with exchangers who enmesh and mutually subordinate one another; with spouses, moieties, and regions that appropriate and incorporate one another's potencies; and, indeed, with the ways people responded to my presence in their midst. Appropriation of the other in each of these contexts—as in the context of the (post)colonial—is an act of both self-assertion and differentiation.

◄o►

For anthropologists, the remote village has long been the site *par excellence* of traditional culture—an outside, a place in which to locate the Other, a site of redemption at some remove from the metropole and the global system (cf. Starn 1991; Gupta and Ferguson 1997b). While I understand the romance and appeal of such a vision, and can imagine its promotion having had (at an earlier moment) politically progressive possibilities, today such a project often serves to feed reactionary political agendas (such as those I described in the introduction). Moreover, such a romantic vision fundamentally fails to come to terms with the agendas and aspirations of peoples like Kabre who are today, and have long been, an integral part of the modern world. I prefer to see the village as a site—and also, in many ways, an effect—of the modern, one that is as privileged as any other, one that has shaped the modern as much as it has been shaped by it, and one that brings to the modern—that always uneven, often discordant, ever refracting, forever incomplete cultural/political project—its own vernacular modernity.

Notes

Chapter One

1. By "modernity," I mean those everyday forms of culture, politics, and economy associated with the rise of industrial capitalism in Europe of the sixteenth, seventeenth, and eighteenth centuries and disseminated globally by European imperial expansion—forms, however, which have no essence (Rabinow 1989: 9) and whose content is unstable and shifting (Pratt 1998). For useful discussions of the concept of modernity, see Berman 1982, Harvey 1989, Giddens 1990, Lash and Friedman 1992, Pred and Watts 1992, Gilroy 1993a, and Comaroff and Comaroff 1993.

2. See, respectively, *Atlantic Monthly,* February 1994; *New York Times Magazine,* 2 March 1997; *New York Times,* 15 April 1996; *Washington Post,* 3 July 1996.

3. The political violence that caused half a million Togolese to flee Lomé in the early 1990s led the embassy to keep track of all Americans in Togo in the event that a renewed outbreak of violence would necessitate quick evacuation.

4. While "Kabiyé" is used throughout much of Togo today—because Eyadéma, Togo's president, is from a village in the southern massif where that is the term of reference—I employ the term "Kabre" that is used by those in the communities of the northern massif among whom I lived and worked.

5. See, for example, "Fleeing Mutilation, Fighting for Asylum," *Ms.*, July/ August 1996.

6. Within anthropology, of course, such a now patently postcolonial position has a venerable history. Anthropologists have long been committed to seeing culture and history in the plural, and to representing—giving voice to—other cultural worlds and realities. For example, Evans-Pritchard's studies of Azande witchcraft, Benedict's work on Native American cultural logics, and Lévi-Strauss's analyses of Amazonian mythology and totemic thought, among others, have all been attempts not only to understand and describe non-Eurocentric thought and lifeways but also to celebrate them—and to strategically use these other truths to criticize Western theories and epistemologies and, indeed, Western society itself.

7. See also Strathern 1984, 1987a, 1987b, 1991, 1992a, 1992b.

8. A related position and critique may be found in the works of those anthropologists who derive inspiration from phenomenology (Riesman [1974] 1977, 1986; Munn 1986; Jackson 1989, 1996, 1998; Stoller 1989, 1997; Werbner 1989; Weiss 1996). Drawing on the work of Heidegger, Husserl, James, Merleau-

Ponty, and Schutz, among others, these anthropologists argue that social life and personhood in the societies where they work is intersubjective, that culture is "embodied," and that notions of agency, space, and time should be theorized with such understandings in mind. They also, like Strathern, critique the way Western social theory has attempted to come to terms with personhood and agency in non-Western cultures. I have found Michael Jackson's (1989, 1996, 1998) work, in particular his focus on the relational dimensions of personhood, especially helpful.

9. There were in fact rather pronounced inequalities in the distribution of work group labor over the course of the year among different households. But these differences correlated neatly with household size—bigger households with more mouths to feed called the work group more often than smaller households with fewer mouths to feed (see Piot 1988)—and thus did not lead to the production of inequalities among different households or producers.

10. See especially *African Political Systems* (Fortes and Evans-Pritchard 1940), for the acephalous/centralized opposition that was to frame the research of a generation of Africanist anthropologists.

11. See Middleton (1960, 1963, 1965), a structural functionalist, for a much earlier and virtually identical argument. And notice in the following quotes the affinities between the logic of Donham's argument and that of Middleton. First, Middleton (1965: 43): "The Lugbara traditionally lack any form of kingship or even chiefship. They also lack any clearly formulated law. There were, traditionally, neither courts nor machinery for enforcing legal decisions made in the light of codified jural offenses and punishments. . . . All legitimate authority is controlled by the ancestors, who originated orderly social life. They control relations within the local community, and use mainly religious sanctions to that end." Now, Donham (1990: 43): "It is not, as in capitalist society, that the power of the state is used to set right contracts not fulfilled. The state does not exist. Rather, every misfortune in the younger brother's life . . . will be interpreted by those around him as a consequence of his resisting proper control by his eldest brothers."

12. See Foucault (1980: 118–19) and Eagleton (1991: 10–14) for critiques of theories that explain social practice in terms of the notion of false consciousness; see Mitchell (1988: 18–19) for a critique of theories that rely on a distinction between the real and the symbolic (or ideological); and see Arens and Karp (1989: xi–xxv), Jackson and Karp (1990: 15–29), and Karp (1990) for an Africanist critique of theories that configure power strictly in terms of mastery over persons.

13. While I argue with Donham on the points raised here, I nevertheless also find much of genuine theoretical interest in his work. I have been enormously stimulated by the way he has incorporated history and regional analysis into his work on Maale (Donham 1985, 1990), by his writing on the intersection between anthropology and Marxism (Donham 1990), and by his essays on the varieties of theory in economic anthropology (Donham 1981, 1985).

14. See also, of course, Giddens (1979, 1984), Ortner (1984, 1989), Rosaldo (1989), and Sahlins (1985), among others.

15. Needless to say, there are overlaps and affinities between this approach and that of the Marxists. Both see domination and social asymmetry as central to the societies they analyze; both also center the study of process and history (Ortner 1984, 1989). And Marxists like Donham have attempted to incorporate human agency and "practice" into their analyses (see Donham 1990: 139–189).

16. The problems in defining this term are reminiscent of those encountered by ("formalist") economic anthropologists in defining a concept like "maximization": how to define it without engaging in tautology (Cancian 1968; Donham 1981) and/or without invoking a definition that applies to any and all behavior, and thus explains very little?

17. There are, of course, other West Africanist theoretical positions—most notably in the savanna area, the French tradition centered around Griaule. While I would want to critique this tradition on other grounds—its tendency to exoticize and dehistoricize—I would not criticize it for having individualist assumptions (the main focus of the present critique). As mentioned above (note 8), there is also a significant phenomenological tradition in West Africanist anthropology (Riesman [1974] 1977, 1986; Jackson 1989, 1996, 1998; Stoller 1989, 1997) that, most notably in the work of Michael Jackson, has consistently argued for a relational conception of personhood.

18. I draw here on several collections of essays devoted to the study of personhood in African societies (Dieterlen 1973; Carrithers, Collins, and Lukes 1985; Jackson and Karp 1990) as well as on Riesman's (1986) review of the Africanist literature on notions of the person. See also Zahan 1960, [1970] 1979; Lienhardt 1961; Jackson 1982; Swanson 1985; and Berglund [1976] 1989.

19. See Fiske's (1991: 231–345) work on Voltaic Moose for a similar argument from a cognitivist ("relational models") perspective. Fiske marshals an impressive body of material to show that relational personhood (what he calls "communal sharing"), rather than self-interest, organizes social action in multiple Moose contexts.

20. One of the reasons many feminists and critical race theorists have embraced difference and resisted endorsing sameness is that any sameness standard is invariably defined by the group in power (men, Euroamericans).

21. See, for example, Harvey (1989: 216, 240–242) and Baudrillard (1989: 50–51, 66, 70).

22. Hannerz (1992a: 8–9, 228–231; 1992b: 42–43) invokes a similar set of binary contrasts.

Chapter Two

1. While the body itself is buried in the south, family members take hair and nail clippings from the cadaver back to the north, where they "rebury" the deceased.

2. An earlier anthropology, for instance, might have focused on the way three orders—cosmological, social, and environmental—are conflated in this Kabre world: thus, a violation of social and cosmological norms produces a nat-

ural calamity that can only be reversed by restoring cosmic/social order. For certain anthropologists, such exotic worldviews raised questions about the nature of rationality (and typically led to a defense of alternative ways of ordering reality). Others, of a more sociological bent, have been more interested in the social effects of such moral/religious systems—in the way they sanction and control the behavior of those who transgress social norms, and thus help to maintain social order. Marxist anthropologists, by contrast, have focused on the way elders deploy the sanctions of ceremonial/cosmological systems like this to reinforce and maintain their position of authority within a system of power relations.

3. Sikpetro was the head of the highest-ranking house in the highest-ranking Kabre community (Faren) in the northern massif.

4. For similar myths of origin from the larger Voltaic and savanna area, see Swanson (1985: 13) and Amselle (1990: 103).

5. Oral traditions in the southern massif also recount "landings," and footprints preserved in rock, and it is of some dispute in Togo today which massif can claim first occupation. Northern massif elders—those from Faren and Kuwdé—point out as proof of their claim to priority that when there is drought in the communities of the southern massif, ritual leaders from there go to Faren, while the reverse does not occur.

6. These are precisely the grounds on which he has discriminated against other Togolese groups. Thus, he has repeatedly prevented groups like Tyokossi, eighteenth-century immigrants from Côte d'Ivoire, and Fulani, herders from the north—Burkina Faso, Mali, Niger—who spend much of each year grazing cattle on unoccupied land in northern Togo, from receiving government aid.

7. The ambivalences that inform Frobenius's text throughout are transparent in such a passage. Here, an attempt to praise simultaneously reveals an underlying racism—the implication is that most "black people of Africa" lack what Kabre have achieved.

8. While recent development projects in the plain have had some success in transforming agricultural practices there, they have foundered in the mountains—where the rocky terrain, the narrow terraces, and the often steep slopes mitigate against most interventions.

9. Germany had annexed "Togoland"—a strip of land 150 km wide and 600 km long—in 1884, but not until almost fifteen years later did they penetrate and attempt to "pacify" the interior.

10. There is a puzzling aspect to this story. Many I spoke to claimed that the German killed was a child—*anasara pɛya*. My interpretation of this seemingly fantastic feature of the account is that as a story of Kabre resistance, and of their initial defeat of the Germans, it has become embellished in a way that enhances the Kabre sense of victory. To wit, killing an enemy's child is a greater form of conquest than killing the person himself, since a childless man is dead in perpetuity.

11. This instrumentalist reading of Frobenius's text finds support in his own statements regarding one of the central aims of his work. *Und Afrika Sprach,*

he says, was meant not only for "professors and ethnologists" but also for "district officers in the field, missionaries, traders, and armchair, stay-at-home legislators" (Frobenius 1913: 106). He hoped that it would have "unusual value to the colonial politician who would conduct the affairs of the countries through which we travelled" (1913: vi).

12. For instance, Kabre celebrate "kisimasʋ"—Christmas—not "Weihnacht" or "Noel"; they use "maŋcɛsʋ"—matches—to light their pipes and lamps, not "zundholzchen" or "alumettes"; they take a "lɔrʋ" (lorry) to the south, not a "roll wagen" or a "camion."

13. The French were content to allow Kabre living in this zone to produce on their own and market their surplus.

14. The coup was highlighted by an all-night siege at the president's (Sylvanus Olympio's) residence and a dawn chase which ended, it is told, with Eyadéma shooting and killing Olympio on the steps of the U.S. Embassy.

15. Olympio had a Portuguese name because he was descended from repatriated Brazilian slaves who, once returned to Africa (at the end of the nineteenth century), became wealthy middlemen in the trade with Europe. At independence, these "Brazilians"—who were not only wealthy but also highly educated—were well-positioned to take power (Cornevin 1962: 306; Toulabour 1986: 232–33). Thus, the fallout from the slave trade has continued to shape Togolese culture and politics into the postcolonial period and down to the present.

16. I also heard many stories in the north—he attended a mission school at the base of the mountain where I lived—about the special powers, both good and bad, Eyadéma possessed as a child. He is said, for example, to have bewitched members of his family (hence his name "the people are finished"), and for this reason was sent away to the mission school, where the French missionary's wife took a liking to, and "saved," him.

17. The association between those in power (chiefs, kings, presidents) and the supernatural (spirit possession, clairvoyance, witchcraft) is widespread throughout Africa (Ben-Amos 1976; Heusch 1982; Toulabour 1986; Gottlieb 1989; Stoller 1995; Geschiere 1997).

Chapter Three

1. The theoretical argument of this chapter is influenced not only by Mauss ([1925] 1967), Gregory (1982), and Strathern (1988), but also by Damon (1978, 1990), Munn (1986), Thomas (1991), and Miller (1995), as well as by the essays in Appadurai (1986), Parry and Bloch (1989), Humphrey and Hugh-Jones (1992), and Guyer (1995b).

2. People I knew were fond of telling me how puzzling they found the behavior of Europeans (*anasarana,* lit. "Nazarenes") in responding to gifts—how they accepted gifts when they should have politely refused them, how they reciprocated in ways that were odd, and so on.

3. I attempted at one point—indeed, early on it was one of my major re-

search aims—to see if there was a correlation between land holdings and wealth hierarchy in Kuwdé. My assumption was that those with more fields might be able to loan them out and receive labor and/or products in return (which they could then translate into wealth). However, that did not turn out to be the case. For one thing, the returns on field loans—a small pot of beer once a year—were negligible. For another, some of the wealthiest members in the community had very little land; conversely, some who were land-rich had little wealth. Nnamnawé is a perfect example. His relative landlessness has not prevented him from achieving status and wealth as a cultivator. During the mid-1990s, he was the most productive cultivator in the community and was able at harvest time not only to fill his granary with crops that fed his family throughout the year but also to sell surplus food in the markets.

4. *Sɔɣɔlɪm* has no easy translation into English. It means a mixture of need, choice, intention, will, desire, and pleasure, and is used in both exchange and nonexchange contexts. Needless to say, these are not the universal needs or "wants" of neoclassical theory but are forever culturally- and locally-specified.

5. While each of the exchange forms mentioned here has similar social consequences (i.e., they produce social relations), each nevertheless has distinct formal features. An outright gift (*haʊ,* to give), such as a gift of beer, in principle requires no return—though, in fact, such gifts usually produce return gifts, at some later point in time. Barter (*kʊlʊɣʊsʊɣʊ*) involves the direct and immediate exchange of one product for another. When borrowing (*sɪmɪlʊɣʊ,* to borrow) an animal or a field, the borrower keeps the item for a period of time (often several years) before returning it to its owner. In the case of animals, the offspring are then divided among the loaner and the borrower.

6. If the offense is not undone, it is said that the victim will contract leprosy—a disease associated with the operation of witches.

7. It is interesting that Karabu's, and others', narratives about the start of *ɪkpantʊrɛ* often include situations like these where gift-giving arises out of an initial state of hostility. Before too hastily endorsing the classical view here, however—which would use this as evidence of the solidarity-enhancing function of *ɪkpantʊrɛ*—I would suggest a couple of alternative interpretations. One is that, for Kabre, giving a gift to an enemy is less a way of making something solidary than of reversing an already existing hierarchical relationship. Each of the initial conditions—squirting someone with breast milk, insulting someone—is shameful and itself establishes a "respect," or hierarchical, relationship between the parties involved. By giving that person a gift, the shamed one reverses the hierarchy. Secondly, the frequency with which such stories are mentioned may have more to do with the special emotional charge that invests a relationship in which the heat of anger is turned to friendship, than with systemic needs like solidarity.

8. Though not directly germane to the present discussion, I should mention that this system of exchanges can also engender a good deal of conflict. Kabre men, for instance, are very much caught between the contradictory pulls of obligation to their (mostly male) *ɪkpantʊna* on the one hand, and to their wives

and families on the other. It is never easy to fulfill both at the same time, a fact that leads to a good deal of domestic conflict and, sometimes, divorce. (See Piot 1991 for a more complete description of this "contradiction.")

9. This system of exchange is in many ways similar to, though also in important ways different from, that of the Tiv of Nigeria, famously described in the writings of Paul Bohannan (1955, 1959). See Piot (1991) for a more complete analysis of the relationship between Tiv and Kabre "spheres of exchange," and for a more in-depth discussion of the Kabre three-sphere system.

10. The major difference between the *ikpantʊrɛ* of men and that of women is that, while the latter participate in the bottom two spheres of food and wealth exchanges, they do not (formally) participate in the top sphere of marriage exchange. Otherwise, women engage in *ikpantʊrɛ* as much as men do and in many of the same ways—though often exchanging female rather than male objects.

11. According to those I asked in Kuwdé, the similarities and differences between and among these pairs of animals derive from their habits. Chickens and goats stay close to the homesteads and are easy to tend, while guinea hens and sheep are hardheaded and flee. Mice and cows, unlike other animals, live in homestead and bush alike.

12. See Piot (1996) for a more detailed discussion of how Kabre assign value to things.

13. Foster (1990a, 1990b, 1995) and Strathern (1984, 1987a, 1987b) have described a similar set of themes in Melanesian exchange practices. They show, for instance, how in creating a distinction between giver and receiver, exchange is an act of separation and differentiation. This insight, of course, flies in the face of much exchange theory, which has assumed the opposite—namely, that people exchange to overcome difference.

14. By "commodity," I mean that which is alienable and whose exchange is governed by quantitative rather than qualitative criteria—by "exchange-value."

15. A discourse of "needs/desires" dominates Kabre discussions about why they go to market (just as it does for why they barter). Thus, if someone needs a hoe blade, or some palm oil, or some sorghum, he/she may go to market to find it. This is not just true of buyers, however. Sellers sell, they say, only because they have a need to buy. A woman sells palm oil, for instance, so that she can buy sorghum; a man sells a chicken because he needs to buy a hoe blade; and so on. From the Kabre perspective, then, people are never exchanging a product for money but rather one product for another—when selling the one, they always have in mind the purchase of that other. (The money is only a short-term facilitator of the exchange.) This, of course, converts what looks like a commodity exchange (of money-for-product) into something much more like barter (*kʊlʊɣʊsʊɣʊ*) in the community (and accounts for the fact that Kabre women have no problem going to the Sunday market in Asiri where barter is practiced). However, unlike barter exchange in the community, market exchange brings together two people who *both* have needs—both buyers and sellers (for the seller is selling in order to buy). Thus, in the market, Kabre say,

transactions are always of things of equal value (because both sides in each exchange are fulfilling needs by engaging in it), and therefore market exchanges never lead to indebtedness or hierarchy between individuals.

16. In a stimulating article, Geschiere (1992) describes similar processes of the penetration of the market, and market metaphors, into the domestic domain in various Cameroonian societies. Needless to say, this association of the market and commoditization with the domestic marks an important distinction between these African societies and certain Euroamerican categories (where the domestic-private and the market are kept separate).

17. For example, the Kula Ring is today many times larger, and has a greater volume of gift exchange, than when Malinowski studied it in the 1910s (Leach and Leach 1983). See also Gregory (1982: 112–209, 1987) for other Melanesian instances of the same phenomenon, and Monaghan (1996) for a recent example from Mexico.

18. I am indebted here to Karin Barber's (1995) fascinating work on the meaning and symbolism of money among the Yoruba of Nigeria.

Chapter Four

1. The belief in childhood androgyny is found in societies throughout West Africa (Zahan 1960, [1970] 1979; Griaule 1965; Griaule and Dieterlen 1965).

2. The division of the animal also provides an embodied image of the self-as-relations and as product of its sources. As such, sacrifice, and the circulation of the body of the animal/initiate back to these sources, is an act of memory and acknowledgment.

3. Those familiar with the work of Marilyn Strathern (1988) will recognize here my debt to her language.

4. There is a wealth of richly detailed, theoretically challenging work on initiation ritual in Africa. Works from which I have drawn inspiration include Zahan 1960; Paulme 1971; Comaroff 1985: 84–120; La Fontaine 1985; Ottenberg 1989; Kratz 1994; and Beidelman 1997.

5. *Asɔkaa* also make appearances in the marketplaces, as do *sɪŋkarɪŋ* and *kɛŋnaa*. These market appearances, however, are not so much intended to identify initiates with these spaces (indeed, the market is a female domain) as to allow the initiates to present themselves in a public place so that all may see "that their time has arrived."

6. The word for "blood" and "semen" is the same, *calɪm*. When I asked people in what sense the two were alike, since one is red and the other white, they said that semen is lighter in color because it is blood that has been "filtered"—like the lighter-colored (more potent) variety of *sɪlɪm* (sorghum beer) that is produced by repeated filtering.

7. Indeed, *sɪŋkarɪŋ* are strongly associated with androgyny. Their dress combines male and female elements: "female" initiation beads and arm bracelets, a "male" flute and bow. Their behavior similarly flips between male and female:

they work the fields with men while also helping women with food preparation; when they do the latter, however—e.g., when they pound in a woman's mortar—they are mocked by onlookers, a response whose aim is clearly to further the process of separating them from femaleness.

8. I should note here—as it draws attention to the limits of the type of epistemology such an analysis relies on—that when they impersonate animals, Kabre are not merely engaging in a type of play (or a "playing at" being animals). Nor do they see themselves as merely creating tropes—employing animal signifiers to symbolize the transformations in a self that is centered in an ontological field (cf. Jackson 1989: 108; Werbner 1989: 66–74; Devisch 1993: 280–83). Rather, they are decentering the self and erasing the boundary between it and that which is outside. Kabre say that when they put on the horns of the antelope, initiates *become* these wild animals and, in so doing, appropriate their physical and mystical powers—through the head. It is for this reason that bystanders at the ceremonies are overcome with tremendous fear when they see initiates with their horns on.

9. Through their role in the *haɗaa,* and in other work groups, *asɔkaa* also "feed" others throughout the community. That is, it is they who put more labor into the community-wide work groups than any other age group. As well, *asɔkaa* and *keŋnaa* play an instrumental role in feeding the nation as a whole, for it is they who migrate south to labor in the yam and corn fields of southern farmers that supply much of the food to those who live in the cities. It should not be surprising, then, that when I witnessed the ceremonies during the 1980s, they played to the themes of male solidarity, strength, and cultivating ability.

10. There are certain affinities between this material and Chodorow's (1974, 1978) psycho-social model of gender differentiation (see also Benjamin 1988). While it would be interesting to explore the way in which the Kabre ceremonial complex maps the psychological onto the cultural, and vice versa, I would nevertheless resist efforts to reduce one to the other. Such attempts typically fail to come to terms with the complexity of either the cultural or the psychological processes at work.

11. Moreover, the political events of the early 1990s, and the ensuing return of many southerners to the north, gave rise in 1995 to a resurgence of some of the warrior themes of the slaving era. I was told that bows and arrows that had not been seen for years reemerged at the time of *waaɣa* and that the races and dances assumed a more aggressive, warlike tone.

12. Certain individual ceremonies have also been compressed. Thus, the confinement of both *afalaa* and *akpema* (female initiates) in their mothers' huts at the beginning of their initiations used to last an entire week, but today lasts only a single day. This, I was told, is both because initiates who are in school are unable to spend a full week in confinement and because southerners who return to the north for these ceremonies often cannot stay for more than a few days. Nor, however, do their hosts in the north necessarily want them to, for they have a difficult time coming up with the food to feed them for an ex-

tended period: "When they stayed for weeks at a time, it brought famine to the house!" I heard again and again as an additional reason for limiting the length of the ceremony.

13. While the ceremonies of *afalaa* in the two massifs are otherwise similar, only those *afalaa* in the southern massif wrestle.

14. This method of selection of course creates personal ties between Eyadéma and his soldiers that help explain the tremendous loyalty that is a trademark of the Togolese army.

15. Kabre men who live in the south and marry southern women follow the same brideservice and harvest gift system. However, many southern men marry women who grow up in the north and are therefore unable to work in the fields of their fathers-in-law. In this case, they make a single lump-sum payment of ten to fifteen thousand CFA and a large sack of grain—which, again, is said to "feed" the man's future wife.

16. The Kabre word for a female initiate, *akpeŋ,* seems to register the ambivalence about which I am speaking and to mark the fact that her alienation from her natal family is always only partial. *Akpeŋ* is a nominal whose root derives from the verb *kpem,* "to go home," a derivation whose meaning was explained to me as follows: even though a girl leaves her parents' homestead at initiation/marriage, she is never permanently separated from it; she is only "borrowed" by her husband's family for a period of time, to bear children and work for them. At death, she is returned to be buried in her natal family's tomb. Nor are her children fully lost to her family, for, despite the fact that they will grow up, work, and inherit in their father's homestead, they are still said to be "owned" by their mother's brother (*ekpele,* a term also derived from the verb "to go home").

17. He wins them over in other ways as well. On another ritual occasion, for example, male initiates meet their parents-in-law in one of the sacred forests where the latter tell mildly insulting jokes about the former. The initiates attempt to respond in clever and funny ways. If they succeed, they are admired by their parents-in-law, thus furthering the process of winning them over.

18. Elsewhere (Piot 1993) I have written at greater length about the way Kabre are preoccupied with processes of concealment and revelation. Thus, while a person's money remains hidden during life, it is brought out into the open the day after death for all to see and judge whether the deceased saved or spent foolishly; similarly, a central aim of divination is to bring that which is concealed (the activities of spirits and ancestors in the unseen world) into the open; and so on. Initiation, I am suggesting, is a similar process of making visible—making known—that which was previously unknown.

19. Indeed, for Kabre, *creating* distinctions, rather than overcoming them, is the task that initiation has set for itself.

20. This argument has many permutations. Thus, one might suggest that through these ceremonies (and through their continuation into adulthood, for it is men who perform all ceremonies to the spirits in the sacred forests), men

have co-opted the public domain of ritual and consigned women to the private, less prestigious, domestic domain (Rosaldo 1974; Ortner and Whitehead 1981; Llewelyn-Davies 1981). Or, again, one might wonder whether, since women have more powerful access to "nature" (they menstruate, give birth, nurse), and therefore have—or could claim—a certain superiority, men have had to compensate by creating a cultural apparatus that allocates power to them too (Read 1952, 1982; Herdt 1981; Bloch 1987). And so on.

However, each of these theories—which have wide currency in the anthropological literature on initiation—contains assumptions that lie at some distance from the Kabre materials. Thus, there is no neat correlation between gender differences and public/private domains. Men as well as women are associated with the domestic, and women, like men, are associated with the public. As to the culture/nature binary, Kabre do not have a category of that which is "natural." Indeed, the most apparently natural of processes—the fertility of humans and crops—are thought to be dependent on the operations of spirits and on processes that are cultural and social through and through. As the account with which I opened chapter 2 indicates, for example, even the rain's coming is seen as dependent on human agency. It is difficult in the Kabre case, then, to sustain the distinctions on which such interpretations rely.

Chapter Five

1. My use of the term "house" (ɖɛɣa) follows closely that of Kabre themselves. Thus, in referring to the ɖɛɣa, Kabre mean either the physical collection of huts—what I also call the homestead—or the social group (the family or household) domiciled there (cf. Fortes 1949; Goody [1956] 1967, 1958; Schloss 1988; Gottlieb 1992). The latter typically consists of a man, his wife or wives, and their unmarried children. While several households may be found in a single Kabre homestead, such is normally not the case. For example, in Kuwdé, in 1983, 31 out of 43 homesteads were occupied by a single household; the remaining 12 were occupied by two households each (Piot 1988). The term ɖɛɣa is also extended to larger groups of dispersed families that share a common ancestor, as well as to the two moieties—into which all the houses in the community are divided—that perform rituals for the community as a whole. The houses within these latter, however, do not claim descent from a common ancestor.

2. The government no longer taxes those who farm ("paysans")—though it does tax civil servants. However, it does conduct a national census every ten years, and, at least among northern Kabre, still uses the system of numeration established during the colonial period.

3. RPT is the acronym for Eyadéma's ruling party, Rassemblement du Peuple Togolais.

4. See Piot (1988) for a more detailed description of the productive and developmental cycle of the domestic group.

5. Moreover, those with whom I spoke pointed out to me that food is behind wombs and blood as well, for both are the products of food (and of the specific feeding relationships spouses have with one another).

6. The practice of fostering children is extremely common in Kabre communities and, since parent-child relationships are primarily defined in terms of the feeding relationship, fostered children take their place alongside the other children of the homestead as full members of the family—with access to property, to ritual privilege, and so on. Indeed, I saw no evidence that fostered children were treated any differently from others.

7. The importance of food as a metaphor for relationship extends beyond the house as well, for virtually all relationships are mediated through food gifts and at almost every occasion on which people gather in groups—whether for work or for sacrifice to the spirits and ancestors—food (beer, meat, porridge) is shared with those who attend.

8. There was another problem as well that prevented me from obtaining fully accurate genealogies: some of those I interviewed were hesitant to speak the names of dead ancestors, for fear that the latter would be upset that they were being spoken about indiscriminately. Such silences, of course, left significant gaps in some of my genealogies.

9. The body of a woman should be placed in fetal position on its right side facing west; men, by contrast, are placed in fetal position on their left sides facing east. After the interrer has positioned the body in the tomb, house elders are summoned to examine it before the tomb is sealed tight with a flat rock.

10. There are others as well. Men are associated with the east and women with the west, because, as Kabre put it, when the sun comes up in the east, men leave for the fields, and when it sets in the west, women begin cooking the evening meal. The right hand is female, because women cook with the right hand, while the left hand is male, because men pull weeds with their left hands while working in the fields.

11. One additional example of the value Kabre attach to the notion of difference: When I asked why a brother marrying a sister within the same house—incest/endogamy—was taboo, people responded by saying: "If you married your sister, your father and your father-in-law would be the same person—that's not good"; or: "If your children married one another, you would be both their father and their mother's brother at the same time. Who, then, would help out with a funeral in the family?" The problem with—the scandal of—incest, then, is not that it is biologically problematic, but rather that it collapses social differences, differences that are seen as essential to the very constitution of the family.

12. The linguistic classification of Dogon has long been disputed. While linguists early on classified Dogon as Mande-speakers (Delafosse 1904), they have more recently classified them as Gur/Voltaic (Westermann and Bryan 1952; Greenberg 1963; Bendor-Samuel 1971). Lending support to the latter identification, Voltaic Moose claim that Dogon are descended from indigenous inhabitants of Mooseland (Fiske 1991: 346–47). Moreover, the Dogon bear

such clear similarities, both cultural and historical, to the broad band of acephalous societies that anthropologists have studied throughout this large savanna region (Tallensi, LoDagaa, Konkomba, Batammaliba) that I find it useful to think about them in relation to these other Voltaic groups. When I read Griaule and Dieterlen on the Dogon, for instance, I feel that I am in many ways reading about Batammaliba (Blier 1987) or Kabre.

13. Note too that this model of connection through difference is altogether different from much Euroamerican differences discourse. For many Euroamericans, difference often poses irresolvable problems for the social body. Take ethnicity as an example. Either ethnic difference is affirmed (the nationalist option) and connection is problematic (and/or impossible), or difference is rejected (the assimilationist, "melting pot" option) and connection then becomes possible. Kabre (and other Voltaic and closely-related peoples) have chosen a third option: affirm difference and engage others through those differences. Indeed, in the domains I have been analyzing, such engagement is impossible without difference. See Gottlieb (1992) for a related, though not identical, enunciation of the significance of the principle of difference among the Beng of Côte d'Ivoire.

14. Euroamerican gender oppositions are typically rooted in a belief in various (natural, biological) essences. As a result, the terms of the opposition (male/female) are thought to be unchangeable and mutually exclusive. Because such oppositions legitimize various hierarchies in Euroamerican culture, feminists in particular have wanted to make apparent the constructed, contingent, ideological nature of such oppositions (and to show the ways in which individuals contest, subvert, and escape them). In an even more radical critique, certain postmodern feminist scholars (Butler 1990; Fuss 1989) have suggested that the very terms of the opposition male/female cannot be coherently separated (that which is taken as an attribute of "male" could just as easily be shown to be "female" and vice versa). Thus, they suggest, the whole binary system is as much the product of analytical/scholarly constructs as of existing cultural models. Such constructs are also complicit with power, they suggest, for power gets deployed through the binaries. The Kabre material, I want to suggest, offers an example of an alternative—nonessential, more fluid, less hierarchical—system of gendered binaries.

15. The bleeding appears deliberate: not only does it symbolically replicate the experience of birth—of a baby's bloody emergence from the birth canal—but also it counters the dryness of a cadaver, and so (along with the interrer's bending of the limbs before the body is inserted into the tomb) serves to prepare the body for birth. Babies, I was told, should be "wet" and limber, by contrast with old people (and cadavers), who are "dry" and stiff.

16. A metaphorical connection between birth and death is also established through the plant (*ası-welaɣa*) that is dropped into the tomb to purify it before it is sealed. The only other time this plant is used is after a birth, when it is rubbed over the mother and baby to purify them.

17. Kabre have an "Omaha"-style kinship terminology. Consistent with such

terminologies generally, the Kabre term *ekpele* refers not only to mother's brother but also to mother's brother's son and daughter, and mother's brother's son's son. While the "real" *ekpele* (the mother's brother) is usually dead by the time his sister's child dies, another member of the house—another *ekpele*—will stand in for him at the opening of the money box.

18. See Piot (1996) for an analysis of this particular historical practice. The mother's brother has other prerogatives as well. The first of his sister's children to die is buried at his house rather than at the child's father's. As well, the mother's brother can ask that one of his sister's sons (usually the oldest) come to live with, and work for, him. Further, if there is no one to take over his house at his death, he will request that a nephew move in and take his place.

19. As well, until the colonial period, a sister's son used to inherit a mother's brother's "movables"—grain, animals, and money—upon the latter's death.

20. See Piot (1988) for a more detailed description of the relationship, and conflicts, between Kabre fathers and sons.

21. Before birth, he "feeds" his future wife with harvest gifts (thus making her womb), and, later, when she becomes pregnant, he feeds the fetus with his semen during intercourse.

22. Girls—sisters' daughters—do not go through a similar ceremony because it is through the marriages of sisters' daughters that a house develops a connection (*liḍi,* lit. "the roots of a tree") to—and has a claim on the offspring of—the houses into which they marry. Houses thus need to maintain, rather than terminate, their ties with sisters' daughters (cf. Sacks 1982).

23. Women, of course, also establish relations with a third house—the house into which they marry—though, unlike their mother's and father's natal houses, this third house never has a claim of "ownership" over them.

24. Many of these histories are inscribed onto the physical "body" of the homestead itself. Changes in household composition, cash-cropping successes in the south, success on the hunt and with the harvest, a house's relationship with the spirits and ancestors, the death of a family member—all these are recorded, made visible, through changes in the physical structure and appearance of the homestead exterior itself. Thus, homesteads expand and contract, add shiny tin roofs, mark a death in the family by turning granary roofs upside down, record the successes of their members on the hunt through the display of feathers and animal skulls on the walls of the entrance, erect new shrines and take down old ones, and so on. As with persons, houses make their identities, their histories, "visible"—so that others may see.

Chapter Six

1. See Froelich (1963: 93), Sauvaget (1981: 22), and Verdier (1982: 113–14).

2. I should note that spirits also appear to be central to the identity of Tallensi and Lowiili communities. For example, Goody ([1956] 1967: 91) suggests that Lowiili settlements are best understood as "parishes" (ritual areas associ-

ated with spirit shrines). Fortes also clearly recognized the importance of community-wide rituals to major spirits—what he referred to as the "Great Festivals." Thus, he states that "Tallensi are well-known to their neighbors for the ritual festivals which they celebrate" (1936: 593); and "Weeks in advance, the approaching festivals are the dominant theme of conversation for man, woman and child" (1936: 598); and again: "Among the most striking mechanisms of this equilibrium [between Tallensi clans] are the ritual festivals. The various settlements are always classified in terms of them, and the natives never tire of dilating enthusiastically upon them" (1936: 598).

3. The mediating role Cacarɛya taa plays follows from its identity: it is androgynous (its members participate in certain ceremonies with Tɔutɛɛ [the male clan] and in others with Komatɛ [the female clan]), childlike (like children, it is recalcitrant and possesses mystical powers, especially clairvoyance [kɪnaʊ], that it sometimes misuses), and a "stranger" (it came from Faren and retains ties with that community—performing ceremonies there at the initiation and death of its members).

4. Kabre dualisms are constantly flirting with a third term (Lévi-Strauss [1963] 1967). Indeed, it would appear that without the third term, the pair is unstable and will dissolve. To give just one additional example of this principle: the relationship between husband and wife in the house will end in divorce if no children are born. Moreover, note that children are said to possess the same characteristics as Cacarɛya taa, the mediator house—they are "strangers," and are also androgynous.

5. It is said that women used to dance but that their mystical power was such that they committed atrocities with it and were subsequently banned from dancing. One woman, for example, is said to have given birth on the dance ground and then to have eaten her baby; another gave birth to guinea hens. These narratives (which invert normal female/motherly behavior) clearly serve to articulate and reinforce the separation effected by ɖɔyɔntʊ between men/ death and the fertility of women.

6. The sorghum grains should begin to dry on their stalks—with the help of the wind—before they are harvested in November and stored in house granaries. Similarly, the wind is needed for dry season hut-building—to dry the thick mud walls of huts quickly and thus avoid lengthy delays.

7. Cɪmʊɣʊ is also associated with two other important activities. It is the first day when men enter their granaries, and thus the day families begin to eat the best grain from the new harvest. It is also a time when women receive gifts of salt from various male relatives and friends around the community. Both activities—the opening up of granaries and the gift of salt—are symbolically consistent with other activities of the rainy season, and indeed serve to mark the entry into that season: the rainy season is a time of decontainment (of rain, wind, and wombs) and is associated with the female color white, and salt, as opposed to the dry season, which is associated with acts of containment (of death, the wind, and wombs), the male color red, and the consumption of red palm oil. When I asked people about what seemed to me to be the obvious sex-

ual symbolism of the *cɪmʊɣʊ* activities of men entering womblike granary holes and giving white salt to women, they laughed and acknowledged that such was probably also the case. They also added that at the ceremonies at the ancient homesteads on this day, the elders put (male) arrows into a hole in the top of a round (female) gourd (*tokuu*) at each house. All of these activities are, of course, consistent with the idea that the wet season is symbolically a time of fertility and life.

8. The transformations that occur as *cotu* (locust bean paste) is being made are seen as analogous to those undergone by pregnant women: like the process undergone by a baby in the womb, the mashed locust beans are wrapped tightly in leaves and placed in a basket (a womblike container) where they generate heat as they ferment. Because of these similarities, menstruating women are tabooed from making, or coming into contact with others who are making, *cotu*.

9. The symbolism of flute-playing here seems quite obviously phallic: flutes are wooden, phallic-shaped objects played only by men—on this occasion, to make the sorghum grow tall and erect.

10. Thus, the final two ceremonies of the year—*kamʊɣʊ* and *sɪŋkarɪŋ*—are performed on the same day in all northern massif communities.

11. Yams are planted in tall mounds of earth. The tuber itself grows under the soil, while the leaves—which are cut from the tuber at harvest—bush out on top of the mound. Since throwing the stems away, rather than reinserting them in the hole, is said to bring the wind out, it is prohibited prior to this time.

12. Of all crops, yams are the most explicitly personified—there are two varieties, one "male," the other "female"—and yam mounds are strikingly similar to the tombs where humans are buried.

13. Note that the process by which the spirits are captured is similar to the way persons enmesh and appropriate one another through gifts. A spirit is brought into relationship with humans, and the spirit's powers appropriated, through a gift of food (the animal sacrificed) that will bring a return (aid/protection). Moreover, the reciprocal hierarchies that define person-to-person exchange also operate in human-spirit exchanges: when the spirit gives rain, humans are in debt to that spirit until the time when humans sacrifice—when the debt is reversed.

14. To wit, this is the time when the order in which the different communities perform the ceremonies, which corresponds to the hierarchy of communities, is first abolished (*kamʊɣʊ* and *sɪŋkarɪŋ* are performed on the same day in all communities) and then recreated (from *ɗɔɣɔntʊ* until *kamʊɣʊ*, the ceremonies are performed in each community on consecutive weeks, following the rank order of communities).

15. The principle of separation operates within each season as well: those objects, symbols, crops, and activities associated with a particular ceremony should not reappear at the time of any other ceremony. Thus, it is taboo to eat locust beans before *kucontuɣu*, or red oil before *kamʊɣʊ*, or the new sorghum before *sɪŋkarɪŋ*, or to go into male granaries before *cɪmʊɣʊ*, and so on.

16. As already suggested, revision of the ceremonies and their meanings

also takes place as they engage various historical contexts—Samasi raiding, the arrival of the Germans, the political events of the 1990s.

17. At the end of the colonial era, when their compensation dried up, chiefs began charging litigants to hear disputes. Thus, in Kuwdé and Boua today each party to a dispute pays five hundred CFA to the chief.

18. Fortes, recall, argued that Tallensi communities were organized around a set of genealogically based lineages and clans, held together through a "segmentary" logic—Durkheim's "mechanical solidarity."

19. I retain the Kabre term "house" rather than using Fortes's terms, "lineage" and "clan." While resembling Tallensi clans in some ways (they are named, totemic, and convene for rituals), Kabre houses differ significantly in other ways (they are not exogamous and many of the smaller units—"segments"—within each do not share a common genealogy).

20. In the male moieties of Kuwdé and Faren (I do not know about those in other communities), two houses alternate at the top. Typically, upon the death of the head of the house in charge, the other house takes over (for the ensuing generation). Such paired, alternating relationships are of course consistent with the dyadic nature of Kabre social life in other domains as well—of exchange between *ıkpantʋna,* of FZD marriage, and even of work groups. This latter example is telling: while work groups consist of anywhere from five to thirty men (depending on the type of group) who rotate around one another's fields, each person will only work the fields of those individuals who showed up to work his own field. As one man put it to me, "When deciding whether to work someone else's field, I don't think about the group. I think about whether that person worked me." Thus, the group is no more than the sum of a series of dyadic relationships.

21. A similar "organic" division of social labor organizes the community health system. Thus, each house "owns" (possesses the special knowledge it takes to find and make) a different medicine for the treatment of a specific disease, and provides that medicine to others.

22. Indeed, in spite of his somewhat naturalizing view of Tallensi social relations—as rooted in genealogically based lineages—Fortes nevertheless also held what might be described as a Saussurean, antifoundationalist position. Thus, he conceived of Tallensi social structure as relational through and through: as consisting of lineage segments that had identity only through opposition to other segments.

23. It is interesting that Fortes claims that Tallensi clans have a depth of 8–12 generations, since such genealogical depth is reported from no other acephalous Voltaic society I know of—where 2–4 generations is the norm. Thus, the Tallensi lineage system—often taken as typical of African systems generally—would appear to be an anomaly even in its own local environment. Even more ironic—since Fortes's depiction of Tallensi is frequently taken as representative of some pure, timeless African kinship system—is the fact that the system he observed had been deeply affected by, and was very much a product of, colonial rule. To wit, in 1911 the British had dynamited the spirit

shrines of those Tallensi living in the hills (because of their resistance to colonial rule), and relocated them to the plains area where Fortes worked in the 1930s (Hart 1978). With time, such relocation exacerbated an already extreme state of pressure on the land and magnified the importance of land claims. Such claims, of course, could be established through genealogies, thus likely accounting for the unusual length of, and uncharacteristic importance placed upon, the genealogies Fortes was collecting.

24. Of course, I am aware of the risks involved in comparing Tallensi in the 1930s and 1940s with Kabre in the 1980s and 1990s. While I would not underestimate the transformations that fifty years of colonialism and postcolonialism have wrought on Kabre social structure, nor the effect of the differing locations of Kabre and Tallensi within the political economies of British and French West African colonialism, nevertheless Kuwdé elders I spoke to insisted that the organic nature of the relationship between houses has changed little since their childhood.

25. Unlike in other places in Africa, colonial governments in this coastal hinterland were apparently little concerned with fixing and controlling territorial boundaries. According to Kabre elders, for instance, the Germans were more preoccupied with names and naming than with fixing territorial boundaries— "they were always asking us the names of people and places"—and when they found no names, they made them up. Indeed, the name "Kabre" was created by the Germans at the moment of first contact. Of course, naming is also a form of classification. But while names map and fix peoples and localities in their own right, they do not preclude the movement of people into and out of places, nor do they necessarily lead to rigid boundary maintenance. However, an unintended effect of the colonial presence on Kabre was to remake some of the internal divisions within communities. Thus, Kuwdé and Boua elders told me that prior to the colonial period Boua had two *haḍaa* (community-wide work groups), and Kuwdé one, but that after the colonial census the residents of both communities reorganized the *haḍaa* and doubled their number so that they matched the census divisions. It was apparently easier to raise tax money within rather than between these work collectives. Here, then, is an example of the way an instrument of colonial power led to a locally initiated redrawing of group boundaries, which in turn became the basis of a new form of work and sociality.

Chapter Seven

1. Witches, it is rumored, roam the national roadways and cause many of the deadly accidents that all too frequently strike taxis as well as trucks.

2. Recall here that the animal may *not* be purchased in the market. The prescription ensures that mountain and bush communities engage in exchange, and thus maintain a relationship with one another.

3. Another set of differences among communities exists at the level of female productive activities. Thus, the women of each community produce products that are different from, and thus come to be exchanged for, female prod-

ucts from other communities. For instance, women from Kuwdé produce baobab nuts, which they sell in the markets in order to buy red palm oil from the women of Kawa, locust bean paste from the women of Tchi-Kawa, cooking pots from the women of Wazilao, and so on. In principle, each evening meal contains each of these products, and thus represents a microcosm of the regional system as a whole and of the differences that define it. See Piot (1992) for a fuller description of this regional system of production and exchange.

4. This resituating of markets into the plain also opened them to long-distance traders, especially those who worked the Hausa-Ashanti route that passed through Djougou and Kétao.

5. "Comaroffian" in the sense that they emphasize—more than other theorists (Gramsci 1971; Williams 1977; Eagleton 1991; Laclau and Mouffe 1985; Guha 1997)—the formal, non-agentive, unconscious aspects of hegemony (as opposed to the substantive and more agentive workings of ideology). Thus, when European missionaries began to challenge and debate Tshidi Tswana about their views as to the source of the rain (Tswana rainmakers and deities), Tswana were being subtly colonized by European forms of debate about matters usually beyond debate—and this despite the fact that they overtly and consciously (ideologically) rejected the missionaries' specific arguments (Comaroff and Comaroff 1991: 206–13). So, too, for Kabre: while Kabre consciously deny that wealth trumps ritual/spirits, the former nevertheless exerts a subtle, colonizing influence over Kabre everyday forms and values.

6. Note, however, that the tension between ritual and wealth, and the mountain's anxiety about the wealth of the bush, has little to do with the inherent value of money or wealth. Rather, it is rooted in the limited access those from the mountain have to such wealth, and, what is most irksome to many, the fact that it is their "children" rather than they who are privileged by this system.

7. I use the terms "mimesis" and "discourse" in theorizing Kabre diasporic identity in order to displace some of the more classic Africanist approaches to the question of identity. Namely, I am suggesting that the mimetic and the discursive organize a sense of Kabre-ness as much as, for example, common kinship or coercive ritual mechanisms.

8. Indeed, as described in chapter 5, it is in the north that gender norms are being challenged—in response to global forces, especially structural adjustment.

9. However, as mentioned above, in the southernmost communities of the diaspora, those between Atakpamé and Kpalimé, Kabre live and farm on land that is owned by Ewe. And there it is Ewe who organize the rituals that bring the rain and fertilize the land, and to Ewe that Kabre defer ritual authority.

10. A series of incidents over the years—disputes with elders over his support for various northern projects—had contributed to his estrangement from those in Kuwdé.

11. Tin roofs, of course, have multiple significations (cf. Gottlieb 1992: 135–36). As the above-mentioned dispute between Halitoké and his brother makes clear, they are not only symbols of southern deference; they also enable southerners to maintain rights in their northern homesteads.

Chapter Eight

1. Criticizing conventional understandings of resistance has become something of an academic cottage industry of late. Some of the more compelling critiques include Arens and Karp (1989), Abu-Lughod (1990), Mitchell (1990), Mbembe (1992), Bhabha (1994), Comaroff and Comaroff (1997), and Gupta and Ferguson (1997a).

2. Scholars of the African diaspora (Gilroy 1987, 1993a, 1993b; Gates 1988; Mercer 1988; Hall 1990) have made similar observations about the way members of the diaspora have subverted the colonization process. The following passage from Mercer (1988: 57) is typical:

> Across a whole range of cultural forms there is a "synchretic" dynamic which critically appropriates elements from the master-codes of the dominant culture and "creolises" them, disarticulating given signs and re-articulating their symbolic meaning. The subversive force of this hybridizing tendency is most apparent at the level of language itself where creoles, patois and black English decenter, destabilize and carnivalize the linguistic domination of "English"—the nation-language of master-discourse—through strategic inflections, re-accentuations and other performative moves in semantic, syntactic and lexical codes.

3. In any case, identifying foreign goods as having a unitary identity—as either "Western" or "African"—is increasingly difficult in today's transnationalized, post-Fordist world. What, for instance, is the identity of a piece of cloth that is manufactured in Holland, but designed by African women (the "Nanas Benz," who run the cloth market in Lomé, and whose name derives from the cars they purchase with money made in the lucrative cloth trade, travel to Holland each year to select the patterns), and universally thought of as "African"?

4. Such an appropriative dynamic is manifest in colonial and postcolonial cultural productions across the continent. See, for example, Comaroff (1985) on Southern African Independent (Zionist) churches, Stoller (1995) on Songhai spirit possession, Waterman (1990) on Nigerian juju music, Kraemer ([1987] 1993) and Steiner (1994) on colonial and postcolonial art, and Comaroff and Comaroff (1997) on Tswana clothing styles. As well, Barber's (1997) edited volume on African popular culture is filled with examples of cultural appropriation and mixing.

5. Note here that taking seriously Kabre cultural concerns with potency and fertility enables one to move beyond the empty formalism of those classical theories I detailed above—theories that would reduce the cultural to the mechanical: "cohesion," "power," "interest." Such theories fail to do justice to the spirit, and to those spirits, that animate Kabre and give meaning to their world (cf. Chakrabarty 1997).

6. To wit, Kabre labor power was, and continues to be, brutally exploited.

References

Abu-Lughod, Lila. 1990. "The Romance of Resistance: Tracing Transformations of Power through Bedouin Women." *American Ethnologist* 17 (1): 41–55.

———. 1997. "The Interpretation of Culture(s) After Television." *Representations* 59: 109–34.

Amselle, Jean-Loup. 1990. *Logiques Métisses: Anthropologie de l'Identité en Afrique et Ailleurs.* Paris: Payot.

Appadurai, Arjun, ed. 1986. *The Social Life of Things: Commodities in Cultural Perspective.* Cambridge: Cambridge University Press.

———. 1990. "Disjuncture and Difference in the Global Cultural Economy." *Public Culture* 2 (2): 1–24.

———. 1991. "Global Ethnoscapes: Notes and Queries for a Transnational Anthropology." In *Recapturing Anthropology: Working in the Present,* ed. R. Fox. Santa Fe, N.M.: School of American Research Press.

———. 1997. *Modernity at Large: Cultural Dimensions of Globalization.* Minneapolis: University of Minnesota Press.

Appiah, Anthony. 1992. *In My Father's House: Africa in the Philosophy of Culture.* New York: Oxford University Press.

Appiah, Anthony, and Henry Louis Gates, eds. 1995. *Identities.* Chicago: University of Chicago Press.

Apter, Andrew. 1992. *Black Critics and Kings: The Hermeneutics of Power in Yoruba Society.* Chicago: University of Chicago Press.

———. 1993. "Atinga Revisited: Yoruba Witchcraft and the Cocoa Economy, 1950–1951." In *Modernity and Its Malcontents: Ritual and Power in Postcolonial Africa,* ed. J. Comaroff and J. Comaroff. Chicago: University of Chicago Press.

Arens, W., and Ivan Karp. 1989. "Introduction." In *Creativity of Power: Cosmology and Action in African Societies,* ed. W. Arens and I. Karp. Washington, D.C.: Smithsonian Institution Press.

Asad, Talal, ed. 1973. *Anthropology and the Colonial Encounter.* Atlantic Highlands, N.J.: Humanities Press.

———. 1991. "Afterword: From the History of Colonial Anthropology to the Anthropology of Western Hegemony." In *Colonial Situations: Essays on the Contextualization of Ethnographic Knowledge,* ed. G. Stocking. Madison: University of Wisconsin Press.

Auslander, Mark. 1993. "'Open the Wombs!': The Symbolic Politics of Modern Ngoni Witchfinding." In *Modernity and Its Malcontents: Ritual and Power in*

Postcolonial Africa, ed. J. Comaroff and J. Comaroff. Chicago: University of Chicago Press.

Barber, Karin. 1995. "Money, Self-Realization, and the Person in Yoruba Texts." In *Money Matters: Instability, Values and Social Payments in the Modern History of West African Communities,* ed. J. Guyer. Portsmouth, N.H.: Heinemann.

———, ed. 1997. *Readings in African Popular Culture.* Bloomington: Indiana University Press.

Bastien, Misty. 1993. "'Bloodhounds Who Have No Friends': Witchcraft and Locality in the Nigerian Popular Press." In *Modernity and Its Malcontents: Ritual and Power in Postcolonial Africa,* ed. J. Comaroff and J. Comaroff. Chicago: University of Chicago Press.

Battaglia, Debbora. 1990. *On the Bones of the Serpent: Person, Memory and Mortality in Sabarl Island Society.* Chicago: University of Chicago Press.

Baudrillard, Jean. 1989. *America.* New York: Verso.

Beattie, John. 1980. Review Article. "Representations of the Self in Traditional Africa: La Notion de Personne en Afrique Noire." *Africa* 50 (3): 313–20.

Beidelman, T. O. [1986] 1993. *Moral Imagination in Kaguru Modes of Thought.* Washington, D.C.: Smithsonian Institution Press.

———. 1997. *The Cool Knife: Imagery of Gender, Sexuality, and Moral Education in Kaguru Initiation Ritual.* Washington, D.C.: Smithsonian Institution Press.

Ben-Amos, Paula. 1976. *The Art of Benin.* London: Cambridge University Press.

Bendor-Samuel, John. 1971. "Niger-Congo, Gur." In *Current Trends in Linguistics,* vol. 7, ed. T. A. Sebeok. The Hague: Mouton.

Benjamin, Jessica. 1988. *The Bonds of Love: Psychoanalysis, Feminism, and the Problem of Domination.* New York: Pantheon Books.

Berglund, Axel-Ivar. [1976] 1989. *Zulu Thought: Patterns and Symbolism.* Bloomington: Indiana University Press.

Berman, Marshall. 1982. *All That Is Solid Melts Into Air: The Experience of Modernity.* New York: Simon and Schuster.

Bezon, A. 1955. "Sondage Démographique Comparatif en Pays Kabre (Togo)." *Medecine Tropicale* 15 (4): 437–55.

Bhabha, Homi. 1994. *The Location of Culture.* New York: Routledge.

Blier, Suzanne. 1987. *The Anatomy of Architecture: Ontology and Metaphor in Batammaliba Architectural Expression.* Cambridge: Cambridge University Press.

Bloch, Maurice. 1982. "Death, Women and Power." In *Death and the Regeneration of Life,* ed. M. Bloch and J. Parry. Cambridge: Cambridge University Press.

———. 1987. "Descent and Sources of Contradiction in Representations of Women and Kinship." In *Gender and Kinship: Essays Toward a Unified Analysis,* ed. J. Collier and S. Yanagisako. Stanford: Stanford University Press.

Bohannan, Paul. 1955. "Some Principles of Exchange and Investment among the Tiv." *American Anthropologist* 57: 60–70.

———. 1959. "The Impact of Money on an African Subsistence Economy." *Journal of Economic History* 19: 491–503.

Bohannan, Paul, and George Dalton, ed. 1962. *Markets in Africa.* Evanston, Ill.: Northwestern University Press.

Bourdieu, Pierre. 1977. *Outline of a Theory of Practice.* Cambridge: Cambridge University Press.

———. [1980] 1990. *The Logic of Practice.* Stanford: Stanford University Press.

Bourdieu, Pierre, and Loic Wacquant. 1992. *An Invitation to Reflexive Sociology.* Chicago: University of Chicago Press.

Butler, Judith. 1990. *Gender Trouble: Feminism and the Subversion of Identity.* New York: Routledge.

———. 1993. *Bodies that Matter: On the Discursive Limits of "Sex."* New York: Routledge.

Cancian, Frank. 1968. "Maximization as Norm, Strategy, and Theory: A Comment on Programmatic Statements in Economic Anthropology." In *Economic Anthropology: Readings in Theory and Analysis,* ed. E. Leclair and H. Schneider. New York: Holt, Rinehart and Winston.

Carrithers, Michael, Steven Collins, and Steven Lukes, eds. 1985. *The Category of the Person: Anthropology, Philosophy, History.* Cambridge: Cambridge University Press.

Chakrabarty, Dipesh. 1992. "Postcoloniality and the Artifice of History: Who Speaks for 'Indian' Pasts?" *Representations* 37: 1–26.

———. 1994. "Marx after Marxism: History, Subalternity, Difference." *positions: east asia cultures critique* 2 (2): 446–63.

———. 1997. "The Time of History and the Times of the Gods." In *The Politics of Culture in the Shadow of Capital,* ed. L. Lowe and D. Lloyd. Durham, N.C.: Duke University Press.

Chatterjee, Partha. 1993. *The Nation and Its Fragments: Colonial and Postcolonial Histories.* Princeton: Princeton University Press.

Chernoff, John. 1979. *African Rhythm and African Sensibility.* Chicago: University of Chicago Press.

Chodorow, Nancy. 1974. "Family Structure and Feminine Personality." In *Woman, Culture and Society,* ed. M. Rosaldo and L. Lamphere. Stanford: Stanford University Press.

———. 1978. *The Reproduction of Mothering: Psychoanalysis and the Sociology of Gender.* Berkeley: University of California Press.

Clay, Brenda. 1992. "Other Times, Other Places: Agency and the Big Man in Central New Ireland." *Man* 27 (4): 719–34.

Clifford, James. 1983. "On Ethnographic Authority." *Representations* 1: 118–46.

———. 1988. *The Predicament of Culture: Twentieth Century Ethnography, Literature, and Art.* Cambridge: Harvard University Press.

———. 1997. *Routes: Travel and Translation in the Late Twentieth Century.* Cambridge: Harvard University Press.

Clifford, James, and George Marcus, eds. 1986. *Writing Culture: The Poetics and Politics of Ethnography.* Berkeley: University of California Press.

Cohen, David William, and E. S. Odhiambo. 1992. *Burying SM: The Politics of*

Knowledge and the Sociology of Power in Africa. Portsmouth, N.H.: Heinemann.

Comaroff, Jean. 1980. "Healing and the Cultural Order: The Case of the Barolong boo Ratshidi of Southern Africa." *American Ethnologist* 7: 637–57.

———. 1985. *Body of Power, Spirit of Resistance: The Culture and History of a South African People.* Chicago: University of Chicago Press.

Comaroff, Jean, and John L. Comaroff. 1991. *Of Revelation and Revolution: Christianity, Colonialism and Consciousness in South Africa,* vol. 1. Chicago: University of Chicago Press.

———, eds. 1993. *Modernity and Its Malcontents: Ritual and Power in Postcolonial Africa.* Chicago: University of Chicago Press.

Comaroff, John L., and Jean Comaroff. 1992. *Ethnography and the Historical Imagination.* Boulder, Colo.: Westview Press.

———. 1997. *Of Revelation and Revolution: The Dialectics of Modernity on a South African Frontier,* vol. 2. Chicago: University of Chicago Press.

Coombe, Rosemary J., and Paul Stoller. 1994. "X Marks the Spot: The Ambiguities of African Trading in the Commerce of the Black Public Sphere." *Public Culture* 7 (1): 249–75.

Cooper, Frederick, and Ann Stoler, eds. 1997. *Tensions of Empire: Colonial Cultures in a Bourgeois World.* Berkeley: University of California Press.

Coquery-Vidrovitch, Catherine. 1972. "Research on the African Mode of Production." In *Perspectives on the African Past,* ed. M. Klein and W. Johnson. Boston: Little, Brown.

Cornevin, Robert. 1961. "Connaissance des Kabre depuis Frobenius." *Le Monde Non-Chrétien* 59–60: 95–99.

———. 1962. *Histoire du Togo.* Paris: Editions Berger-Levrault.

Coronil, Fernando. 1996. "Beyond Occidentalism: Toward Nonimperial Geohistorical Categories." *Cultural Anthropology* 11 (1): 51–87.

Crenshaw, Kimberlé, Neil Gotanda, Gary Peller, and Kendall Thomas, eds. 1995. *Critical Race Theory: The Key Writings that Formed the Movement.* New York: New Press.

Damon, Frederick. 1978. "Modes of Production and the Circulation of Value on the Other Side of the Kula Ring." Ph.D. thesis, Princeton University.

———. 1990. *From Muyuw to the Trobriands: Transformations Along the Northern Side of the Kula Ring.* Tucson: University of Arizona Press.

Delafosse, Maurice. 1904. *Vocabulaires Comparatifs de plus de 60 Langues en Dialectes Parlés à la Cote d'Ivoire de dans les Régions Limitrophes.* Paris: Levraux.

Delord, Jacques. 1961. "Notes et Commentaires sur les Kabre de Frobenius." *Le Monde Non-Chrétien* 59–60: 101–73.

Derrida, Jacques. [1972] 1982. "Différance." In *Margins of Philosophy.* Chicago: University of Chicago Press.

Devisch, René. 1993. *Weaving the Threads of Life: The Khita Gyn-Eco-Logical Healing Cult among the Yaka.* Chicago: University of Chicago Press.

Dieterlen, Germaine, ed. 1973. *La Notion de Personne en Afrique Noire.* Paris: Editions du Centre Nationale de la Recherche Scientifique.

Dirks, Nicholas. 1990. "History as a Sign of the Modern." *Public Culture* 2 (2): 25–32.

———. 1992. Introduction. In *Colonialism and Culture,* ed. N. Dirks. Ann Arbor: University of Michigan Press.

Dirlik, Arif. 1997. "The Postmodernization of Production and Its Organization: Flexible Production, Work and Culture." In *The Postcolonial Aura.* Boulder, Colo.: Westview Press.

Donham, Donald. 1981. "Beyond the Domestic Mode of Production." *Man* 16: 515–41.

———. 1985. *Work and Power in Maale, Ethiopia.* Ann Arbor: University of Michigan Press.

———. 1990. *History, Power, Ideology: Central Issues in Marxism and Anthropology.* Cambridge: Cambridge University Press.

Drewal, Margaret. 1992. *Yoruba Ritual: Performers, Play, Agency.* Bloomington: Indiana University Press.

Dubois, W.E.B. [1903] 1989. *The Souls of Black Folk.* New York: Penguin Books.

Dupre, G., and P. P. Rey. 1973. "Reflections on the Pertinence of a Theory of the History of Exchange." *Economy and Society* 2: 131–63.

Eagleton, Terry. 1991. *Ideology: An Introduction.* London: Verso.

Ellis, Stephen. 1993. "Rumour and Power in Togo." *Africa* 63 (4): 462–76.

Escobar, Arturo. 1995. *Encountering Development: The Making and Unmaking of the Third World.* Princeton: Princeton University Press.

Evans-Pritchard, E. E. 1937. *Witchcraft, Oracles and Magic among the Azande.* Oxford: Clarendon Press.

———. 1940. *The Nuer.* London: Oxford University Press.

———. 1956. *Nuer Religion.* London: Oxford University Press.

Ewing, Katherine. 1990. "The Illusion of Wholeness: Culture, Self, and the Experience of Inconsistency." *Ethos* 18 (3): 251–78.

Fabian, Johannes. 1983. *Time and the Other: How Anthropology Makes its Object.* New York: Columbia University Press.

Ferguson, James. 1990. *The Anti-Politics Machine.* Cambridge: Cambridge University Press.

Fernandez, James. 1982. *Bwiti: An Ethnography of the Religious Imagination in Africa.* Princeton: Princeton University Press.

Fiske, Alan. 1991. *Structures of Social Life: The Four Elementary Forms of Human Relations (Communal Sharing, Authority Ranking, Equality Matching, Market Pricing).* New York: Free Press.

Fortes, Meyer. 1936. "Ritual Festivals and Social Cohesion in the Hinterland of the Gold Coast." *American Anthropologist* 38: 590–604.

———. 1940. "The Political System of the Tallensi of the Northern Territories of the Gold Coast." In *African Political Systems,* ed. M. Fortes and E. E. Evans-Pritchard. London: Oxford University Press.

———. 1945. *The Dynamics of Clanship among the Tallensi, Being the First Part of an Analysis of the Social Structure of a Trans-Volta Tribe.* London: Oxford University Press.

———. 1949. *The Web of Kinship among the Tallensi.* London: Oxford University Press.

———. 1953. "The Structure of Unilineal Descent Groups." *American Anthropologist* 55 (1): 17–41.

———. 1957. "Malinowski and the Study of Kinship." In *Man and Culture,* ed. R. Firth. New York: Harper and Row.

———. 1958. "Introduction." In *The Developmental Cycle in Domestic Groups,* ed. J. Goody. London: Cambridge University Press.

———. 1973. "On the Concept of the Person among the Tallensi." In *La Notion de Personne en Afrique Noire,* ed. G. Dieterlen. Paris: Centre National de la Recherche Scientifique.

———. 1987. *Religion, Morality and the Person: Essays on Tallensi Religion.* Edited by J. Goody. Cambridge: Cambridge University Press.

Fortes, Meyer, and E. E. Evans-Pritchard, eds. 1940. *African Political Systems.* London: Oxford University Press.

Foster, Robert. 1990a. "Value Without Equivalence: Exchange and Replacement in a Melanesian Society." *Man* 25: 54–69.

———. 1990b. "Nurture and Force-feeding: Mortuary Feasting and the Construction of Collective Individuals in a New Ireland Society." *American Ethnologist* 17: 431–48.

———. 1995. *Social Reproduction and History in Melanesia: Mortuary Ritual, Gift Exchange, and Custom in the Tanga Islands.* Cambridge: Cambridge University Press.

Foucault, Michel. 1980. "Truth and Power." In *Power/Knowledge: Selected Interviews and Other Writings,* 1972–1977, ed. Colin Gordon. New York: Pantheon.

Friedman, Jonathon. 1990. "Being in the World: Globalization and Localization." In *Global Culture: Nationalism, Globalization and Modernity,* ed. M. Featherstone. London: Sage.

Frobenius, Leo. 1913. *Und Afrika Sprach: Unter den Unstraflichen Aethiopien,* vol. 1. Berlin: Benjamin Blom.

———. [1913] 1961. "Les Kabre." *Le Monde Non-Chrétien* 59–60: 101–73.

Froelich, Jean-Claude. 1963. "Les Kabre, Les Lamba, Les Naoudemba." In *Les Populations du Nord Togo,* ed. J. C. Froelich, P. Alexandre, and R. Cornevin. Paris: Presses Universitaires de France.

Fuss, Diana. 1989. *Essentially Speaking.* New York: Routledge.

Gable, Eric. 1995. "The Decolonization of Consciousness: Local Skeptics and the 'Will to be Modern' in a West African Village." *American Ethnologist* 22 (2): 242–57.

Gates, Henry Louis. 1988. *The Signifying Monkey: A Theory of African-American Literary Criticism.* New York: Oxford University Press.

Geschiere, Peter. 1988. "Sorcery and the State: Popular Modes of Action among the Maka of Southeast Cameroon." *Critique of Anthropology* 8 (1): 35–63.

———. 1992. "Kinship, Witchcraft and 'the Market'." In *Contesting Markets:*

Analyses of Ideology, Discourse and Practice, ed. R. Dilley. Edinburgh: University of Edinburgh Press.

———. 1997. *The Modernity of Witchcraft: Politics and the Occult in Postcolonial Africa.* Charlottesville: University Press of Virginia.

Giddens, Anthony. 1979. *Central Problems in Social Theory.* Berkeley: University of California Press.

———. 1984. *The Constitution of Society.* Berkeley: University of California Press.

———. 1990. *The Consequences of Modernity.* Stanford: Stanford University Press.

Gilroy, Paul. 1987. *'There Ain't no Black in the Union Jack': The Cultural Politics of Race and Nation.* Chicago: University of Chicago Press.

———. 1993a. *The Black Atlantic: Modernity and Double Consciousness.* Cambridge: Harvard University Press.

———. 1993b. *Small Acts: Thoughts on the Politics of Black Cultures.* London: Serpent's Tail.

Gluckman, Max. 1962. "Introduction." In *Essays on the Ritual of Social Relations,* ed. M. Gluckman. Manchester: Manchester University Press.

Goody, Jack. [1956] 1967. *The Social Organisation of the Lowiili.* Oxford: Oxford University Press.

———. 1959. "The Mother's Brother and the Sister's Son in West Africa." *Journal of the Royal Anthropological Institute* 89: 61–88.

———. 1971. *Technology, Tradition and the State in Africa.* London: Oxford University Press.

———. 1978. "Population and Polity in the Voltaic Region." In *The Evolution of Social Systems,* ed. J. Friedman and M. J. Rowlands. Pittsburgh: University of Pittsburgh Press.

———. 1995. *The Expansive Moment: Anthropology in Britain and Africa, 1918–1970.* Cambridge: Cambridge University Press.

Goody, Jack, ed. 1958. *The Developmental Cycle in Domestic Groups.* London: Cambridge University Press.

Gottlieb, Alma. 1988. "Menstrual Cosmology among the Beng of Ivory Coast." In *Blood Magic: The Anthropology of Menstruation,* ed. T. Buckley and A. Gottlieb. Berkeley: University of California Press.

———. 1989. "Witches, Kings and the Sacrifice of Identity *or* the Power of Paradox and the Paradox of Power among the Beng of Ivory Coast." In *Creativity of Power: Cosmology and Action in African Societies,* ed. W. Arens and I. Karp. Washington, D.C.: Smithsonian Institution Press.

———. 1992. *Under the Kapok Tree: Identity and Difference in Beng Thought.* Bloomington: Indiana University Press.

———. 1998. "Do Infants Have Religion?" *American Anthropologist* 100 (1): 122–35.

Gottlieb, Alma, and Philip Graham. 1993. *Parallel Worlds: An Anthropologist and a Writer Encounter Africa.* New York: Crown Publishers.

Gramsci, Antonio. 1971. *Selections from the Prison Notebooks.* Edited and translated by Q. Hoare and G. Nowell Smith. New York: International Publishers.

Greenberg, Joseph. 1963. *Languages of Africa.* Bloomington: Indiana University Press.

Gregory, Christopher. 1982. *Gifts and Commodities.* New York: Academic Press.

Griaule, Marcel. 1965. *Conversations with Ogotemmeli.* Oxford: Oxford University Press.

Griaule, Marcel, and Germaine Dieterlen. 1965. *Le Renard Pale.* Paris: Institut d'Ethnologie.

Guha, Ranajit. 1997. *Dominance without Hegemony: History and Power in Colonial India.* Cambridge: Harvard University Press.

Gupta, Akhil, and James Ferguson. 1992. "Beyond 'Culture': Space, Identity, and the Politics of Difference." *Cultural Anthropology* 7 (1): 6–23.

———. 1997a. "Culture, Power, Place: Ethnography at the End of an Era." In *Culture, Power, Place: Explorations in Critical Anthropology,* ed. A. Gupta and J. Ferguson. Durham, N.C.: Duke University Press.

———. 1997b. "Discipline and Practice: 'The Field' as Site, Method, and Location in Anthropology." In *Anthropological Locations: Boundaries and Grounds of a Field Science,* ed. A. Gupta and J. Ferguson. Berkeley: University of California Press.

Guyer, Jane. 1993. "Wealth in People and Self-Realization in Equatorial Africa." *Man* 28: 243–65.

———. 1995a. "Wealth in People as Wealth in Knowledge: Accumulation and Composition in Equatorial Africa." *Journal of African History* 36: 121–40.

———, ed. 1995b. *Money Matters: Instability, Values and Social Payments in the Modern History of West African Communities.* Portsmouth, N.H.: Heinemann.

Hall, Stuart. 1990. "Cultural Identity and Diaspora." In *Identity: Community, Culture, Difference,* ed. J. Rutherford. London: Lawrence and Wishart.

Hannerz, Ulf. 1992a. *Cultural Complexity: Studies in the Organization of Meaning.* New York: Columbia University Press.

———. 1992b. "The Global Ecumene as a Network of Networks." In *Conceptualising Society,* ed. A. Kuper. London: Routledge.

———. 1996. *Transnational Connections: Culture, People, Places.* New York: Routledge.

Hansen, Karen. 1994. "Dealing with Used Clothing: *Salaula* and the Construction of Identity in Zambia's Third Republic." *Public Culture* 6 (3): 503–23.

Harris, Olivia, and Kate Young. 1981. "Engendered Structures: Some Problems in the Analysis of Reproduction." In *The Anthropology of Pre-Capitalist Societies,* ed. J. Kahn and J. Llobera. London: Macmillan.

Hart, Keith. 1978. "The Economic Basis of Tallensi Social History in the Early Twentieth Century." In *Research in Economic Anthropology,* ed. G. Dalton. Greenwich, Conn.: JAI Press.

Harvey, David. 1989. *The Condition of Postmodernity: An Enquiry into the Origins of Cultural Change.* Cambridge, Mass.: Basil Blackwell.

Hendrikson, Hildi, ed. 1996. *Clothing and Difference: Embodied Identities in Colonial and Post-Colonial Africa*. Durham, N.C.: Duke University Press.

Herdt, Gilbert. 1981. *Guardians of the Flutes: Idioms of Masculinity*. New York: McGraw Hill.

Héritier, Francoise. 1981. *L'Exercice de la Parenté*. Paris: Gallimard.

Heusch, Luc de. 1985. *Sacrifice in Africa*. Bloomington: Indiana University Press.

Hogendorn, Jan, and Marion Johnson. 1986. *The Shell Money of the Slave Trade*. London: Cambridge University Press.

hooks, bell. 1989. *Talking Back: Thinking Feminist, Thinking Black*. Boston: South End Press.

Humphrey, Caroline, and Steven Hugh-Jones, eds. 1992. *Barter, Exchange and Value: An Anthropological Approach*. Cambridge: Cambridge University Press.

Hutchinson, Sharon. 1996. *Nuer Dilemmas: Coping with Money, War, and the State*. Berkeley: University of California Press.

Hymes, Dell. [1969] 1974. *Reinventing Anthropology*. New York: Vintage.

Iliffe, John. 1995. *Africans: The History of a Continent*. Cambridge: Cambridge University Press.

Jackson, Michael. 1982. *Allegories of the Wilderness*. Bloomington: Indiana University Press.

———. 1989. *Paths Toward a Clearing: Radical Empiricism and Ethnographic Inquiry*. Bloomington: Indiana University Press.

———. 1990. "The Man Who Could Turn into an Elephant: Shape-Shifting among the Kuranko of Sierra Leone." In *Personhood and Agency: The Experience of Self and Other in African Cultures*, ed. M. Jackson and I. Karp. Washington, D.C.: Smithsonian Institution Press.

———, ed. 1996. *Things as They Are: New Directions in Phenomenological Anthropology*. Bloomington: Indiana University Press.

———. 1998. *Minima Ethnographica: Intersubjectivity and the Anthropological Project*. Chicago: University of Chicago Press.

Jackson, Michael, and Ivan Karp, eds. 1990. *Personhood and Agency: The Experience of Self and Other in African Cultures*. Washington, D.C.: Smithsonian Institution Press.

Jameson, Frederic. 1991. *Postmodernism; or, The Cultural Logic of Late Capitalism*. Durham, N.C.: Duke University Press.

Jewsiewicki, Bogomul. 1997. "Painting in Zaire: From the Invention of the West to the Representation of the Social Self." In *Readings in African Popular Culture*, ed. K. Barber. Bloomington: Indiana University Press.

Karp, Ivan. 1990. "Power and Capacity in Iteso Rituals of Possession." In *Personhood and Agency: The Experience of Self and Other in African Cultures*, ed. M. Jackson and I. Karp. Washington, D.C.: Smithsonian Institution Press.

Kelly, John D., and Martha Kaplan. 1990. "History, Structure and Ritual." In *Annual Review of Anthropology* 19: 119–50. Palo Alto, Calif.: Annual Reviews, Inc.

Kopytoff, Igor, ed. 1987. *The African Frontier: The Reproduction of Traditional African Societies.* Bloomington: Indiana University Press.

Kraemer, Fritz. [1987] 1993. *The Red Fez: Art and Spirit Possession in Africa.* London: Verso.

Kratz, Corinne. 1994. *Affecting Performance: Meaning, Movement and Experience in Okiek Women's Initiation.* Washington, D.C.: Smithsonian Institution Press.

Kuper, Adam. 1982. "Lineage Theory: A Critical Retrospect." *Annual Review of Anthropology* 11: 71–95.

———. 1988. *The Invention of Primitive Society: Transformations of an Illusion.* London: Routledge.

Laclau, Ernesto, and Chantal Mouffe. 1985. *Hegemony and Socialist Strategy: Towards a Radical Democratic Politics.* London: Verso.

La Fontaine, Jean. 1985. *Initiation: Ritual Drama and Secret Knowledge across the World.* New York: Penguin.

Lan, David. 1985. *Guns and Rain: Guerillas and Spirit Mediums in Zimbabwe.* Berkeley: University of California Press.

Lash, Scott, and Jonathon Friedman, eds. 1992. *Modernity and Identity.* Oxford: Basil Blackwell Ltd.

Leach, Jerry, and Edmund Leach, eds. 1983. *The Kula: New Perspectives on Massim Exchange.* Cambridge: Cambridge University Press.

Lévi-Strauss, Claude. [1962] 1966. *The Savage Mind.* Chicago: University of Chicago Press.

———. [1963] 1967. "Do Dual Organisations Exist?" In *Structural Anthropology.* New York: Doubleday.

Lienhardt, Godfrey. 1961. *Divinity and Experience: The Religion of the Dinka.* Oxford: Clarendon Press.

Llewelyn-Davies, Melissa. 1981. "Women, Warriors, and Patriarchs." In *Sexual Meanings: The Cultural Construction of Gender and Sexuality,* ed. S. Ortner and H. Whitehead. Cambridge: Cambridge University Press.

Lorde, Audre. 1984. "The Master's Tools Will Never Dismantle the Master's House." In *Sister Outsider: Essays and Speeches.* Trumansburg, N.Y.: Crossing Press.

Lucien-Brun, B. 1974. *La Colonisation des Terres Neuves du Centre-Togo par les Kabré et les Losso.* Paris: ORSTOM.

Lyotard, Jean-François. 1984. *The Postmodern Condition: A Report on Knowledge.* Minneapolis: University of Minnesota Press.

Mamdani, Mahmood. 1996. *Citizen and Subject: Contemporary Africa and the Legacy of Late Colonialism.* Princeton: Princeton University Press.

Manning, Patrick. 1990. *Slavery and African Life: Occidental, Oriental and African Slave Trades.* Cambridge: Cambridge University Press.

Marcus, George. 1992. "Past, Present and Emergent Identities: Requirements for Ethnographies of Late Twentieth-Century Modernity Worldwide." In *Modernity and Identity,* ed. S. Lash and J. Friedman. Cambridge, Mass.: Blackwell.

Marguerat, Yves. 1994. *Population, Migrations, Urbanisation au Togo et en*

Afrique Noire; articles et documents (1981–1993). Lomé: Presses de l'Université du Benin.

Marquiessac, H. de. 1932. "Enquete et Sondage Démographique en Pays Kabre (Nord Togo)." *Societé de Pathologie Exotique Bulletin* 9: 986–92.

Marx, Karl. [1857] 1973. *Grundrisse: Introduction to the Critique of Political Economy.* New York: Vintage Books.

———. [1867] 1977. *Capital,* vol. 1. New York: Vintage Books.

Matison, J., and R. Mack. 1984. *The Only Barter Book You'll Ever Need.* New York: Bantam.

Matory, Lorand. 1994. *Sex and the Empire That Is No More: Gender and the Politics of Metaphor in Oyo Yoruba Religion.* Minneapolis: University of Minnesota Press.

Mauss, Marcel. [1925] 1967. *The Gift: Forms and Functions of Exchange in Archaic Societies.* New York: Norton.

Mbembe, Achille. 1992. "The Banality of Power and the Aesthetics of Vulgarity in the Postcolony." *Public Culture* 4 (2): 1–30.

Mbembe, Achille, and Janet Roitman. 1995. "Figures of the Subject in Times of Crisis." *Public Culture* 7 (2): 323–52.

Meigs, Anna. 1990. "Multiple Gender Ideologies and Statuses." In *Beyond the Second Sex: New Directions in The Anthropology of Gender,* ed. P. Sanday and R. Goodenough. Philadelphia: University of Pennsylvania Press.

Meillassoux, Claude. 1964. *Anthropologie Economique des Gouro de Cote D'Ivoire.* Paris: Mouton.

———. 1972. "From Reproduction to Production: A Marxist Approach to Economic Anthropology." *Economy and Society* 1: 93–103.

———. 1973. "The Social Organisation of the Peasantry: The Economic Basis of Kinship." *Journal of Peasant Studies* 1: 81–90.

———. 1981. *Maidens, Meal and Money: Capitalism and the Domestic Community.* Cambridge: Cambridge University Press.

Mercer, Kobena. 1988. "Diaspora Culture and the Dialogic Imagination." In *Blackframes: Critical Perspectives on Black Independent Cinema,* ed. M. Cham and C. Watkins. Cambridge: MIT Press.

Middleton, John. 1960. *Lugbara Religion: Ritual and Authority among an East African People.* London: Oxford University Press.

———. 1963. "Witchcraft and Sorcery in Lugbara." In *Witchcraft and Sorcery in East Africa,* ed. J. Middleton and E. Winter. London: Routledge.

———. 1965. *The Lugbara of Uganda.* New York: Holt, Rinehart and Winston.

Miller, Daniel. 1995. "Consumption and Commodities." In *Annual Review of Anthropology* 24: 141–61. Palo Alto, Calif.: Annual Reviews, Inc.

Mitchell, Timothy. 1988. *Colonising Egypt.* Cambridge: Cambridge University Press.

———. 1990. "Everyday Metaphors of Power." *Theory and Society* 19: 545–77.

Mitchell, Timothy, and Lila Abu-Lughod. 1993. "Questions of Modernity." *Items* 47 (4): 79–83.

Monaghan, John. 1996. "Fiesta Finance in MesoAmerica and the Origins of a

Gift Exchange System." *Journal of the Royal Anthropological Institute* 2 (3): 499–516.

Moore, Henrietta. 1994. *A Passion for Difference: Essays in Anthropology and Gender.* Bloomington: Indiana University Press.

Moore, Sally Falk. 1986. *Social Facts and Fabrications: "Customary" Law on Kilimanjaro, 1880–1980.* Cambridge: Cambridge University Press.

———. 1994. *Anthropology and Africa: Changing Perspectives on a Changing Scene.* Charlottesville: University Press of Virginia.

Mosko, Mark. 1992. "Motherless Sons: 'Divine Kings' and 'Partible Persons' in Melanesia and Polynesia." *Man* 27 (4): 697–718.

Mudimbe, V. Y. 1988. *The Invention of Africa: Gnosis, Philosophy, and the Order of Knowledge.* Bloomington: Indiana University Press.

Munn, Nancy. 1986. *The Fame of Gawa: A Symbolic Study of Value Transformation in a Massim (Papua New Guinea) Society.* Cambridge: Cambridge University Press.

Murphy, William. 1980. "Secret Knowledge as Property and Power in Kpelle Society." *Africa* 50: 193–207.

———. 1991. "Creating the Appearance of Consensus in Mende Political Discourse." *American Anthropologist* 92: 24–41.

Nadelson, Leslee. 1981. "Pigs, Women and the Men's House in Amazonia: An Analysis of Six Mundurucu Myths." In *Sexual Meanings: The Cultural Construction of Gender and Sexuality,* ed. S. Ortner and H. Whitehead. Cambridge: Cambridge University Press.

Nandy, Ashis. 1983. *The Intimate Enemy: Loss and Recovery of Self Under Colonialism.* Delhi: Oxford University Press.

Netting, Robert. 1968. *Hill Farmers of Nigeria: Cultural Ecology of the Kofyar of the Jos Plateau.* Seattle: University of Washington Press.

———. 1974. "Agrarian Ecology." In *Annual Review of Anthropology* 3: 21–56. Palo Alto, Calif.: Annual Reviews, Inc.

O'Laughlin, Bridget. 1977. "Production and Reproduction: Meillassoux's 'Femmes, Greniers et Capitaux'." *Critique of Anthropology* 8: 3–32.

Ortner, Sherry. 1984. "Theory in Anthropology Since the Sixties." *Comparative Studies in Society and History* 26: 126–66.

———. 1989. *High Religion: A Cultural and Political History of Sherpa Religion.* Princeton: Princeton University Press.

———. 1995. "Resistance and the Problem of Ethnographic Refusal." *Comparative Studies in Society and History* 37 (1): 173–93.

Ortner, Sherry, and Harriet Whitehead. 1981. "Introduction: Accounting for Sexual Meanings." In *Sexual Meanings: The Cultural Construction of Gender and Sexuality,* ed. S. Ortner and H. Whitehead. Cambridge: Cambridge University Press.

Ottenberg, Simon. 1989. *Boyhood Rituals in an African Society: An Interpretation.* Seattle: University of Washington Press.

Parry, Jonathon, and Maurice Bloch. 1989. *Money and the Morality of Exchange.* Cambridge: Cambridge University Press.

Paulme, Denise, ed. 1971. *Classes et Associations d'Age en Afrique de L'Ouest.* Paris: Librairie Plon.

Perry, Donna. 1997. "Rural Ideologies and Urban Imaginings: Wolof Immigrants in New York City." *Africa Today* 44 (2): 229–60.

Philips, John. 1990. "The African Heritage of White America." In *Africanisms in American Culture,* ed. J. Holloway. Bloomington: Indiana University Press.

Pillet-Schwartz, Anne-Marie. 1984. *Les Migrations Rurales des Kabyè et des Losso (Togo).* Paris: ORSTOM.

Piot, Charles. 1988. "Fathers and Sons: Domestic Production, Conflict and Social Forms among the Kabre." In *Research in Economic Anthropology,* ed. Barry Isaac. Greenwich, Conn.: JAI Press.

———. 1991. "Of Persons and Things: Some Reflections on African Spheres of Exchange." *Man* 26: 405–24.

———. 1992. "Wealth Production, Ritual Consumption and Center/Periphery Relations in a West African Regional System." *American Ethnologist* 19 (1): 34–52.

———. 1993. "Secrecy, Ambiguity and the Everyday in Kabre Culture." *American Anthropologist* 95 (2): 353–70.

———. 1995. "Symbolic Dualism and Historical Process among the Kabre of Togo." *Journal of the Royal Anthropological Institute* 1 (3): 611–24.

———. 1996. "Of Slaves and the Gift: Kabre Sale of Kin During the Era of the Slave Trade." *Journal of African History* 37: 31–49.

Prakash, Gyan. 1990. "Writing Post-Orientalist Histories of the Third World: Perspectives from Indian Historiography." *Comparative Studies in Society and History* 32 (2): 383–408.

———. 1994. "Subaltern Studies as Postcolonial Criticism." *American Historical Review* 99 (5): 1475–90.

Pratt, Mary Louise. 1992. *Imperial Eyes: Travel Writing and Transculturation.* New York: Routledge.

———. 1998. "Peripheral Modernity and the Idea of the Global." Paper presented at Mellon Seminar on "Transnationalism and Public Culture," Duke University.

Pred, Allan, and Michael Watts. 1992. *Reworking Modernity: Capitalisms and Symbolic Discontent.* New Brunswick, N.J.: Rutgers University Press.

Rabinow, Paul. 1989. *French Modern: Norms and Forms of the Social Environment.* Chicago: University of Chicago Press.

Radcliffe-Brown, A. R. 1952. "The Mother's Brother in Southern Africa." In *Structure and Function in Primitive Society.* New York: Free Press.

Read, Kenneth. 1952. "Nama Cult of the Central Highlands, New Guinea." *Oceania* 23: 1–25.

———. 1982. "Male-Female Relationships among the Gahuku-Gama: 1950 and 1981." *Social Analysis,* special issue 12.

Rey, Pierre-Philippe. 1975. "The Lineage Mode of Production." *Critique of Anthropology* 3: 27–29.

———. 1979. "Class Contradiction in Lineage Societies." *Critique of Anthropology* 4: 41–60.

Riesman, Paul. [1974] 1977. *Freedom in Fulani Social Life.* Chicago: University of Chicago Press.

———. 1986. "The Person and the Life Cycle in African Social Life and Thought." *African Studies Review* 29 (2): 71–138.

Rosaldo, Michelle. 1974. "Woman, Culture, and Society: A Theoretical Overview." In *Woman, Culture, and Society,* ed. M. Rosaldo and L. Lamphere. Stanford: Stanford University Press.

Rosaldo, Renato. 1989. *Culture and Truth: The Remaking of Social Analysis.* Boston: Beacon Press.

Sacks, Karen. 1982. *Sisters and Wives: The Past and Future of Sexual Equality.* Urbana: University of Illinois Press.

Sahlins, Marshall. 1981. *Historical Metaphors and Mythical Realities: Structure in the Early History of the Sandwich Islands Kingdom.* Ann Arbor: University of Michigan Press.

———. 1985. *Islands of History.* Chicago: University of Chicago Press.

Said, Edward. 1978. *Orientalism.* New York: Pantheon.

———. 1993. *Culture and Imperialism.* New York: Vintage Books.

Sanday, Peggy. 1990. "Introduction." In *Beyond the Second Sex: New Directions in the Anthropology of Gender,* ed. P. Sanday and R. Goodenough. Philadelphia: University of Pennsylvania Press.

Sapir, J. David. 1970. "Kujaama: Symbolic Separation among the Diola-Fogny." *American Anthropologist* 72: 1330–48.

Sauvaget, Claude. 1981. *BOUA Village de Koudé: Un Terroir Kabyè (Togo septentrional).* Paris: ORSTOM.

Schloss, Marc. 1988. *The Hatchet's Blood: Separation, Power, and Gender in Ehing Social Life.* Tucson: University of Arizona Press.

Seddon, David, ed. 1978. *Relations of Production: Marxist Approaches to Anthropology.* London: Frank Cass.

Shaw, Rosalind. 1997. "The Production of Witchcraft/Witchcraft as Production: Memory, Modernity, and the Slave Trade in Sierra Leone." *American Ethnologist* 24 (4): 856–76.

Shipton, Parker. 1989. *Bitter Money: Cultural Economy and Some African Meanings of Forbidden Commodities.* Washington, D.C.: American Anthropological Association.

Starn, Orin. 1991. "Missing the Revolution: Anthropologists and the War in Peru." *Cultural Anthropology* 6 (1): 63–91.

Steiner, Christopher. 1994. *African Art in Transit.* London: Cambridge University Press.

Stoller, Paul. 1987. *In Sorcery's Shadow: A Memoir of Apprenticeship among the Songhay of Niger.* Chicago: University of Chicago Press.

———. 1989. *The Taste of Ethnographic Things: The Senses in Anthropology.* Philadelphia: University of Pennsylvania Press.

———. 1995. *Embodying Colonial Memories: Spirit Possession, Power and the Hauka in West Africa.* New York: Routledge.

———. 1996. "Spaces, Places, and Fields: The Politics of West African Trading in New York City's Informal Economy." *American Anthropologist* 98 (4): 776–88.

———. 1997. *Sensuous Scholarship.* Philadelphia: University of Pennsylvania Press.

Strathern, Marilyn. 1984. "Subject or Object? Women and the Circulation of Valuables in Highlands New Guinea." In *Women and Property—Women as Property,* ed. R. Hirschon. New York: St. Martin's Press.

———. 1987a. Introduction and Conclusion. In *Dealing with Inequality: Analysing Gender Relations in Melanesia and Beyond,* ed. M. Strathern. Cambridge: Cambridge University Press.

———. 1987b. "Producing Difference: Connections and Disconnections in Two New Guinea Highland Kinship Systems." In *Gender and Kinship: Essays Toward a Unified Analysis,* ed. J. Collier and S. Yanagisako. Stanford: Stanford University Press.

———. 1988. *The Gender of the Gift: Problems with Women and Problems with Society in Melanesia.* Berkeley: University of California Press.

———. 1991. *Partial Connections.* Savage, Md.: Rowman and Littlefield.

———. 1992a. *Reproducing the Future: Anthropology, Kinship and the New Reproductive Technologies.* New York: Routledge.

———. 1992b. "Parts and Wholes: Refiguring Relationships in a Post-Plural World." In *Conceptualising Society,* ed. A. Kuper. London: Routledge.

———. 1995. "Gender: Division or Comparison?" In *Practicing Feminism: Identity, Difference, Power,* ed. N. Charles and F. Hughes-Freeland. London: Routledge.

Swanson, Richard. 1985. *Gourmantché Ethnoanthropology: A Theory of Human Being.* New York: University Press of America.

Tait, David. 1961. *The Konkomba of Northern Ghana.* Oxford: Oxford University Press.

Taussig, Michael. 1980. *The Devil and Commodity Fetishism in South America.* Chapel Hill: University of North Carolina Press.

———. 1993. *Mimesis and Alterity: A Particular History of the Senses.* New York: Routledge.

Terray, Emmanuel. 1972. *Marxism and Primitive Societies.* New York: Monthly Review Press.

Thomas, Nicholas. 1991. *Entangled Objects: Exchange, Material Culture and Colonialism in the Pacific.* Cambridge: Harvard University Press.

———. 1994. *Colonialism's Culture: Anthropology, Travel and Government.* Princeton: Princeton University Press.

Toulabour, Comi. 1986. *Le Togo Sous Eyadéma.* Paris: Karthala.

Tsing, Anna Lowenhaupt. 1993. *In the Realm of the Diamond Queen: Marginality in an Out-of-the-Way Place.* Princeton: Princeton University Press.

Vansina, Jan. 1990. *Paths in the Rainforests: Toward a History of Political Tradition in Equatorial Africa.* Madison: University of Wisconsin Press.

Verdier, Raymond. 1982. *Le Pays Kabiyé: Cité des Dieux, Cité des Hommes.* Paris: Karthala.

Wagner, Roy. 1977. "Analogic Kinship: A Daribi Example." *American Ethnologist* 4: 623–42.

——. 1981. *The Invention of Culture.* Chicago: University of Chicago Press.

——. 1986a. *Asiwinarong: Ethos, Image and Social Power among the Usen Barok of New Ireland.* Princeton: Princeton University Press.

——. 1986b. *Symbols that Stand for Themselves.* Chicago: University of Chicago Press.

Waterman, Christopher. 1990. *Juju: A Social History and Ethnography of an African Popular Music.* Chicago: University of Chicago Press.

Weiss, Brad. 1996. *The Making and Unmaking of the Haya Lived World: Consumption, Commoditization, and Everyday Practice.* Durham, N.C.: Duke University Press.

Werbner, Richard. 1989. *Ritual Passage Sacred Journey: The Process and Organization of Religious Movement.* Manchester: Manchester University Press.

West, Cornel. 1990. "The New Cultural Politics of Difference." In *Out There: Marginalization and Contemporary Cultures,* ed. R. Ferguson, M. Gever, T. Minh-ha, and C. West. Cambridge: MIT Press.

Westermann, D., and M. A. Bryan. 1952. *Languages of West Africa.* London: Oxford University Press.

Wilks, Ivor. 1975. *Asante in the Nineteenth Century: The Structure and Evolution of a Political Order.* Cambridge: Cambridge University Press.

Williams, Raymond. 1976. *Keywords.* London: Fontana.

——. 1977. *Marxism and Literature.* Oxford: Oxford University Press.

Wilmsen, Edwin. 1989. *Land Filled with Flies: A Political Economy of the Kalahari.* Chicago: University of Chicago Press.

Wolf, Eric. 1982. *Europe and the People Without History.* Berkeley: University of California Press.

Yagla, W. O. 1978. *L'Edification de la Nation Togolaise.* Paris: L'Harmattan.

Yoshimoto, Mitsuhiro. 1994. "Images of Empire: Tokyo Disneyland and Japanese Cultural Imperialism." In *Disney Discourse: Producing the Magic Kingdom,* ed. E. Smoodin. New York: Routledge.

Young, Crawford. 1994. *The African Colonial State in Comparative Perspective.* New Haven: Yale University Press.

Young, Robert. 1990. *White Mythologies: Writing History and the West.* London: Routledge.

——. 1995. *Colonial Desire: Hybridity in Theory, Culture and Race.* London: Routledge.

Zahan, Dominique. 1960. *Societés d'Initiation Bambara: Le N'Domo, Le Koré.* Paris: Mouton.

——. [1970] 1979. *The Religion, Spirituality and Thought of Traditional Africa.* Chicago: University of Chicago Press.

Zukin, Sharon. 1995. *The Cultures of Cities.* Oxford: Blackwell.

Index

Abu-Lugod, Lila, 23, 172, 173, 198n. 1
agriculture. *See* cultivation
Amselle, Jean-Loup, 23, 24, 28, 182n. 4
androgyny, 78–79, 84, 186nn. 1, 7
Appadurai, Arjun, 21, 22–23, 71, 166, 174, 183n. 1
Appiah, Anthony, 1, 20, 172
Apter, Andrew, 1, 68, 143, 168
Arens, William, 180n. 12, 198n. 1
Asad, Talal, 24, 131
Auslander, Mark, 68

Barber, Karin, 2, 186n. 18, 198n. 4
Bastien, Misty, 68
Baudrillard, Jean, 22–23, 181n. 21
Beidelman, T. O., 84, 145, 186n. 4
Benjamin, Jessica, 187n. 10
Berglund, Axel-Ivar, 18, 181n. 18
Berman, Marshall, 179n. 1
Bhabha, Homi, 6, 147–48, 198n. 1
Blier, Suzanne, 107, 118, 191n. 12
Bloch, Maurice, 14, 122, 183n. 1, 189n. 20
Bohannan, Paul, 36, 71, 72, 185n. 9
Bourdieu, Pierre, 15–16, 147
Butler, Judith, 20, 123, 147, 191n. 14

Cartry, Michel, 8
Chakrabarty, Dipesh, 6, 198n. 5
Chaterjee, Partha, 6
Chernoff, John, 94, 153
Chodorow, Nancy, 187n. 10
Christianity, 27–28, 49, 51, 177
Clifford, James, 25, 42

Cohen, David William, 1
colonialism
    and anthropology, 24–25, 33, 42–43, 115, 131–32
    and calendrical ceremonies, 144
    and chiefs, 148–49
    and community boundaries, 131–32, 154–55, 196nn. 24, 25
    during German rule, 37–40
    and initiation ceremonies, 84–86, 90
    and the Kabre diaspora, 40–44, 156–60, 162–63
    local responses to, 70, 85–86, 89–90, 155, 182n. 10
    and witchcraft, 68
Comaroff, Jean, 1, 19, 21, 24, 131, 135, 163, 173, 174, 179n. 1, 186n. 4, 197n. 5, 198nn. 1, 4
Comaroff, John, 1, 21, 24, 131, 135, 163, 173, 174, 179n. 1, 197n. 5, 198nn. 1, 4
Coombe, Rosemary, 21
Cooper, Frederick, 131
Coquery-Vidrovitch, Catherine, 11, 12
Coronil, Fernando, 20
cosmopolitanism, 22–24, 26, 132
cowrie shells
    as currency, 36
    and divination, 73–74
    and initiation dress, 84
    and slavery, 36, 71–72
Crenshaw, Kimberlé, 20
critical race theory, 20, 181n. 20